PENGUIN BOOKS

WILL AND ME

'A superbly written, infectiously high-spirited narrative . . .
crammed with fascinating anecdotes, finely turned phrases and
genuine shafts of insight . . . it's a hard book to put down'
Terry Eagleton, *Irish Times*

'I can honestly say that I haven't enjoyed a work on Shakespeare
so much since reading Kott thirty years ago' Jonathan Bate

'Funny and fluent' Fiona Shaw

'The living chronicle of a relationship: his own passionate and
turbulent love affair with Shakespeare . . . In him Dromgoole
has found a universal guru, a balm for his hurt mind, a human
hero and a cheeky accomplice' *Independent on Sunday*

'A gloriously readable account of his lifelong rough-and-tumble
passion for Shakespeare' *Daily Telegraph*

'Fresh, funny, self-mocking and alive' *Scotsman*

'It mixes loving yet temperate appreciation with telling and often
hilarious memoir, cumulatively creating a refreshingly original
explanation of why this bard actually is immortal' *The Times*

'A passionate, often very funny account' *Economist*

ABOUT THE AUTHOR

Dominic Dromgoole is Artistic Director of the Globe Theatre.
He has been a passionate Shakespearean since birth.

DOMINIC DROMGOOLE

Will and Me

How Shakespeare Took Over My Life

PENGUIN BOOKS

PENGUIN BOOKS

Published by the Penguin Group
Penguin Books Ltd, 80 Strand, London WC2R ORL, England
Penguin Group (USA) Inc., 375 Hudson Street, New York, New York 10014, USA
Penguin Group (Canada), 90 Eglinton Avenue East, Suite 700, Toronto, Ontario, Canada M4P 2Y3
(a division of Pearson Penguin Canada Inc.)
Penguin Ireland, 25 St Stephen's Green, Dublin 2, Ireland
(a division of Penguin Books Ltd)
Penguin Group (Australia), 250 Camberwell Road, Camberwell, Victoria 3124, Australia
(a division of Pearson Australia Group Pty Ltd)
Penguin Books India Pvt Ltd, 11 Community Centre, Panchsheel Park, New Delhi – 110 017, India
Penguin Group (NZ), 67 Apollo Drive, Mairangi Bay, Auckland 1310, New Zealand
(a division of Pearson New Zealand Ltd)
Penguin Books (South Africa) (Pty) Ltd, 24 Sturdee Avenue, Rosebank, Johannesburg 2196, South Africa

Penguin Books Ltd, Registered Offices: 80 Strand, London WC2R ORL, England

www.penguin.com

First published by Allen Lane 2006
Published in Penguin Books 2007
1

Copyright © Dominic Dromgoole, 2006
All rights reserved

The moral right of the author has been asserted

Typeset by Rowland Phototypesetting Ltd, Bury St Edmunds, Suffolk
Printed in England by Clays Ltd, St Ives plc

ISBN: 978-0-141-02007-5

For
Sasha, Siofra, Grainne and Cara
who made the world better and brighter
And for
Jen, Pat, Sean and Jessica,
who brought me into it

Contents

Foreword   viii

The Life   1

The Walk   213

Acknowledgements   293

Foreword

Ten years ago, on the brink of a huge new relationship, I was walking around a book fair in Glastonbury, with my beloved. My eye fell on something which made me feel like a pirate falling on a casket of treasure. In a tatty box, padded out with cheap cloth, were forty small booklets bound in battered red leather, the gold lettering on their spines faded with age and use. It was easy to see the ghost of each title, however faint: *Othello*, *Hamlet*, *King Lear*, *Twelfth Night*, and on . . . In mounting disbelief, I looked at each, and counted them all up. They were all there, all the plays, all the poems. It was the celebrated Temple edition from the end of the nineteenth century. Each beautiful little book – big enough to fill a large hand, small enough to slip into a back pocket – and they were all there. It was a miracle. I looked at the price, and they were cheap, around forty pounds, but not cheap enough for my impoverished state. With a heavy heart, I had to leave them there. Yet a couple of months later, on Christmas Day, I unwrapped my final present and there they all were again. My passion and excitement had been noted and remembered. It was my favourite ever gift.

Only a few years ago, my young family moved somewhere new. There were many boxes to unpack, including several with gifts from my mother-in-law. Piles of crockery, linen and household necessities were drawn out. At the bottom, there was a stack of red books, dully designed from the 1950s. There were twenty of them, each containing two of Shakespeare's plays. It was the Windsor edition, stolid with schoolteacher introductions, pedantic footnotes and Victorian melodramatic drawings. We drew them out with surprise and pleasure and placed them carefully before we had arranged anything else. Immediately a sense of security and warmth settled on the house.

All my life I've encountered different versions of the *Complete Works*. The classic single volume, a thousand pages long, two columns to each page, packed with close type like the Bible, has popped up everywhere. The first copy I learned speeches from was of that ilk; the same type has hung around all the different houses I've passed through; on holidays or long walks the fat copy has been carried for an innate sense of direction. There was the beautiful Riverside edition that came out in the mid-eighties, a broad and elegant book, with wafer-thin pages that fell from your hand like water; the recent Oxford edition bristling with textual rigour and surprise; and, for the intellectually exacting and the seriously wealthy, there were the collected Arden editions with their kooky folkloric covers and their insanely exhaustive footnotes. Wherever it is, whether in home, school, shop, workplace, yacht, airplane or space rocket, the *Complete Works* has the most remarkable effect. It lends weight and ballast to its surroundings. It works like a benign bomb hurling out, not destruction, but invisible waves of laughter and wisdom and cultural and human value. It animates every object in its vicinity with an extra preciousness, and an extra worth.

It is a book which has guided me through my life, its weight of exhilaration and insight hovering beside me as I blunder from one thing to another. This book is a record of that journey in that company. It is not like many another Shakespeare book (and there is no shortage of others at the moment). It pretends to no scientific or objective authority in its understanding of Shakespeare. I had thought of writing one such, but soon realized that the field was so crowded, and with so many wonders, that to attempt anything of that nature would be like entering an elite Sudoku championship with no head for numbers. The book has no shortage of convictions or insights about Shakespeare's life and his work, but they emerge from my enthusiasm and my own instincts as a theatre man, rather than from long hours in Reading Rooms.

One of the joys of working on Shakespeare is encountering the enthusiasm and excitement of others. It is an international passion, and recent years have thrown up a bumper crop of its fruits. Stephen Greenblatt's *Will in the World* is a wonderful, almost poetic meditation on the relationship between the life and the work; James

Shapiro's *1599* is a thrilling re-creation of one pivotal year in the history of England and the life of Shakespeare; Frank Kermode's *The Age of Shakespeare* is full of telling insights about how the time and the words danced together; Stanley Wells' *Shakespeare: For All Time* has a wonderful rendition of how Shakespeare's plays have fared in the world after his death. Beyond those books and several others, there have been many excellent biographies; an underrated one from Anthony Holden, one packed with fact and new perspectives from Katherine Duncan Jones, and the peerless one, full of rubbish and glories, from Anthony Burgess. I wholeheartedly recommend all these books for anyone interested in the subject. Yet this was not the sort of book that I set out to write.

My story is of how I have stumbled, shambled and occasionally glided through a life with Shakespeare as a guide. And how, having entered the same field of endeavour, the theatre, I have been afforded certain understandings into how his plays work, and how his life may have panned out. One can't claim to be right in these matters – the world of Shakespeare is too comprehensive, too exploded and too relative for those who want to be tinnily right. We simply throw our understandings into the air and see what lands with whom, and whether it makes them happy.

The Life

poetry in the cot

Shakespeare was printed on me early. My father was, and is, a great believer in poetry. The rhythms, the form, the music all hold magic properties for him. It still bubbles up out of him, and no poetry as much as Shakespeare. He knows whole scenes off by heart and, if there's no one to stop him, will reel them off. He lowers his head slightly, darkens his brow and, with a deep, steady tread, walks you through the verse. He hits the consonants hard and regular, pressing each word into you with a measured force. It is a mesmerizing act, as if summoning up some inner energy to suit the provenance of the words. A druidic performance. Whenever he does it, even now when I can appreciate the level of con in the act, it still sends a shiver straight through me.

He wasted no time in impressing it on us. He kicked off when we were still in the cot. He started with Racine and Corneille. Book in hand, he walked gently to and fro, to and fro, in our shared bedroom, pouring seventeenth-century French alexandrines into our empty faces and soothed ears. The absurdity of what he did struck even him before too long. Probably when we started to squawk 'What?' from our bunk beds. So he Anglicized his offerings and centred them round Shakespeare.

There are Arabic storytellers in the marketplace in Marrakech, the Jmaa El Fnaa. Crowds of up to 300 surround these hooded figures, as they pace back and forth, back and forth, their faces monkishly hidden. In a light, almost shrill tone they chant out the tales of the Arabian Nights, improvising in perfect rhythm around a stock memory of several thousand lines. The last true inheritors of Homer. Their audiences sit and stand spellbound, as the performances continue for hours.

Though I'm sure my father packed in his renditions after ten minutes, I imagine him as one of those figures. His feet padding softly to and fro to an iambic beat, entrancing the six ears of my brother, my sister and me. Letting us close our eyes and drift away on the soft cushion and heartbeat of blank verse. I sang the blues to my own children. Badly. But it pillowed them to sleep in the same way, and its warm sorrows wiped their own cares clean.

Whenever I hear Shakespeare spoken I compare it to my father's way. It rarely measures. When I hear a bad, old-school actor bombasting his way through it, it sounds like lazy, stupid violence. When I hear an arrogant youth break it up into television mutters, it breaks my heart they are so many miles beneath what they are feigning to be above. But when it is spoken in a warm, steady human voice, with accuracy and with love, then I feel at home again.

middle England, radio waves and my mother's inheritance

Shakespeare stains every surface of English life. He is woven into our history, our most private selves, even our landscape. Since our primary tool for understanding and expressing all these is our language, and since he dominates that language so completely, it is foolish to underestimate his influence. Many of the words we use he invented; many of the clichés we fall back on were his new-minted truths; and many of the sentiments we live by he first thought, or coined with a brilliance none since has matched. Shakespeare's great volcanic eruption of words carved out the verbal landscape within which we have lived ever since. Other languages and other cultures have vitalized and reinvigorated that wordscape, but, thus far, they are only pitching their tents on Shakespeare's broad plain.

He is everywhere, popping up in odd places at odd times, with a ubiquity that would tire, if he was not always so elusive and out of reach. He has danced through significant moments in my life, and illuminated nooks and crannies of my parents' lives as well. Since Shakespeare permeates so far, he works as a wonderful aide-mémoire. Ask anyone about each of their contacts with his work, and, unbidden, disparate memories will pop up like magic mushrooms in a September meadow. Certain experiences are common to everyone: their first visit to a play, their first encounter on television, on a cinema screen, on the radio, the school play, studying at school, hearing quotations and phrases. Ask everyone who they were with at each moment they encountered Shakespeare, and what their relationships were, and a web of family warmth and family resentment, first love and tired indifference, filial gratitude and parental responsibility will start to spread around them. However dull the production or tedious the lesson, the contact with Shakespeare torches the moment and fixes it in the mind.

My mother and father's contacts with Shakespeare formed much of our childhood mythology. And beyond them my grandparents. My mother's father came from Witney, near Stratford. Fastidiously reserved, and always old, in the days when people grew old, before they started going on cruises and dyeing their hair and drinking alcopops, he would sit for long hours in a chair reading his Shakespeare and watching cricket on the television. When he spoke of Shakespeare, his face would spark up and his voice would tremble. He went to Stratford many times as a boy and talked to me of seeing the same crude Elizabethan boy's desk in the Stratford Grammar School that I saw seventy years later on a childhood trip. He took many walks and bike rides around that area in the early 1900s. He used to say that, if Shakespeare hadn't existed, someone else would have emerged from that area producing poetry and plays of similar quality, since the land was so uniquely beautiful.

Beyond the processed tweeness of the Cotswolds, there is a heart-soothing quality to that landscape, with its low, rolling valleys and gently curving hills, rich in woodland, in wild scrubby grass and scutty weeds and flowers. It's not only the modern world that treats this area as a lost Arcadia – even in the seventeenth century, they were harking back to a time of greater innocence there. The Forest of Arden, a zone of geographical and internal myth for Shakespeare, since it was his mother's maiden name, was once supposed to have spread like a belt across the middle of England. Within its shade nature and magic abided together, concocting between them the soul of England. Shakespeare's friend Drayton, a fellow Warwickshire poet, wrote of the goddess Diana hunting there with her 'dishevelled Nymphs attired in youthful green'.

There's a wonderful anglomorphic tendency in poets from the Middle Ages on. 'Sir Orfeo' puts the Orpheus myth in Winchester, Drayton grafts Greek gods into Warwickshire, and Shakespeare throughout his career has no shame in bringing all kinds of myth and humanity – Greek, Roman, Venetian – into the circle of his English wit. There's even a barmy nearby myth that Adam and Eve were resident in the Vale of Evesham in Gloucestershire. It's ridiculous, though recent research has proved it not too far wide of the mark. The African savannah where the human was incubated over tens of thousands of years, and where mitochondrial Eve herself would have shambled about, was supposedly most like the gentle English landscape of today. Beside the Highlands of Scotland, it looks toytown; beside any of the world's greater dramatic landscapes, it looks Teletubbies. In nature's more stupendous stage sets, the human looks lost, desolate and alone. But in the English Midlands, the horizon is far away, but can be walked. A figure can be seen within it. Within its gentle shapes, we look on speaking terms with nature.

As my grandfather lay dying in a grotty nursing home in Dorchester, an aunt provided him with a large black and white print of stone breakers. It hung on the wall over his bed. He told us he had seen such stone breakers working on the road between Witney and Stratford where he used to walk and bicycle as a boy. Such memories were treasured, since the end of his childhood was blasted away by the maelstrom of the First World War. He survived the Somme, but lost his closest and best-loved brother there. He never mentioned his presence in the war. My mother didn't know he had fought until after his death. He lived out the purpose of the popular war song: 'And when they ask us, how dangerous it was / Oh we'll never tell them, no we'll never tell them'. Long after his death, my mother found a brief account of his early life. It finishes with an adapted quote from *Julius Caesar*, 'Whilst in France on the Somme in 1916 I cycled over to see my brother on two successive Sundays. After the second visit, I knew I would never see him again. He was killed by a long-range shell in the rear trenches. There was a knock on my brother's door on the night of his death. His name appears on the Witney war memorial. He was the noblest Davis of them all.' In his brief memoir, when my grandfather needed words to lean on to describe the most wordlessly painful moment of his life, he leaned on Shakespeare. By coincidence the words that Mark Antony goes on to use to describe the slain Brutus further,

> His life was gentle, and the elements
> So mix'd in him that Nature might stand up
> And say to all the world 'This was a man!'

were used at my other grandfather's funeral. For a generation of men who had seen a slew of tyrants come and go across the world stage – Mao, Stalin, Hitler, Hirohito, Franco, Mussolini – it's not surprising that the words of praise for an honorable assassin should have such a rich resonance.

After the war, my grandfather met his wife and carried out a courtship attending Shakespeare plays at the Birmingham Rep. It would have been very new – just opened by Barry Jackson, a theatrical manager of the early twentieth century, who brought standards of consistency and commitment to his theatres, wiping away the scrappiness of Victorian and the decadence of Edwardian theatre. They always talked of Shakespeare plays they had seen there, remembering exquisite productions and an extraordinary company of actors that included a young Ralph Richardson, later to be one of the great Shakespearean actors of the century, and Gwen Ffrangcon Davies (a particular favourite of my grandfather). His stories about this delicate young ingénue with a ferocious spirit were great, but hard to credit until Ffrangcon Davies turned up on *Desert Island Discs* almost seventy years later. She was touching 100, shortly before her death. Her Juliet was legendary, and she was asked if she still remembered any Shakespeare. She immediately charged off into a breathtaking version of:

> Gallop apace, you fiery-footed steeds,
> Towards Phoebus' lodgings; such a waggoner
> As Phaeton would whip you to the west,
> And bring in cloudy night immediately. –
> Spread thy close curtain, love-performing night!
> That rude day's eyes may wink, and Romeo
> Leap to these arms, untalked of and unseen . . .
> Come night; – come Romeo, – come thou day in night
> For thou will lie upon the wings of night
> Whiter than new snow on a raven's back. –
> Come gentle night – come loving black browed night,
> Give me my Romeo . . .

She sounded fourteen. Her old voice lost its wobbly quavering and refound the clarity of youth. As breathless, joyful and fertile of mind as any young girl in love. It was a door in time.

In the early years of their marriage, my grandparents did a lot of amateur acting, and when they later moved to Bristol they joined a Shakespeare Society. This was in the days when culture was judged as crucial to health as iron in the diet: long before it was shunted away towards minority and inaccessible arts channels. Culture was the means by which the working class bettered themselves and the middle class kept their house in order. For my grandparents and my parents, culture was something you were given with your daily glass of milk, and at the centre of that health-giving was Shakespeare. My mother was born into the seemingly stable between-wars home of a headmaster and his wife. That stability was a mask, with private passions buried beneath public respectability. The rigid mask of English reserve was prevalent everywhere in the 1930s, as wild behaviour, Moulimixed with an overpowering sense of historical foreboding, set hearts racing behind starched shirts. It must have been a weird time to be a child, as the English carried on with their *thés dansants* and bowls and Shakespeare Societies, while over the horizon the world brimmed over with fascism and communism and anarchism and all the strange mutations of the modern. Somehow the English pottered on, blithe and bonny, until that mask was shattered by the arrival of the Second World War.

It's hard to know if Shakespeare would be quite so tightly hard-wired into the English psyche had it not been for World War II. He would certainly still be there. But it's hard to know if we would grip on to him so fiercely. For my mother and her parents, during those dark days of blitz and bombing, English culture was one of the main reasons for fighting Hitler's Germany, and many felt that Shakespeare was synonymous with that culture. The radio was listened to avidly. Patriotic songs and sentiments poured out to solidify the spirit of the nation. In the finer strain of Shakespeare's thoughts – 'This royal throne of kings, this sceptred isle' from *Richard II* or 'Now all the youth of England are on fire' from *Henry V* – people found an older and more solid authority to substantiate their faith in what they were doing.

Each culture needed an icon at that time to help explain their reasons for sacrificing their sons. America's icon of democracy was the hard-bitten cynic, the Humphrey Bogart archetype. The man who had emerged from the Depression and the New Deal stripped dry of illusions and with no time for bullshit. The man who says a sharp and final No! to any half-baked scheme to make humans buy into some fantasy of communal endeavour. The United Kingdom had Shakespeare, the fountain of the democratic spirit itself, the writer who gives such universal respect to all his characters, whether brothel-creepers or sainted kings, that he exemplifies in play after play how all humans stand together. An intellectual could appreciate his respect for freedom and for the individual life. A less cerebral approach could enjoy how often he celebrates going abroad and putting the boot into the continentals.

Shakespeare in the patriotic vein was much quoted at the time. Laurence Olivier and Ralph Richardson and many other famous actors were discharged from the forces so they could travel with the Old Vic Company around England to army camps and elsewhere. Churchill, and all the propagandists fighting against the insane modernist simplifications of Goebbels, saw the theatre at that moment as a source of strength, a stiffener of sinews. The right for us to enjoy watching men in tights warbling verse, and elderly ladies faking youth in lurid wigs, was what we were fighting for. In 1944, while V2 rockets were still bombarding London, Olivier's *Henry V* opened in the cinema. It was an extraordinary piece of propaganda. The flying missiles – arrows thickening the air as they flocked towards the French – reversed the direction of the missiles heading so perilously at that moment towards the English. Also there was the glorious rhetoric of the St Crispin's Day speech:

> Old men forget; yet all shall be forgot,
> But he'll remember with advantages
> What feats he did that day: then shall our names,
> Familiar in their mouths as household words, –
> Harry the King, Bedford and Exeter,
> Warwick and Talbot, Salisbury and Gloster, –

and how each quoted city name would resound in the hearts of the English and fill them up with a fresh sense of pride for their past, their present and their future,

Be in their flowing cups freshly remember'd.
This story shall the good man teach his son;
And Crispin Crispian shall ne'er go by,
From this day to the ending of the world,
But we in it shall be remembered,
We few, we happy few, we band of brothers;
For he today that sheds his blood with me
Shall be my brother; be he ne'er so vile,
This day shall gentle his condition:
And gentlemen in England now a-bed
Shall think themselves accursed they were not here;
And hold their manhoods cheap while any speaks
That fought with us upon Saint Crispin's day.

This was so resonant of Churchill's 'never in the field of human conflict, was so much owed by so many to so few' speech in praise of the young pilots who fought in the Battle of Britain that the parallel was there for all to see. Churchill understood the weird corner of the English heart that wants to be Horatius on the bridge defending Rome from thousands of enemy, the us-against-the-world impulse. He also knew no one had articulated it better than Shakespeare and stole from him mercilessly. But even he can't match the cheeky, light, fresh heroism of the young Henry. There is something so endearingly childish about that 'Harry the King', you want to jump out of your seat and join in. It's written into our genetic code, that speech, and those sentiments. Love it or loathe it, it's part of us and still stirs the blood and pricks the tears. The women of Normandy have an extraordinary phrase for the beginning of their menstruation, 'Les Anglais ont débarqué' (the English have landed). It's testimony to a millennium of the English expressing those sentiments in action.

The *Henry V* film was loved and applauded by all apart from my grandmother, who disliked Olivier, contending that he wasn't an actor, 'just a show off'. The Old Vic had been bombed in London in 1942, and one of the places the company visited was the Theatre Royal in Bristol. My grandfather would buy tickets for these productions with money earned by my mother from appearing in radio plays as a child actor. The obligation of the rest of her family to her gave her a special thrill.

The *Complete Works* sat in the centre of my mother's home. It was the family bible. It had a soft red leather cover, Moroccan leather, and was weather-beaten by devoted usage, yet it exuded comfort and value. It was permanently available to anyone, and my mother used to love to dip in. *Saturday Night Theatre*, an early series of prestigious radio broadcasts, was an event for her whole family. They would all gather round the old wooden monstrosity, built like a tank, as buzzy and excited as if they were going out. They dressed up for the occasion. It would often be a Shakespeare production. This may seem absurd from a distance, a family gathering in stiff suits and skirts, cups of Horlicks in hand, to listen to the crackly distant music of Shakespeare coming alive in their living rooms, but millions gathered in millions of front rooms to do the same thing. The listening was sophisticated and picky; different directors would be keenly antici-pated; others who indulged in too many extra sound effects would be quickly lambasted. There was one production of *Julius Caesar* when my mother delighted her father by reciting many of the lines alongside the radio. He offered a gentle compliment but was clearly glowing. To see a relish for Shakespeare igniting in a child is an assuring joy. You know they are walking into a world of kindness and plenty.

When my mother started secondary school, she went to see a lower-school production of *A Midsummer's Night Dream*. She was sick with envy at the girl who played Puck, and the envy cemented her desire to be close to the action. Something about speaking those lines boldly in front of other people looks to a child like a form of enfranchisement, a further step on the ladder of being fully human. She speaks often of her first lessons on Shakespeare with a Miss Brown. She'll never forget opening her book of *Julius Caesar* and being asked to read the first lines to the class:

Hence! Home you idle creatures, get you home

It was another rite of passage. She remembers the class, the light in the room, the other pupils, Miss Brown's tight bun.

Later, they moved on to *The Merchant of Venice*, a play whose characters she found less gripping, but she was starting to fall in love with the poetry:

> How sweet the moon light sleeps upon this bank
> Here will we sit and let the sounds of music
> Creep in our ears. Soft stillness and the night
> Become the touches of sweet harmony.
> Sit, Jessica. Look how the floor of heaven
> Is thick inlaid with patines of bright gold;
> There's not the smallest orb which thou beholdst
> But in his motion like an angel sings,
> Still quiring to the young eyed cherubims
> Such harmony is in immortal souls
> But, whilst this muddy vesture of decay
> Doth grossly close it in, we cannot hear it.

We all need a sugar rush of sweetness to bounce our spirits up higher at different times. As a kid it's Coke from a slim glass bottle on a hot day; as a youth it's the milky sluice of a long first kiss; a little later it's the cooing and crooning of a popular melody; but at a certain moment only a good rush of sublime poetry will do. When your soul is starting to flex its muscles and wants to be taken for a walk, only poetry can match its pace.

Slowly, through the gentle nudging of Miss Brown – a covert subversive like so many tightly wrapped English teachers – my mother started to understand where Shakespeare was taking her, and how joyous the journey was going to be, away from the war, and ration books, and families squabbling. Imagination and compassion, the two tent-poles of humanism, bloomed in her. And it was through those virtues that she was able to throw off the dogma and the strictures of the organized religion in which she had been brought up. It was a long process and it cost thought, but Shakespeare answered her instincts. Instincts that didn't involve old men with long white beards, mild women in blue with inclined heads or golden young men with bleeding stigmata.

In concert with atheism came love, the fact of it arriving at the same moment as the understanding of it. The fact of it came via dashing young renegades in uniform wanting to show her the gorillas in Bristol zoo for the afternoon; the understanding came via the sonnets. She was almost as passionate about this verse form as she was about chaps. They stimulated for her, as they have for a thousand literary detectives since, a passionate interest in Shakespeare's life and loves. Who was the young man being addressed? How deep did the relationship go? Who was the dark lady? They also acted as a window for her own passions.

She began her professional life as an actress working in regional rep, including one not-so-glamorous year in Weston-Super-Mare. Then she escaped from postwar Britain to Africa, working in a potty small theatre in Nairobi called the Donovan Maule. Situated above a grocer's shop, it was patronized by the aristocratic white trash of Kenya's notorious Happy Valley set in all their excessive finery. Then, returning to Bristol, she joined the Rapier Players at the Little Theatre, and started to hang around the posher set at the Bristol Old Vic. The big swinging dick of that crowd was Peter O'Toole, who sat in the centre of a fertile gang that included Tom Stoppard and Harold Pinter and John Boorman. It was O'Toole who first told her about a radical production of *Julius Caesar* he had seen at Oxford which bore so little relation to the original play that they hadn't even put Shakespeare's name in the programme. And of the man who had directed it. Soon after, my mother met that director, my father. One of their first points of contact was Shakespeare. My mother was dazzled by my father's knowledge and love of Shakespeare, my father vice versa. For their honeymoon, rather than a grand tour through Europe, their mutual passion sent them to Stratford to see O'Toole as Shylock. They always spoke about his beauty, and the vicious energy of his sibilant voice as he spat out: 'Hath not a Jew eyes . . .'

The acting was done by the time my parents married, and for her next few years everything was obliterated by the arrival of my brother and sister and me.

shipwrecks, Israel and the misunderstandings of children

It's hard to know how a man as landlocked as Warwickshire Will came to have such sympathy with the shipwrecked. It's a trope that runs from *The Comedy of Errors* through *Twelfth Night*, to *Pericles* and *The Tempest*. It was a common feature in many of the lurid adventure stories of the day, quickie hack pamphlets about encounters in strange corners of the world after rickety boats had failed in stormy seas. 'My Hell with the Cannibals', 'My Heaven with the Dusky Maidens', that sort of thing – not a million miles from the alien abduction stories of today.

It may also have been a specific emotional dislocation for the disasters that befell Will's family. For some reason his father, John Shakespeare, an upwardly mobile glover who pursued position and influence with great eagerness through Will's early life, suddenly went into free fall in the late 1570s, when his son was fifteen. Having been an alderman, piled high with chains and robes and silly hats, he was removed from the town council. Whether this was for non-payment of debts, or for breaking the law (apparently he was crossing the lines of the day by both butchering his animals and converting them into swanky gloves), or for his covert papistry, is uncertain. But what is sure is that a weight of disgrace settled on the previously prosperous household. Shakespeare thus joined the great line of playwrights and novelists whose fathers have failed them in early adulthood. Dickens, Chekhov, Ibsen and Arthur Miller all had fathers whose heady ambitions led to bankruptcy and disgrace. Each later took their parent's entrepreneurial energy and social imagination and transformed it. Yet for the young Will, preening himself within the shelter of his father's position and hopeful for a life of bourgeois comfort, the effect must have been shattering when he was plucked out of his grammar school and made to work himself. It was his own shipwreck.

Yet washing up on strange shores and having to improvise a new existence isn't only a metaphor for those whose parents have gone bust. It is true for any moment of loss or confusion. The first day at school, arriving in a new metropolis, embarking on a new love affair. There's a potential shipwreck round every corner. My family created a situation that was closer to the literal.

We were in Israel in 1967, and I was a thoughtful and tubby three-year-old. My memories of Israel are my first visual ones. The contrast between Tel Aviv and the small Somerset farm I grew up on was so striking it's not surprising the images are secure. They are fragments and confused but they are there. Most vivid was our arrival. The sound of a thousand voices belting out the Israeli national anthem as our ship pulled into Haifa; the way the song and the soaring emotion within it seemed to pull the ship into dock; the tune itself and the Shalom Aleikham that always followed; the fierce tears and greedy clutching when people remet. Beyond that are the scattered banalities a three-year-old recalls – new, square, brutish blocks of flats; oranges on a kibbutz; meat off a barbecue; the heavy heat of the sun; my brother returning from a Hebrew-speaking school in tears having been bullied all day. It probably would have remained a light smear on the memory, a strange summer, had it not been for the war.

My father was directing *Othello* at the Habimah, Israel's National Theatre. It was the third summer in a row that he had disappeared there to direct. My mother was sick of being left alone with three puling children for long summers with little to offer beyond a bus trip to Burnham-on-Sea. She had insisted that this year we all travelled out. We were happy to all be together, and the cruise out was brimming over with joy. We met the captain twice, which felt as if God himself had chubbed our cheeks. And Israel was full of the company of actors, which is some of the best company in the world. We were allowed to poke around back-stage, which for a child is a special pleasure. At one moment you can be on the set, acting the part and walking around in someone else's imagination, the next moment you pass through a door to tatty flats and black masking, and see how that imagination has been constructed. For a child to be both within and without a magic trick, and to have an insight into how it works is dangerously empowering.

My father always treated his rehearsal rooms as a temple. The exclusion of outsiders was as firm as the most extreme mosque. For some, it's a seminar room (the deadliest); for some a party (the most fun, with the most variable results); for some it's a therapy session (avoid like the bubonic plague); and for many it's a knocking shop (be selective). But for the best it is often a temple. Something special and magical takes place in there, and the air around it has to be carefully looked after to ensure anything is possible. This doesn't mean everyone prays or takes off their shoes and pads around with Peter Brookish Obi-Wan faux religiosity. It means you treat it with respect and humility. And you don't allow kids in. Which only maximized our desire to build a tunnel.

We met the other actors, who treated Shakespeare with the same devotional enthusiasm as my parents. Israel in 1967 had the innocent enthusiasm for the classics of a country that was improvising its own identity. How you played and how you received *Othello* in some way defined who you were. It was a long way from the tourist trundle of productions in Stratford. And all this was going on so close, and with such passion, and yet behind such firmly closed doors. We floated around in frustrated limbo outside.

Maybe it was that limboid state that meant the brewing of a war passed us by. Maybe it was just the natural blithe ignorance of infants. We may have noted a growing bellicosity in the air. But when the panic struck, it struck in a rush. We were at the airport. There were crowds. There was screaming. A great mass of hysterical bodies was swirling around and within itself playing a frantic game of musical airplanes. There were three times too many people for the number of seats to get out. Everyone was using everything at their disposal – violence, tears and money – to claim them before the music stopped. Even from this distance, I can recall a strong sensibility of 'Oh no, not this again' that enraged the hall, a bubbling anger against history. We might well have found no way out, had not my brother been carrying a very English, very Victorian teddy bear. Six or seven brutes in blazers from the British Embassy spotted it. They forced their way through to us, formed a rugby scrum around us and literally mauled their way through the crowd, scattering non-Brits fore and aft in their determination to get women and children out first. I seem to remember sitting down on a light airplane next to an elderly Viennese lady, a Peggy Ashcroft type, who gave me chocolates. I remember enjoying the excitement, the warmth of everyone and the chocolates. It was only once the plane was in the air that my brother and my sister and I noticed my father wasn't there.

We were told that he had stayed behind to look after his Mercedes. Though we knew he was proud of his car, even we must have thought that reflected slightly skewed values. Maybe we had a sense it wasn't the whole truth. Maybe we thought he was staying behind for Shakespeare and a fuller feast on the delights we had only nibbled. Maybe we could guess even then that work can be a greater intoxicant than love; and that one's loyalty to one's art can in a moment of crisis be greater than one's loyalty to one's family. It wasn't until much later that I learned another truth.

We flew into Cyprus, where there was no welcome for us and little comfort. We were without money, or friends, or much sense of where we were. For a week we were installed in a military barracks, sharing a room with about twenty others. At the end of that week, my brother, who was older, more conscious and less thrilled by the whole thing than I, heard on the radio that an Irishman had been killed in the war. He exploded in grief. Since there was no way to contact my father, there was no way to stem the tide of his tears. Soon after, we were evicted from the barracks – now overfull – and found ourselves sleeping on a beach. My mother maintained a brave face through about two days of this, until we ran out of food, when she dissolved into tears as well. There we were, four washed-up bits of flotsam on a Mediterranean shore, never knowing when the broken pieces of a family jigsaw would be put back together.

We were a little and collapsed version of Viola, or Ferdinand, or Pericles, or Antipholus, or any of Shakespeare's shipwrecked children, washed by the sea, and by our tears. As Shakespearean as it comes, and redeemed by a Shakespearean moment of charity. A French communist walked by and saw us – three children merrily burying their weeping mother in the sand. He acted with the suddenness of the good – unloading a bundle of money on us and forcing us back to his home, where we stayed for a further two weeks. It was an idyllic time, the freedom of an island, the sun and the sea, the escape from tension, and the absence of patriarchal authority. It was probably the first great lesson in how quick and light is the twist of the coin that can turn despair to joy. Extreme reversals of fortune always play strangely in the theatre. When Shakespeare's comedies miraculously resolve at the end, with children finding parents, brothers united with sisters, and husbands wives, a tidal wave of disbelief runs through an audience. Through their brains. Yet in their hearts and their instincts, they know how moments of extreme despair are often redeemed by accidental grace, or benign coincidence. This is one of the several tensions running through the end of any comedy, disbelief and recognition in the same moment.

Meanwhile, my father continued with rehearsals for as long as he could, then found employment entertaining the troops. Not knowing quite what would suit Israeli conscripts, he fell back on what he knew best. So soldiers, weary from the whizz flash bang of modern warfare, would return from a battlefield of tanks and artillery to find my father, standing on the back of a truck, giving his very fine version of 'Once more unto the breach, dear friends, once more . . .' from *Henry V*. As beautiful things often prosper in unlikely settings, it was deeply appreciated. The cadence of gathering storm within that speech, its forced insertion of courage into the nerve-ends that flap the feeblest, could still thrill the blood and stiffen the sinews, in the war of another century and another continent. My father told of how, after one performance, a man was pointed out to him sitting on the sidelines. He was a bull of a man, spoken of with reverence by the others. He had fought with great courage that day, done terrible things, and stayed calm while all beside fell to pieces. My father watched him as he undid the laces on his boots. One lace broke and pulled away in the man's hand. Slowly his whole body began to roll a little, then heave, then shake, as big fat tears coursed down his cheeks. At the end of the war my father was given a gold medal by the Habimah theatre company, a small star of Israel with a cross in the centre.

When we were reunited, it was with joy, yet in a different Israel from the one we had left. Even the faulty antennae of a self-absorbed three-year-old could pick that up. The wonderful, plangent sorrow of the mass singing, the fragile throb that arced through their national anthem, had been replaced by a loud triumphalism, by a brute force. The warmth and easy physical sharing of the kibbutz spirit was replaced by an excited confidence, a thrill in victory. Everyone we met, it seemed, had won the war. They had been in the crucial plane or the crucial tank, or at the crucial meeting. I loved it. There were guns and there was machismo by the bucketful. More than enough for a boy who liked to hold up his arms and make machine-gun noises. We joined in with the feeling of mass contribution. I felt my actions on the beach in Cyprus had swung it. That something precious had been lost in victory couldn't have occurred to me.

Twenty-five-odd years later, I was drinking in the pub beneath a theatre I ran in London, the Bush, a small but influential theatre that produced an exclusive diet of new plays. An elderly actor joined us for a natter. After he heard my name, he started reminiscing about his own time at the Habimah. 'Your father worked there a couple of years before me. Oh, yes, they all remembered him. Remembered him well. There was one girl who couldn't get over him. What was her name? Can't remember. She was Desdemona, that's it. He was screwing his Desdemona.' I assumed that peculiar facial expression where you pretend to have known for years something that has just landed like a bomb on your head. 'Yeah . . . he was,' I feebly offered. Old lies were crumbling inside my head. Somehow, drawing on that huge reservoir of infantile daftness that never seems to leave us, I had managed to go on buying the ludicrous story about staying behind to look after the Mercedes until I was almost thirty. My later rationalization that he had stayed behind for his art lessened in value. The real reason was at once more tawdry, and more joyous. He was in love with his Desdemona. The correspondences with *Othello* – war, Cyprus, a barracks, and now sexual jealousy around a Desdemona – flared up more brightly still.

Even that was not the end of the understanding. We peel and peel away the skins from the events of our youth in the effort to find some truth. I challenged my father later over lunch with the story about the Desdemona. He wouldn't deny that some shenanigans had occurred, but he said they were long over by the time we left for Cyprus. He said the reason he stayed was perverse, but automatic: 'I stayed because some obscure obtusity on my part would not allow me to seem to run away from anything.' Later in the same meal, where we were eating hot Thai food, he accidentally spooned two lethal chillies into his mouth. His face went red, then purple, then swelled up; sweat poured from his upper brow and tears down his cheeks. He looked as if he was about to explode. The waiters and the fellow diners started to get concerned about him. I started to worry about cardiac arrests. Eventually, after much heavy breathing, and cold water, he returned to normal. The restaurant breathed a sigh of relief. He then separated out his chillies from the rest of his curry, and proceeded to eat them slowly one by one. 'You've got to be kidding,' I said. 'I don't back down before a plate of oriental food,' he replied.

There's a perverse flintiness in the British and the Irish spirit, a refusal to be moved from one's path, no matter what trauma or mess is strewn in one's way. It was expressed most recently by the staunchly unimpressed manner in which the many cultures of London returned to work after various thugs had made such a terrible jigsaw of human flesh and human happiness on tubes and buses. Much of it is drawn from Shakespeare, who sucked much of it himself out of the marrow of Seneca, the Roman playwright who was the first great mouthpiece of stoicism. It is the exercising of a muscle which my father flexed in a war-torn London as a child, in a martial Israel as a man and with a plate of chillies with his grown son.

war, a Welsh village and a way through

It's a curiosity for such an essentially pacifist writer as Shakespeare that his name has come to be so attached to war. He wrote extensively of battle and understood its terrifying appeal. He knew about the adrenaline rush, the pursuit of fugitive honour and the sense of a unity beyond camaraderie. He also knew its cost, and how comprehensively it degraded the human. He could hardly avoid the realities of war – he had a burning and eruptive civil conflict going on all around him between Catholics and Protestants, and beyond that there was no shortage of biffing carrying on with the Netherlands and the Spanish. But he also knew and hugely valued the virtues of peace. Though he can't help but get caught up in the excitement of the fight, he never lets any but his most barmy characters sing hymns to it. He never takes sides with or against any of his creations, but when he allows a Faulconbridge or a Hotspur to blow off steam about how desperate they are to get into a fight and do a little biffing, you know he is observing with fond amusement the skinhead in the corner of the pub. When one of his elder statesmen puts the case for peace and prosperity, you know Shakespeare is echoing the views of the man he is happy to spend long hours drinking wine with. It is the latter strain of poetry that convinces. In the last act of *Henry V*, after all the violence has let its blood, and as Henry is preparing for the different trials of courtship, Shakespeare produces as close to a moral resolution as he ever does. The Duke of Burgundy pleads:

> . . . let it not disgrace me
> If I demand, before this royal view,
> What rub or what impediment there is

Why that the naked, poor and mangled Peace,
Dear nurse of arts, plenties and joyful births,
Should not in this best garden of the world,
Our fertile France, put up her lovely visage?
Alas she hath from France too long been chas'd!
And all her husbandry doth lie on heaps,
Corrupting in its own fertility.
Her vine, the merry cheerer of the heart,
Unpruned dies; her hedges even-pleach'd,
Like prisoners wildly overgrown with hair,
Put forth disorder'd twigs; her fallow leas
The darnel, hemlock and rank fumitory,
Doth root upon, while that the coulter rusts
That should deracinate such savagery;
The even mead, that erst brought sweetly forth
The freckled cowslip, burnet and green clover,
Wanting the scythe, all uncorrected, rank,
Conceives by idleness, and nothing teems
But hateful docks, rough thistles, kecksies, burs,
Losing both beauty and utility.
And as our vineyards, fallows, meads and hedges,
Defective in their natures, grow to wildness;
Even so our houses and ourselves and children
Have lost, or do not learn for want of time,
The sciences that should become our country . . .

He's writing on home turf here, about gardens and weeds and the fruit of the earth. The sense of husbandry denied, of nature running to seed, carries an extra moral weight from the Stratford boy. The speech does not hector, or screech, but carries a steady moral aplomb. A friend performed it at a Foreign Office do, in front of all the ambassadors to Britain. It was a cute choice. Despite this strain of pacifist sentiment, it is at times of war, when emotions are at their fiercest, and values sought out most urgently, that people seem to hunger for Shakespeare most greedily. It is a paradox his legacy has had to negotiate.

It was the Second World War which gave my father the 'obscure obtusity' that stopped him from running from battle in Israel and helped him get to the end of a blastingly hot curry. It also planted a passion for Shakespeare in him which would never stop blooming. For him the seed was inserted in a small, plain church hall in North Wales.

He had been evacuated there at the beginning of the war. He landed with a warm and generous-spirited family, full of a love of culture and a passion for poetry and song. From early in his visit their village was galvanized by one thing. Not the possibility of being flattened by German bombs, but the promised arrival of theatre stars in their village hall for a performance of *Macbeth*. The entire community became sick with over-excitement like small children on the day before a birthday. The great Lewis Casson and the even greater Sybil Thorndike were coming to their parish. It was a tour to bolster morale for the war effort, and it sent this particular community into a skittish whirl. They all read the play beforehand, argued over it in pubs, discussed it over the dining table. By the time the company arrived, the audience felt as if they had lived through the play several times already. That quality of anticipation can be a curse, but it can also be a huge boost. A feverish audience is always preferable to a dull one, and an exceptional one can provide a rocket fuel which sends an evening up to the stars.

There was no set, beyond some wobbly flats, and little lighting beyond bright or dark, but from the moment the actors were on, my father was transfixed. He sat there breathless, his guts twisting and turning in clenched excitement, thrilled by the story, terrified by its development, shocked by its conclusion, yet wanting it never to end. No matter the lack of scenery, or the shabbiness of the costumes: the actors said something was real, and the audience believed it. Macbeth saw a dagger, and my father saw it; Macbeth said,

<blockquote>
Now o'er the one half-world
Nature seems dead and wicked dreams abuse
The curtain'd sleep; witchcraft celebrates
Pale Hecate's offerings; and wither'd murder
Alarum'd by his sentinel, the wolf,
Whose howl's his watch, thus with his stealthy pace,
</blockquote>

With Tarquin's ravishing strides, towards his design
Moves like a ghost.

And for my father the lights went out, the roof came off, and all the stars hid their light, to leave a black night free for wolves and murderers to prowl in. It shaped a terror within him that he has never entirely rid himself of. For weeks afterwards he could not sleep and lay staring into the darkness, petrified of what the night might bring. It left him with a new appetite, for fear, for imagery, for sensation, for delight. It also locked in a desire to act and to be involved in the Shakespeare circus. People think children's shows have to be happy, full of vacant, smiling faces, worthy moral values and clappy songs. Rollocks. Children don't want happiness at the theatre. They want to be scared shitless and then see the lights come up. They want a nightmare that ends.

It sometimes seems half the world must have been in North Wales at that time, so many claim to have seen those legendary productions. They created an army of phantom fans. Beyond the batty and very British defiance of banging out 350-year-old plays to help a war effort, there must have been something electrifying for the actors. Largely West End boulevard performers, creaking around year by year in commercial dramas with tennis racquets and drinks cabinets and important telegrams, they must have been liberated by the return to the basics of the empty space, the voice like a sword and the shared imagination of an excited crowd.

His trip to Wales was a liberation for my father. His own father was a discreetly glamorous man, but he had buried his own artistry and culture beneath ten feet of solidified Victorian reserve long before my father was born. He gave little room to it in his house. There was a twinkle in his eye, but it was submerged beneath a fanatical attachment to the values of Empire and Britishness. Which was peculiar for a second-generation Irishman. That twinkle manifested in a streak of rebellion and wildness in his sons, encouraged by their mother, but it remained buried in him. For forty years I admired his face as you would a Roman statue, dignified and unmoving. On his death bed at the ripe old age of 104, he croakily asked me to bring Shakespeare's sonnets in for him, and asked me to recite certain specific ones. It was a surprise to me that he had that much literature in him. When I started reading to him he creased up in terrible sobs, his old body doubled over in childish tears. I hardly knew where to put myself. It felt like the dissolution of decades of repressed feeling. His wife, my father's mother, had died thirty years before. The poems were his silent communion with her. He said, after apologizing for his tears, that he couldn't bear to die, because he would miss his wife so. She had stayed alive in his imagination. When he went, she went.

When my father went to Wales, the poetry of the place, deliberate and accidental, revealed something to him. Shakespeare was the conduit for that energy. He returned to London during the second year of the war and started reading him avidly, and when the war was over sought out productions. Almost as many people as the tens of thousands who claim to have been in North Wales to see those crude touring shows also claim to have paid tuppence ha'penny to sit in the top gallery at the New Theatre in St Martin's Lane after the war. Here the Old Vic company, bombed out of their usual residence, settled for a series of productions in the late 1940s. For a brief and glorious period Laurence Olivier, John Gielgud and Ralph Richardson gave nation-defining performances of Shakespeare's great plays. Just as Shakespeare had locked the country into a sense of purpose during the war, so these definitive productions after it was over helped the country understand why the sacrifice had been worthwhile. All our sports might have been adopted by other countries, who had run away with all the trophies; the seat of international exchange might have moved from London to New York, leaving us impoverished and begging; the empire might have folded in on itself, leaving a map less pink; it might have been impossible to get a tin of processed meat without a ration card; all that might have been wrong and fucked up and miserable, but our theatre knights could still turn a thought on a breath in the middle of a Shakespearean line and break a thousand hearts at the same time. It was one thing the English could still do better than anyone else. When you read the exquisite and burnished prose of Kenneth Tynan describing these shows, you feel that passion and pride. However buried it is under Tynan's acidulous ostentation, you feel a pride that England was still free, and still itself. Tears were shed when Richardson as Falstaff met Olivier as Shallow in a

Gloucester garden in *Henry IV Part 2*. The whole nation had heard the 'chimes at midnight', and they had come through the other side to a new morning. To spend some of that morning in a West Country apple orchard with two characters representing all the bumbling, pompous, smalltown, baffled beauty of the English soil was to know afresh that there are some things that no Holocausts nor Hiroshimas nor Dresdens could ever snuff out.

Culture was one of the ways that the country helped put itself back together again after the fragmentation of the war. For my mother, with her family, it was sitting around the radio; for my father it was packing the gallery at the New. Certain bearings had been lost and were beyond recovery. The war dynamited the last etiquettes and mores which had struggled through the Great War and barely survived the twenties and the thirties. Now there was little time for them, and a new generation were out to reinvent the rules. God, who had been limping fairly acutely since the nineteenth century, was using a zimmer frame now. Political dreams had lost their sheen, as Stalin's realities robbed the brightness from the eyes of all but the maddest communists. Culture, literature and Shakespeare in particular were ways of trying to hold on to certain moral moorings since all the rest had been so clinically exploded. Exactly what those values were was up for grabs, and a burgeoning critical industry attacked the subject. Culture was studied with a renewed enthusiasm, as an army of unemployed and displaced theologians sought out a new vocation. And, whatever the confusion over ultimate values, instinct drew everyone to Shakespeare as the centre of that culture.

As soon as he could, my father started acting in school plays, turning in a Peto in *Henry IV* and a Porter in *Macbeth*. But school could not contain the freedom which had been bestowed by the topsy turvy of the war. He left early and bummed around, working hoopla on a fair and disappearing to Paris. Wherever he veered off to, he would be regularly brought home to leafy and staid Dulwich before erupting again. His life found purpose when he joined the Morley College Theatre School, a peculiar blend of young students and elderly professional actors. Their attitude to education was the brutal one of 'the only way to learn is on the job', and they plunged their students quickly into performances, touring Shakespeare around the London parks, and paying them peanuts. The productions were an odd mix of inspired and shoddy. The professional actors were largely on the downward slope of their careers.

At their worst they would stumble around the stage half-drunk, and lose their lines, improvising their way out of trouble in fluent Shakespearean, a language formed from the Moulimixing of all the parts they had played. At their best they would hit a strain of poetry and sing it, unencumbered by the interference of a concept or a director or even a passing thought. In that vein, they could slip into the groove of the author's intentions with a rough purity which buffed up the spirits of the forty or fifty sad faces sitting out in the rain. My father steered his way round their stormy areas and sailed happily through their purple patches, playing Theseus in *A Midsummer Night's Dream* and various parts in *The Winter's Tale*, *The Comedy of Errors* and *Doctor Faustus*. He joined a separate touring company, the Taverners, which travelled around the Northern pubs, playing Caliban from *The Tempest* to smoky rooms packed with pint-fuelled spectators. The enchantment he had felt in his Welsh church hall he was now able to work on others, night after night, in one ill-fitting room after another, much as touring companies had done since before Shakespeare's time, much as the Earl of Leicester's men would have done when they trucked up to Stratford and enchanted the soul of the boy Shakespeare.

Two insights were born out of these experiences for my father which pertained throughout his life and which passed by osmosis and lecture into me. The first arose from a moment in a production of *Doctor Faustus*. My father was in a scene the rhythm of which was constantly being interrupted by someone having to make an unnecessarily long entrance. The director and actors fussed and agonized over this for a day so, until in one rehearsal my father – the most juvenile member of the company – improvised two quick lines in perfect blank verse to cover the moment. The old pros looked at him askance for a brief moment, the thought 'uppity young bugger' floating through their brains, until they considered longer, and trumped it with the thought, 'nice one'. The lines stuck. This has remained with my father as an example of how Shakespeare most probably kicked off his writing career. A frightened but determined young provincial, scared by his peers but assured of his talent, thinking, 'I can do better than that', contributing a line or two here and there, and then the contributions growing to scenes and then soon after plays.

The second came from the company of his actor colleagues, on stage, in the dressing room and in their cups. What thrilled him most was when these small-time, sub-Wolfits launched into a speech away from the stage or any context and just sang it for the pleasure of singing. Without an iota of intellectual understanding they would hurtle into Prospero's great aria from *The Tempest*:

> ... be cheerful, sir.
> Our revels now are ended. These our actors,
> As I foretold you, were all spirits, and
> Are melted into air, into thin air:
> And, like the baseless fabric of this vision,
> The cloud-capped towers, the gorgeous palaces,
> The solemn temples, the great globe itself,
> Yea, all which it inherit, shall dissolve,
> And, like all this insubstantial pageant faded,
> Leave not a rack behind. We are such stuff
> As dreams are made on, and our little life
> Is rounded with a sleep.

As they staggered away from a pub, baying such lines at the moon, my father thrilled to the richness of their delivery, the wine-soaked commitment with which they filled each passing word; the warmth of the 'gorgeous', the frailty of their 'dissolve', the quickstep across the 'not a rack'. It was acting without the brain – or the wrong part of the brain anyway. It was seeking for the same state of grace in which the lines were written, the same simple and lively place, where language bubbles up like a spring. These men taught my father how Shakespeare wrote, and no amount of later academia and contorted thinking would cap their teaching. He wrote with the freedom, the speed and the automatic, unconscious fertility of genius. He packed himself with life and with books – classical, journalistic, gossip, history, whatever he could cram in – let it all stew within, mixed in the tensions of his historical moment and his own emotional broil, and then unburdened himself almost with his eyes closed. He wrote with the same incantatory freedom as was later sung by Burbage, by Garrick, by Kean, by Irving, by Terry, by Gielgud, by Olivier, and by any drunk old boy stumbling home from the pub.

At a riper old age of twenty-one, my father decided that an education wasn't such a bad idea after all, and packed himself off to Oxford. He made an event of himself while he was there, dressing up like a dandy, banging everything that would let him and pulling off various very 1950s stunts. At one point he dressed himself up as an Eastern sage, Dr Mahesh Halai, and addressed the Oxford Union in full silly make-up and flowing whiskers about the virtues of smoking opium, before dining with the university authorities. It was a classic hoax in the nature of the days before television, when 'they knew how to make their own fun'. It earned him a brief notoriety. (His connection with drugs continued. He was the first man on television to smoke a joint, caught in a John Boorman documentary of the early 1960s saying the immortal line, 'Quit yakking, daddy-o, and roll them smokes'). He also carried on acting, though he soon realized it was better to control your own fun by directing as well. He directed a famous production of *Julius Caesar*, the production my mother later heard tell of. He gave himself the show-off role of Mark Antony, and reorganized much of the stage action, and indeed the text to showcase himself in the best possible way. Somehow, with a sort of Orson Welles brio, it worked, and launched him on a new career.

He never stopped acting and toured Europe with companies coming out of Oxford. These productions gave him a steady sense of the depths and the heights of Shakespeare, but an equal relish of how in between those depths and heights there was silly laughter. Playing Nestor in Paris, decked out in full geriatric regalia – long white beard, bad make-up and stick – he had to deliver one of the most meaningless jokes in the canon: 'Let this be granted, and Achilles' horse / Makes many Thetis' sons'. To help the blithely uncomprehending French audience along, he thought he'd help them out with a long senile chuckle. At which point, Agamemnon turned to him and said loudly the unscripted line: 'What are you laughing at, you silly old cunt?' The whole of the Greek council dissolved.

Shakespeare took little further part in his professional life until the job in Israel. But certain feelings have never left him. Though uneasy with any conventional theology, he always steered a usually steady course between two large rocks of a self-created divinity. The first was a sort of mystic pantheism, a Shakespeare- and Wordsworth-fuelled sense of the dance and the pattern in everything, of the full and potent charge in everything from an old wine to a woman's lips to a cheap song. Wordsworth is explicit about this:

>   I have learned
> To look on nature, not as in the hour
> Of thoughtless youth; but hearing oftentimes
> The still sad music of humanity,
> Nor harsh, nor grating, though of ample power
> To chasten and subdue. And I have felt
> A presence that disturbs me with the joy
> Of elevated thoughts; a sense sublime
> Of something far more deeply interfused,
> Whose dwelling is the light of setting suns,
> And the round ocean and the living air,
> And the blue sky, and in the mind of man.

Shakespeare is never so explicit. Even in his lyrical poems, 'Venus and Adonis' and 'The Rape of Lucrece', you very rarely get the sense of a first-person voice. The sonnets are told by an insistent 'I', and an 'I' in the full flush of various passions, but that 'I' feels like a still-forming persona, a man discovering who he is. But every inch of his work is so full of the richness of his own creation, whether in love or grief or rage or a sense sublime, that the same pantheistic energy, the same sense of animistic vivacity coursing through all creation is as present as in Wordsworth.

The second rock was the antithesis of the first, a desperate nullity, a fathomless black hole, discovered in the cruel nihilism of *Macbeth* and the universal despair of *Lear*, and in the great and little disappointments of life. The love that is rejected, the children lost, the hopes frustrated, the daily injustice. All gathered to form an emptiness to check the richness elsewhere. If he could keep both in balance, walk carefully between the nullity of a Iago and the fulness of an Othello, he could steer his way through.

He has never lost a strong theatrical sense of what Shakespeare was, a voice telling a story. I once asked him, at the age when I was worried about such things, whether Shakespeare was a realist. 'Of course he was,' he replied. 'But there are no sets, no naturalism, it's all in verse,' I remonstrated. 'What does that matter?' he said. 'It may be a man standing in an anachronistic costume on a silly painted set looking out at an audience. But it's a real, living man standing there, and he's telling you that his story is real. What could be more real than that?'

Certain actors, Judi Dench as a prime example, have a voice that makes you care for them. With her, it's a little catch in the throat, a curl of sleepy sensuality, a gentle dancing humour. It doesn't matter whether villain or saint, you get pulled towards the humanity. Shakespeare's gift was that, however preposterous the situation, he makes you care for every one of his characters. They all have that catch of humanity in their voice. It's the sine qua non for any piece of dramatic writing. You have to be drawn in to the people (not like them – a Hollywood simplification). Shakespeare's achievement was to let his characters stand on a stage, look at the audience and say this is Venice, this is the Forest of Arden, this is Rome, and make you so excited to share their space that you happily believe them. When my father heard the actors in a dilapidated Welsh church hall tell him they were in an ancient Scotland of witches and warriors and floating daggers he believed them. He never stopped.

Mark Antony, infant nihilism and a boy's big questions

Fragments of Shakespeare surrounded me as a child. It was the age of the commune, and our farm often swelled up with guests. Frisbees skimmed through the air above our fields, and third-rate folk singers twanged their guitars and sang of Vietnam and leaf-fall. The most regular visitors were actors, who often came for a night and stayed for weeks. Two of the most regular were warm old gents called Alfred Burke and Freddie Jones. They, together with O'Toole, were of that generation who had minimal education but had pulled their minds up to a height equivalent to that of any Oxbridge graduate, largely by immersion in Shakespeare. Decades of working, quoting and studying the plays had given them a broad base of wit and humanity. They loved quoting and would always be badgered by us for more.

Yet it wasn't only in the quotation of actors that Shakespeare bubbled up. Somerset itself was still a long way off the modern world. We were the only outsiders in our farming community. Travel was still scarce, televisions rare, technology limited. The first time an automated milking machine arrived in the village everyone came out to look. And the language of the farmers was far from the groovetastic jargon of Carnaby Street. An elderly friend, Fred, would call ants 'emmetts'; a farmer, Ivor, would use the pronoun 'thickee' instead of 'that'; my father was known as 'thickee daft bugger from television', and one of my best friends would always greet me with 'Ow bist tha then, Dom?' There was a muscular simplicity to the language that hadn't changed for centuries. It was a peculiar blend: hippies bombed out on drugs, farmers getting on with their work, actors relishing the quiet and our nuclear family acting as hosts.

Shakespeare wasn't only a decoration for the aural landscape. He dug into the centre of my life as a child. Through all the various flounders of infancy; a sense of uselessness and impotence at school; a confusion about the largest questions; and, worst of all, a terror in the face of death, Shakespeare was there to provoke, and to guide, and to show that it had all been felt, and felt more keenly, before.

The first bit of poetry which stuck doesn't serve as the greatest advertisement for my mental health. Many girls fixate on Juliet, and learn off by heart her love-struck, febrile jitters; boys try on a Hamlet attire and wander around with troubled expressions, trying to work out what on earth 'To be or not to be . . .' actually means. Both sentiments – the fire of young love and the clouds of young confusion – seem psychologically appropriate. For me, the first great source of inspiration was Mark Antony's address to the Roman crowd, over the bleeding corpse of his friend Julius Caesar. Yes, at the age of seven, I was a sucker for the fascistic manipulation of mobs.

This may have had something to do with my status as the school jerk. We went to a local primary, filled with farmer's children. My greatest ambition was to be a farmer, and to be accepted by them, but I couldn't really hack it. Though proficient at actual farming tasks – I was up at dawn most mornings and back at twilight hand-milking our herd of cows – all of the lifestyle options which went with being a young farmer proved too demanding. I couldn't ride a bike. I still can't. My mouth was incapable of proper swearing, preferring 'damn' and 'blast' and 'blummin' to the various compounds of 'clit' which delighted my friends. I had no idea what a clit was. And worst of all, I couldn't play cowpat frisbee, the most popular sport of the time. This involved deftly scooping the dried, hardened surface off an old lump of cow pooh and sending it skimming through the air. Somehow I always got it wrong, and ended chucking lumpen handfuls of wet shit at other people. As I was such a klutz, it's hardly surprising that a great leader of men, acting boldly, at a moment of crisis, was a powerful role model.

There are other reasons why this passage stuck. There was a certain amount of wearing my father's laurels, his Oxford production of *Julius Caesar* having entered the pantheon of family myth. There's something instantly seductive about the rolling cadence of 'Friends, Romans, countrymen . . .' Mark Antony has a heroic glamour defending the honour of his friend in front of a baying crowd and treacherous senators. As a child who had already fallen for the stand-alone courage of Macaulay's Horatius at the Bridge, there was clearly a strong attraction to chaps in tunics who manage to defy large odds in pursuit of honour.

There is something politically suspect behind the blending of honour, heroics and patriotism. It's an intoxicating mix, and preys on the less than savoury side of the English. From the Renaissance through to the Victorian age, the Roman's passion for Roman land and culture has often served as a defining quasi-mirror for English flag flying. There's a spooky mystical music in the Roman's love for Rome, which, in a finer, more spiritual strain, is more sinister and alluring than Henry V's youthful patriotism of drum and pipe. It seems repulsive now from the perspective of maturity. But, coming from an Irish immigrant family who for several generations had worked hard at being more English than the English, and less Irish than a Sikh, I was susceptible to the patriotic game.

So, when my father sat by my bed and gave us all a full-tilt version of this speech, I was flattened. Mark Antony knocked spots off any of the Thunderbirds, and Captain Scarlet to boot. The *Complete Works* was kept beside my pillow, the correct page found, and the right-hand column on the left-hand page stared at intently. As I muttered softly all the while, the speech went in. It stuck. I now had a speech, a character and a situation.

The problem was what to do with it. There were a couple of turns for family friends. Unfortunately my father would usually follow my squeaky rendition by doing it himself much better. I tried it out at school and got thrown into a hedge. Someone excessively dim and friendless was found who would hear me out in return for a game of conkers, but he walked off mid-speech. Finally I settled on a congregation who would placidly accept my speechifying and do a passable impression of the crowd in the forum – our herd of cows. A mix of Jerseys and Guernseys, named after big moments in the space programme, they would mill around me in an excited state, as I boldly told them that I came not to bury Caesar but to praise him. Occasionally I would fix one in the eye, Apolloina or Sputnik maybe, and tell her with heavy irony that Brutus was an honourable man.

35

Though I would get no further applause than a cascade of plop from their backsides, in my imagination they were transformed by my rhetoric into tearful Romans. My brother and sister spied on me from a distance, but the occasional snort of giggles from a ditch would barely interrupt my oratorical flow.

Beyond my posturing to the local bovine sorority, this scene from *Julius Caesar* led to the only painting of any merit I ever achieved. Drawing and painting, like driving a car and riding a bike, are no-go areas for me. But for a few brief weeks at the age of seven or eight, my hand seemed enabled to express what my imagination conceived. The scene was scorched on my inner eye. It was the forum in Rome; Mark Antony stands halfway up some white steps, some white columns behind him; Julius Caesar lies blood-spattered at his feet, on a sandy floor; and a crowd of heads watches. The red of the blood and the yellow of the sand are exceptionally vivid. (Everywhere south of Weymouth was all sand in my imagination.) Mark Antony is caught in a moment of thought; the crowd does not know which way to turn; history is briefly at a crossroads. I brought the picture home and sat and stared at it. Not because it was great – it wasn't – but because by sheer force of attention I had made something separate from myself. It had a life of its own. Everybody manages it at one moment or another. It's the moment you get an intimation of what it means to make art, however clumsy the execution.

The next chunk learned wasn't exactly a prolonged ray of sunshine either. It was my father's favourite passage. A warm, genial, loving man, with a tremendous sense of fun, he always preserved an empty place inside himself. This could have been the result of seeing all his neighbours' homes flattened during the war. There's a silent place in the generation who endured the war, which we can never read. Or it could have been a side-effect of enthusiasm for the left-bank existentialist philosophy of the 1950s. Sartre and Camus were show-stopping philosopher rock gods, and their brand of Gauloises-enshrouded futility must have been pretty irresistible. All that our generation had by way of wise old goalkeepers was David Icke. Whatever the provenance, if my father had a gospel which he drummed into us, it was Macbeth's desolate analysis:

Tomorrow and tomorrow and tomorrow,
Creeps in this petty pace from day to day,
To the last syllable of recorded time;
And all our yesterdays have lighted fools
The way to dusty death. Out, out, brief candle!
Life's but a walking shadow, a poor player
That struts and frets his hour upon the stage,
And then is heard no more; it is a tale
Told by an idiot, full of sound and fury,
Signifying nothing.

Other families got to sing 'Ob-La-Di Ob-La-Da' together.

There's an urban myth, frequently told, almost always by women. It's the tale of the child standing on the table or the wall, and the father standing below. Jump, the father says, I'll catch you, and when the child jumps, he drops his hands and lets the child fall to the earth. There, that's a lesson to you, he says, never trust anyone. It's hard to imagine any father is actually as daft, and as wilfully sadistic, as that. But the urban myth is an expression of a truth. A truth that only becomes apparent when your own children appear. The hope and faith in their faces is one of their chief joys. Imagining all the lazy casual violence this battered world will bring is one of their chief torments. So, in different ways, we want to deflate those expectations, to toughen their skin for the world.

My father had something of that desire in him when he compelled us to learn those words. We were given no theological escape routes. The village church was scoffed at for its ugliness and lack of use. Any form of religion that passed through the house was unpicked mercilessly. Any God there was was little more than an idiot. And the rolling, assured violence with which my father hit that final 'nothing' left us in little confusion about where all stories finished up. Whatever faith or hope or kindness or meaning we've collected in life has been a bonus built on the base of that pessimism.

I learned it, but it wasn't a great one for reciting, neither to the cows, nor to the school bus. Even at that age, the difference between exterior and interior monologue was clear. I didn't need to sail into another hedge to work it out. This was more one that popped up unbidden in the head in that terrifying moment before sleep, the moment when your mind starts whirring just as your body is shutting down. Everything in one side of the brain is screaming stop, go to sleep, while the other side is like a computer screen invaded by spam. Ideas and images and connections pop up deliriously all over the screen. 'My mind is ruling me! I can't rule my mind!' my eldest daughter wails, when this moment hits. The same invasion of mental effervescence harassed me – it still returns to haunt once or twice a year – but as a child it was a daily torture. The questions are starker as a child, the connections more fierce, since they have wider chasms to bridge.

Nothing provoked those nights more than that speech. The mind reeled and twisted back to the beginning of the universe and swooped forwards to the end of the world, all decorated in the same black unknowability. Trivial and terrible questions screamed and shouted for the same space. Would Tottenham Hotspur ever improve as a team? Was I going to die, signifying nothing? Were Sweet better than Slade, and would Showaddywaddy upstage them both? How had the universe begun, and when was the first yesterday? Why had Nicola Dunn slapped me after I gave her a Valentine, when Denise Dunn had given my brother a kiss for his? And how brief was a brief candle? Sleep came as a blessed relief.

My relationship with the play has been queasy ever since. I still find it impossible to say the title of the play, referring to it archly as the Scottish play, frantically touching wood whenever lines are quoted. I was taken to see it in a small theatre in Bristol at the age of ten and had the wits scared out of me. Polanski's film petrified me as a teenager. I wasn't comfortable within my own skin for two months after that. The television version of the studio production with Ian McKellen and Judi Dench practically induced a cardiac arrest. Something profoundly creepy walks beside the play, some unsettling, malevolent energy. Its heart is dark, and I met it early.

Death started flinging stones at my windows at the age of about seven or eight. I remember the triggers and I remember the effect. The effect is still with me, ebbing and flowing in intensity. It never disappears. We have a brief few years of sunshine and unawareness, thinking that life is a party of wine and spliff and punky reggae, and that we'll never stop lazing in the sunshine. Then the lairy, skull-faced gate-crashers march in with their terrible heavy metal records. They never leave. You keep them quiet for a while by feeding them some spiked cider, you even befriend them and beg them to leave. But they never go, and, as dawn finally comes, we walk away with them.

The first stone was abstract, the second hard and real. In the abstract, as a sunny young egomaniac, my mind was made up that I was going to live for ever, and that the centre of the universe wasn't a million miles from, well, me. The foundations of this deception crumbled to pieces one day in an early science lesson at primary school. We were made to draw a diagram involving the eye, a tree and the sun. We were asked to draw arrows between them, explaining their relationship. I confidently drew two arrows emanating boldly from my eye towards both the sun and the tree. I, of course, was the centre of the universe and was creating all these fiddly other things. When the teacher rearranged my diagram, showing the path of light from the sun towards the tree and reflected into my eye, I was bamboozled. I stared and stared. Speechless. I was not the prime mover. Just a reflective thingy bouncing and receiving light from other reflective thingies. It was insupportable. Worse understandings flooded in behind. Like all other reflective thingies, there was an allotted shelf-life. Time would at some point be up.

Once I'd received the information conceptually, it arrived with all its sticky reality. Travelling to football practice for Blackford Villa Under-tens one Thursday evening, our car slowed suddenly. 'Don't look,' my friend's mother said sharply. We looked. A lorry had swerved across the road. A bicycle was mangled under a wheel. A red football shirt and white legs were tangled together. A puddle of red blood was elsewhere. We could not see who it was. When we arrived at the practice, everyone knew it had happened, but no one knew who to. We started playing and waited in terror to see who didn't show up. It was Brian. Whose two brothers were already there. They had ridden on ahead of him. No one could say anything, because no one wanted to admit anything was true. No one wanted to kick the ball, because it might end up near Brian's brothers, and then we would have to look at them. As the dark gloaming descended on the shitty cow field we used for practice, we kicked the ball in aimless fear, our hearts rising up to our mouths. After half an hour, Brian's mother appeared out of the darkness to collect her other two sons. A stocky woman with long black gypsy hair, her winter coat pulled tight around her, she walked straight through our silly game, and gathered her two boys in to her. She carried them both away, clamped to her side. We sat down on the ground in the dark and waited for our own parents.

The shadow of this incident never brightened and remained strong for the next couple of years. Brian's family, a wild mix of gypsy and deep Somerset, adopted me. I travelled to away games with them, sitting snug in the seat which he would have filled, his mother giving us all a healthy slug of cooking sherry on cold days to keep us going, his father freewheeling down endless hills at hair-raising speeds to save on the petrol. In the immediate aftermath of Brian's death, I learned a little about how we cushion tragedy. The words of consolation, the tributes and the cards. I was part of that process, in a very minor way, and was glad to be.

I tailspinned. Not just from the incident with Brian, but from the whole idea of curtailment. We were invited to this happy house, then told to leave. So why invite us in the first place? The Macbeth questions had been the gateway to speculations on dizzying chasms, a spur to imagining the infinites of empty space before, beside and beyond. This was scary but in some way exhilarating. The sheer scale of the questions carried its own thrill. Now they were an introduction to something cold, hard and factual – death. 'A brief candle' was no longer an image to be relished, it was something snuffed out. Sleep soon became impossible, the long hours of the night spent gurning and churning.

How did I deal with it? By fictionalizing it. By performing a death. Terrors were consumed by enacting them. Whenever guests came for dinner they had one of two treats awaiting them before food, the cowboy and the Shakespeare. The first involved me taking a bullet to the chest, reeling back on to the stone floor, then briefly reviving to gasp out, in a butch staccato tone, 'Everybody's got to die some day. I guess today is just my day,' before rolling to the floor with a broken breath. The second was the death of Caesar. No half measures for me, even at that age. If you're going to die, die big. There'd be a bit of 'I am as constant as the Northern star ...' in rolling cadence, before some graphically acted hyper-paranoia as conspirators gathered around me, then a number of imaginary stab wounds, before a last trembling, 'Et tu, Brute? Then fall, Caesar.' Then, a slow decline down the wall, with a little limb jerking. Applause, a little bowing, and bed. All my neurosis bundled into that moment of puerile performance, and all washed away in its own enactment.

The greatest thing about the 'Et tu, Brute?' phrase is the central daftness of having one phrase in Latin in a play full of Romans who otherwise speak fluent Renaissance English. The sheer daffiness makes the phrase iconic. The second greatest thing is the betrayal that skitters nervously through those words. It is the direct betrayal of Caesar's best friend, but also, in the abstract, it is the betrayal of life itself. The gift that is given that then deserts you. The joy that walks away. It is the most complete way of understanding the truth that everything goes.

Stratford, stupefaction and a rowing trip

At my in-laws recently, my wife's uncle turned up with a video. He had transferred on to it some old super-8 films. The first was 'A Day Out in Stratford'. Shot in the late fifties, in sharp, over-bright colours, it featured five or six London friends, proud of their new car and their new camera, flitting around Stratford with those jerky little motions of super-8 millimetre film. They visited Anne Hathaway's cottage, the birthplace, the theatre and strolled round the centre of town. It was full of those funny moments where people are aware of the camera, then unaware, then aware again – revealing them naked and self-conscious by turn. It was also prismatic. A historical record of a town given over to history. A modern television, showing ghostly figures from forty years ago, in a town given over to preserving its identity of 400 years ago.

For 150 years after Shakespeare's death, nobody paid much attention to Stratford. It carried on as a provincial backwater, concerned more with its barley crop than its connection to history's greatest poet. All this changed in 1776. David Garrick, master actor and master con man, came to town. Already a celebrated turn, he was looking for his Bob Geldof moment, needing a cause to hike his star yet higher. He chose Shakespeare and decided to celebrate his favourite playwright with a long festival in his home town. The resulting Jubilee of 1776 was an odd mix of disaster, as rain swept away certain events, riot, as huge barrels of wine and ale were downed, and triumph, as pageants passed through town. Garrick himself gave several specially composed orations dedicated to Will. The most surprising fact about the Jubilee was that not a word of Shakespeare was spoken throughout. His plays and his poems were comprehensively ignored. Thus the relationship between the poet and the way he is remembered in his home town got off to a skew-whiff start. Many feel it's never fully corrected itself.

Since Garrick's Jubilee millions have made the same pilgrimage – A Day Out in Stratford – as my in-laws captured in their shaky film. In spite of the haphazard nature of the Jubilee, it was a seminal step in the process of secular canonization. Since then, his status as an icon has grown more and more secure. And, like any icon, he has attracted more than his fair share of con men and exploiters, happy to cash in on his reputation. There was a lively industry in the nineteenth century in small pieces of Shakespeare's mulberry tree. So many were sold the tree would have to have occupied much of Warwickshire. Shakespeare rapidly acquired the kudos of a medieval saint. Anything that was deemed to have touched him quintupled in value. An effect now industrialized in the plastic busts and key rings that clog up Stratford's shops today. It is now probably England's premier religious site.

My first trip was at ten. Alone with my mother, for three days. This was exceptional, the first time I had been separate from my brother and sister, and the first time alone with either parent. It was rationalized as me being special and picked out. In fact, it was more probably because I was friendless. My brother and sister had been invited on exciting trips with friends; I hadn't. No matter, I was thrilled. Yet, from the beginning of the trip, there was a strong impression of sadness from my mother. We unpacked our things in a uniform little bedroom in a B&B, within a heavy silence. A shy despair filled her eyes as I wittered on about this and that; a smell of loneliness hung in the room as she watched me going to sleep, and a shamed anger tightened her as we went to see the plays in the Memorial Theatre. The reasons for these feelings could be understood later, but were hidden then. As an ex-actress, and now a primary school teacher, it's never comfortable to be in a town devoted to the working actor. And my parents had begun the long, slow drift apart, which would take fifteen years and would eventually end in separation. It was early days, but the ice had begun to shift.

These understandings are true, but only half the picture. The past is never fixed and constantly changes under the pressure of the present.

The realities of childhood morph and twist as we grow older and gain experience. The other half of my mother's sadness I only glimpsed when I took a child of my own to the theatre. There is, quite simply, nothing to beat the company of a child, engaged and excited and innocently in love with life, at the theatre. Their delight in the adventure restimulates an adult appetite that has become jaded. What seems tacky or faded to an adult seems magical and numinous to a child; a bit of commercial merchandise becomes a passport to history; a bad lighting cue is like the sky opening. It is impossible not to join in with their enthusiasm, and to relive that wide-eyed openness to magic. So, why would this be half of my mother's sadness? Because, as with all experiences of happiness that are too good, one mourns moment by moment their passing. The sweetness of the instant cannot last. The height of its present beauty only accentuates the depth of the disappointment that will follow. To see a child so full of joy is life's simplest treasure; to know that a child cannot feel the same for ever its sharpest disappointment.

Stratford was electrifying. It would be hard to imagine anywhere with so much to offer. It was a sweetshop. Full of pickings from my parents' pasts; characters, plays and imaginary places, spoken of through my life, were all around me. All the Ye Olde England stuff – excruciating once you get past the age of twelve – enchanted me. It was a hot few days, and we did all the traipsing, shuffling at the obligatory tourist pace through the fake birthplace, and Anne Hathaway's cottage, and the old schoolroom. My imagination was catapulted back in time by each old wooden table, each low-slung beam or copper bowl. The garden at Anne Hathaway's cottage was like falling into a postcard: hollyhocks, foxgloves, lupins, Canterbury bells, summer flowers all growing together in disarray. We went to his tomb and liked it so much we went back twice more. I devoured every leaflet; I nodded eagerly at every authentically dressed Equity member who said 'Hello, young sir' to me and chucked me on the chin; I peered into the river over the old bridge, and thought thoughtfully about being thoughtful in a thoughtful child way. I was a Catholic in Rome, a Moslem in Mecca.

I had just emerged from a long Sherlock Holmes phase. I had long been a great one for dressing up and assuming contrary identities.

There is a series of photos of me as a podgy child staring into the camera, dressed as a Thunderbird or Batman or an astronaut. The expression is always deadpan and humourless. I think I assumed being a superhero was rather a grave business and shouldn't be spoiled by too much charging around or slack smiling. Sherlock Holmes had consumed me for a couple of years. One of my uncle's weddings was ruined by me storming around a Liverpool church during the service examining people with a magnifying glass and questioning them closely. The residues of Sherlock were still there, even though the cape and the deerstalker had been left behind, and life was still an enormous lattice of whodunnits.

The historical mysteries of Stratford were fuel for that fantasy. The lack of clues about Shakespeare, and the different versions of what his life may have been, impressed themselves on me. His tantalizing presence, so immanent and so evanescent at the same time, was a gripping, unsolved crime. It is the same detective story which still impels legions of eccentric academics to propose that Shakespeare was not Shakespeare at all, but a conglomeration of any other notable Elizabethans – Francis Bacon, the Earl of Oxford, Christopher Marlowe – who can be dragooned in to cover their blinkered embarrassment that the greatest genius of our species was the son of an illiterate glover. I knew nothing of the authorship question at the time, but could see that the lack of real clues required the diligent attention of a master sleuth. I was on the case. Beyond every corner we turned, beneath every table we sat at, behind every bush in the gardens, there may be some little historical memento which could sharpen this blurry image.

We saw two shows, a *Romeo and Juliet* and an *As You Like It*. My state of excitement before the first was bordering on the spontaneous chunder. I remember almost precisely the location of our seats, the heft of the programme, the giggly excitement of the audience. Juliet was a fragrantly exotic Estelle Kohler, Romeo a swarthily handsome Timothy Dalton, and an unbald David Suchet did a fine glowering act as Tybalt. There was a huge humdinger of a fight at the beginning as the Montagues and Capulets piled into each other.

Then I had my first experience of what was to become a constant in all my Shakespeare-going life. Stupefaction. It crept up slowly on me, then became more and more overwhelming. At first I tried to pretend it wasn't happening, but soon I had to admit it. I couldn't understand a blind word anyone was saying. One person charged on to the stage after another and started cheerily shouting, 'Arglebargle, tintytatty, boodahgoodah.' The occasional word penetrated through the mist, a 'love' or a 'fate', or more helpfully a name, 'Romeo' (that'll be him, then) or 'Capulet' (he'll be on their team, then), but generally all was 'pintelprickpogacious'. To begin with I was resentful, since I felt this must obviously be an adult thing. On the page this stuff was comprehensible, but obviously as soon as they got it into the theatre, the adults encoded it to make it harder for children. Then I looked around and saw that a large percentage of the adults in the audience were as stupefied as I was. So why were we all there? I angrily pondered this, but against my injured will I was swept back into the story again, sick with rage at what had happened to Mercutio, indignant about Romeo's exile (Oi, referee, put your specs on, that Tybalt had it coming) and worried sick about how Juliet was going to take it. By the end, although a lot of it was still in the realm of the 'hoorunga, hallay', I was stomach sick with grief at the loss of the two lovers. Shakespeare shares a quality with opera. No matter the minute-to-minute sense, some underground movement, some oceanic swirl, catches you and hurls you merrily about. I was then, as now, hopelessly innocent before it.

The opacity still worries me. Partly it's 400-year-old language, and there's nothing you can do about that. Partly it's the pernicious influence of verse speaking that cares little for sense or clarity as long as you're boldly going ti-tum ti-tum. When Peter Hall launched the RSC it was as much as anything on a programme of clarity – hard, specific clarity. By the time I first went, that was already in decay. But it's less the fault of actors than it is of directors. For a fair while now we've been trying and testing the patience of theatre's devotees with a relentless desire to be interesting. We have forgotten the central contract: an actor works out who their character is, comes on at the appropriate moment and says the lines clearly. Magic occurs. It's hardly rocket science. It is amazing how theatre has conspired to muddy the innocence of that contract, and how directors' neurotic tinkering has led to nothing but a further spread of my childish confusion. Yet, in spite of the opacity, I was in and knew I was in for life. The variety of voices on offer, the boldness of the feelings, the dance of the wit, all mattered more than mere comprehension. That would come later.

The next afternoon was tougher: *As You Like It* in modern dress. The stupefaction returned and there was less tragic surge to compensate. There were also some desperately unfunny people going 'hurdlegurdle' with a cheeky look more of hope than expectation. And *As You Like It* has a hellishly dull fourth act, as confused lovers stumble in and out, crowding out the forest, multiplying exponentially, which I can't imagine I will ever survive. But enough of the magic was still there. Some of the actors from the night before returned, which made me feel part of the family. One of the actors had hurt himself, and there was an understudy, which made me feel part of the excitement. And at the end of the show, instead of a curtain call, there was a big, very seventies disco, with everyone dancing around to pop music. This probably had the actors grinding their teeth with embarrassment, but I thought it was magnificently jolly and informal. A child is an easy sale, and I was sold.

The shows stay clear in the memory, as does the passage from each olde roome into each olde roome, all full of olde thinges. But one moment sticks with me particularly. My mother decided we should hire a boat for the afternoon, and row up and down the Avon. I was game for anything. If she'd suggested we bedecked ourselves with flowers and drowned ourselves, I would have joined in, thinking it all part of the wonderful Shakespeare experience. It was a beautiful afternoon, the sun was out, swans were gliding, willow trees were drooping, and the theatre sat proud and imposing over the river. But what was special was what was in my hands. The oars. I was rowing. I was propelling my mother up and down the river; I was allowed to be in control for an afternoon.

At a bar mitzvah once, I remember closely watching the face of the boy being celebrated. He seemed confused, passive and on the back foot for much of the afternoon. Then during some speeches, an uncle of his made a fool of himself, getting into a tangle with a microphone, unable to make it work. One grown-up after another tried to sort it out, and each failed worse than the one before. It became laughable, and a light grew in the eyes of the boy. He smiled and he understood. He wasn't growing older, he was just on the cusp of realizing that the adults, who had seemed so far away, were the same age as him. It would be false to say that all that occurred to me, with the oar in my hand, as I steered my mother up and down the river and tried to talk grown-up, but I understood something. It was a gentle shift of perspective, the whole trip, the plays, the slow tourist shuffle, the moment with the oars. An induction into adulthood, as for the boy at the bar mitzvah, in the presence of the best high power I knew.

the voice, the verse and a sneak preview of life's lessons

In a recent film, *The Actors*, there's a good gag involving a sad old actor played by Michael Caine. He's the sort of thespian long on dreams and short on achievement. His final desire is to mount a production of *Hamlet* with the actors speaking nothing but the vowels. This, he believes, will revolutionize theatre, returning it to its primitive emotional state. He gives a demonstration of Hamlet soliloquizing: 'oo ee aw o oo ee, a i e e-i-o'. That single line is enough to show why his production will never get on. It's a dream understood by any actor who has sludged and fizzed their way through three years at drama school, contorting his or her mouth into strange shapes at the whim of a voice teacher. The voice is at the heart of acting, and an easy, warm and strong one is central to any achievement.

If actors can get their voice in the right place, and if the play is good, and if the director hasn't fucked it up with too much collapsing scenery, then the words they speak in that strong clear voice will look after them. A director friend has a three-line mantra for actors confused about how to approach their task: 'Find out who you are. Learn your lines. Get out of the way of the play.' It should be written in glow stars on the ceiling above every fretful actor's pillow. The reasoning is simple. The better the play, the less you have to do. The more you do, the more you spoil it. Nowhere is this more pertinent than with Shakespeare. Every evening all over the world in a thousand different Shakespeare productions, simple lines, honest phrases and straightforward sentiments are being tortured, sometimes to death, by actors inflecting, intoning and contorting the language towards their own twisted music. They should follow Shakespeare's advice and 'let be'. He went further than just this advice, unapologetically dictating how his work should be done through his grand effusion, Hamlet:

Speak the speech, I pray you, as I pronounc'd it to you, trippingly on the tongue; but if you mouth it, as many of our players do, I had as lief the town-crier spoke my lines. Nor do not saw the air too much with your hand, thus, but use all gently; for in the very torrent, tempest, and, as I may say, whirlwind of your passion, you must acquire and beget a temperance that may give it smoothness. O, it offends me to the soul to hear a robustious periwig-pated fellow tear a passion to tatters, to very rags, to split the ears of the groundlings, who, for the most part, are capable of nothing but inexplicable dumb shows and noise . . . Be not too tame neither, but let your own discretion be your tutor. Suit the action to the word, the word to the action; with this special observance, that you o'erstep not the modesty of nature; for anything so o'erdone is from the purpose of playing, whose end, both at the first and now, was and is to hold, as 'twere, the mirror up to nature; to show virtue her own feature, scorn her own image, and the very age and body of the time his form and pressure.

This is not only one of the finest passages of prose ever written – matched earlier by more Hamlet when he speaks of 'what a piece of work is a man'; it is not only one of the pre-eminent prescriptions for all art, never mind theatre, it is also a very clear set of instructions on how to produce his work. The key word it pivots on is 'modesty', the essential Shakespearean virtue, a virtue more often than not ignored in life, let alone in acting. And when it is ignored, all doors to understanding his world swing shut. This is not to say the only approach is a bland, neutral, reverential one. The plays need bold characterization, vivid energy and surprising attack. That is finding out who you are. But once found, the language needs love and care, not worrying. Shakespeare will take you where you need to go.

As a child reading it, just as with an actor playing it, the joy of the verse is that it takes you to places you did not know existed. It builds a scaffold inside you; you climb the scaffold step by step, each step seemingly consequent and familiar; then, when you reach the top of the scaffold, you suddenly realize you're in a new and strange place. A child alone; an actor with an audience. New insights, new emotional states, new resolutions. All the guff and stuff we learn through life, through long hours of study, or through meticulous self-examination, Shakespeare tricks us into with his verse.

He honed a technique to achieve this throughout his career. His honing was that of a technician, and largely unconscious. Being a complete man of the theatre – producer, writer, stockholder and, above all, actor – he either acted in or watched every single play he wrote. In performance, his ears heard the biggest laughs and his nose smelled out the most pungent silences. A bit-part player, waiting for his intermittent moments on the stage, he would stand back-stage behind doors and hangings and sneak looks out. Ahead of him were the backs of the actors kitted out in extravagant Renaissance finery. Beyond them 3,000 shining faces, staring in at the play with bright anticipation. He would hear each joke, each lyric swoop, each tragic blow tested out on the critical intelligence of the London crowd. The next time he put pen to paper his knowledge of what worked was refined, and the dead wood stripped away.

Alone, walking around the farm, the *Complete Works* held stiffly out before me, or lying snuggled up under bedclothes, with the book tucked in before my shifting eyes, I shouted or mumbled lines that my brain couldn't compute, but which taught my heart strange and new facts. The first and most obvious stepping stone is an embarrassing one for a chap to fess up to, but it's the one that strikes hardest and brightest at the androgynous pre-teen phase:

O Romeo, Romeo. Wherefore art thou, Romeo?

The magic of that line is peculiarly trans-gender, ageless and international. Little children in Moroccan marketplaces have lampooned the line to me; elderly professors in Moscow have spoken it with moistening eyes. However well or badly it is attacked, it defies destruction. Its basic tool is a bold and open use of big, wide vowel sounds. To employ the Michael Caine tactic it runs with a loud and long O O EO, O EO. Air Or Aa Ow O EO. It's someone throwing the window of their heart wide open. Try and say it without sounding as if you're full of longing and yearning. The very physicality involved in forming the sounds creates the emotions it describes. The way you shape a vowel in your mouth creates an internal movement, which engenders the feeling. Long before I felt the full chill of an unrequited or impossible love, I had the blueprint of that line implanted in me.

Follow that speech through to its end, and you climax with the simple phrase 'Romeo, doff thy name'. Again, it is impossible not to say it without following the movement of the thought to a climax of triumphantly flicking something off. A pretend cap or a metaphorical identity. My wife once played Cleopatra. She says she couldn't hit it – she was too young – until one particular performance, when she was on song. When she hit the track trying to summon the memory of Antony:

> I dreamed there was an Emperor Antony.
> O such another sleep, that I might see
> But such another man!–

she was surprised by the noises coming out of her. The heavy downward gravity of the 'such anothers', the two first vowels, dug up from inside her a depth of yearning she did not know she possessed.

The simplicity of acting the emotions, and the ease of understanding them when young, are often helped by specific stage directions written into the verse. In the absence of directors or often rehearsals, Shakespeare wove into the fabric moments that physicalized each passion. The plays are studded with anatomical descriptions – my heart burns, my hair stands on end, my skin prickles. Constance in *King John*, on hearing of the death of her son, states:

> This hair I tear is mine.

The gesture and the grief are bound together in one phrase, the emotion and the action inseparable. After hearing of the witches' prophecy, Macbeth gives us:

> doth unfix my hair,
> And make my seated heart knock at my ribs . . .

Later he resolves:

> I'm settled, and bend up
> Each corporal agent to this terrible feat.

And later, after he has killed Duncan, on the first knock at the door:

Whence is that knocking?
How is't with me when every noise appals me?

You wonder whether Shakespeare was beginning to worry about his leading actor Richard Burbage's work and felt he needed extra guidance. It's as if he is directing the plays from within, leading his actor towards a physical understanding of the journey he's going through. The body – each sweaty palm, each queasy belly and stuck pulse of it – is brought into the same dance as the cosmos and the body politic.

It makes it easier to understand as a child. It is also closer to the way children speak. One of my children, needlessly censured for crying, said, 'I'm not crying. The tears are leaping into my eyes.' It was a bolt of pure Shakespeare, and serendipitously close to recent thoughts in psychology. Antonio Damasio, a neuroscientist, has written a series of beautiful books, whose details are a trifle opaque, but whose gist I've got a grasp of. It is that emotions are preceded by physiological effects, which then trigger the collection of physical feelings we cluster together as emotions. So a reaction is often physical – doth unfix my hair – and the consequence of the reaction is the emotion – in this case crippling fear. When Shakespeare dictates a physical reaction to an event, he is throwing a stone in a pond, whose automatic, synaptic ripples are the emotions it summons in actors, audience and readers.

Another energy that sucks you into Shakespeare is its urgency in the moment. Throughout the history plays, the same trick is played over and over again. A messenger charges on and says the situation's bad. Ten seconds later a further messenger bursts in to say it's worse. Five seconds after that, a third appears saying it's cataclysmic. This is playground storytelling. Yet it works every time, however corny. No matter that the reported army seems to have travelled 200 miles, won three battles and concluded four treaties in the space of thirty seconds, Shakespeare says it is so, breathlessly, and makes you want to partake in the gathering excitement.

In the comedies, the principle is that everyone lives in the moment. There is a wonderful moment with Viola in *Twelfth Night*, in both the reading and the playing. Having spent some time with Olivia and having earned her unsought love, Viola is chased by Malvolio with a ring, which Olivia has pretended is Viola's. Viola says simply:

I left no ring with her. What means my lady?

The key to this, comically and for truth, is to live in the moment from word to word. Played that way, without archness or cuteness, the whole situation unpeels for Viola with spontaneous freshness, and we participate in her growing understanding. His characters speak their thoughts aloud, and we discover the thought as they do. Hamlet's question 'For in that sleep of death what dreams may come/ When we have shuffled off this mortal coil' surprises Hamlet, and he shares his surprise with us. Juliet trips herself into her question and her answer, 'What's in a name? A rose by any other name would smell as sweet.' The characters ask the question with the audience, and they discover the answer or the confusion together.

No one is fresher, or more inclusive, than Shakespeare's atom bomb of new-found consciousness, Hamlet. Much is made of the scope of Hamlet's mind, its freedom and range, but little is made of the sheer mess he is in at the beginning of the play. He can hardly string a sentence together:

> ... By what it fed on: and yet, within a month, –
> Let me not think on't, – Frailty thy name is woman! –
> A little month; or e'er those shoes were old
> With which she follow'd my poor father's body,
> Like Niobe, all tears; why she, even she –
> O God! A beast, that wants discourse of reason,
> Would have mourned longer – married with my uncle,
> My father's brother; but no more like my father
> Than I to Hercules: within a month . . .

He's all over the shop. Shakespeare's achievement is not to tidy him up. Each zig, each zag of thought is left alone with its own elliptical truth. This is a nutcase trepanned and unravelling before us. This lost, punkish ball of rage is how we get to know him. As a child, this is what thrilled me. I found the composed calm of the 'To be or not to be . . .' passage formal and presented, like an exam for comprehension. But the opening was like falling at speed through a portal into Hamlet's mind.

From the very first moment I read Shakespeare, I knew I was peeping into the private souls of others. Music had given me a little of this, but I could never locate the source of what I was hearing. Art had given none, since it took me a long time to see past the encrustation of the frames to what was within. Movies had given me a little, but again the plasticity of the medium is hard to see beyond. You see the eyes in films, but it's so hard to see through them. They are so plastically impressive. But the hunger for food for the spirit, a lack provoked by an absence of religion, was first tickled into life by meeting the spirits of others in his plays.

The only comparable experience in childhood, which banged the souls of others into me, was the arrival of Tutankhamun's relics. In the non-stop, wrap-around greyness of early seventies England this was an event. These ancient artefacts arrived like a rock star and were written up like the second coming. Like many other children I took a four-hour bus trip up to London with my comprehensive schoolmates. We queued for a further four hours, shuffled round the exhibition, then enjoyed the four-hour bus trip home. It was worth it. In those desperate, hopeless, aesthetically disgusting times, all Osmonds and Dick Emery and Carry On Up Your Tower Block, it was a revelation. Beauty and proportion and opulence and sin and vain magnificence. And, looking into the death masks, all gold and turquoise, one felt the soul of another age.

Away from the world, and hidden in a book, this was what was available through Shakespeare; souls on souls. In any good play before Shakespeare or since, we treasure two or three moments, or maybe only one, where we share an intimacy with a character. We glimpse a little privacy. In Shakespeare, they stream down the hill like orcs in *Lord of the Rings*. Every character that comes on stage is open and revealed to us from the most fly-by messenger to the longest-staying hero. And some of them, most notably Hamlet, burn so bright it's hard to look. In a world of chicken in a basket, and bow-tied comedians, and dinner ladies with afro perms, it's hardly surprising that I was so keen to latch on to the excitement available in the dramatis personae.

The approach to the *Complete Works* was fairly unrigorous at that age. It was a Now That's What I Call Shakespeare line of attack, picking out the best bits and gliding past any difficult or less quickly rewarding sections. I was steered by anthologies, introductions and overheard quotations towards where the match's highlights might be.

One also develops early an instinct for where the mountain peaks will be placed. It's the child's natural instinct for editing. So my appreciation was all peaks of excitement, all climaxes, unmitigated by any appreciation of the delicate foreplay that leads up to them.

I was spoilt for choice. The first line of *The Merchant of Venice*, 'In sooth, I know not why I am so sad', sank its long teeth in. It's slow and drawn out and dripping with the self-pity of youth. I loved it. It's the perfect elegant answer to every parent's angry question: 'What's wrong? Why are you crying?' Beyond my bleated 'I don't know', I could say to myself 'In sooth, I know not . . .' and feel the authority of a sturdy opening line. But I knew the man who said it must be the most almighty drip. What really excited me in *Merchant* was Shylock. Too young to know anything about anti-Semitism or even the argument of the play, I knew this man's brain obviously moved faster than the others'. From the moment Shylock appears, you recognize a rich stew of internal life amongst a number of thin soups. With his hustle and bustle, his alert paranoid rhythms and his complex dialogue with himself, you just want to climb into him and join in.

And beyond Shylock, and Hamlet, there was Falstaff, with his aimless musings and his vainglorious self-puffery; there was Antony, with his sly rhetoric and his private boiling rage; there was Macbeth and his rolling, deadened nihilism; Jaques from *As You Like It*, with his waspish despair as expressed through the 'All the world's a stage . . .' malarkey; Othello, with the soft drumbeat purpose of the 'It is the cause, it is the cause, my soul' passage as he purposes to murder Desdemona; and Romeo, with his drippy passion, which even then I found a bit disappointing beside Juliet's mental energy.

None of these characters I came within a country mile of understanding intellectually. But I knew who they were. Even if my conscious mind was more set on finding the money to buy another CurlyWurly, bartering for Action Men, or the fortunes of Tottenham Hotspur, I felt the echoes of these distant figures in my young bones. Human echoes made of the same muck as I was. Speaking the lines to myself as my eye skittered along each line was putting on the robes and souls of others. What insights I would muster and articulate would come later with study. What was exciting at the time was to be in the presence of this wonderful pantheon of glittering monsters. It was an emotional gymnasium.

the BBC, Olivier and the skull beneath the skin

Holed up for a week recently in a flat in Dalston, doing some very peculiar development work for a film, our eyes kept being drawn to a huge hoarding opposite one window. It was an advertisement for the TV series *Nip/Tuck*. A drama about plastic surgery, it was pristine white, with a couple of photogenic telly actors wearing white coats, holding sharp knives and grinning archly. They were adopting that 'we have a little secret' smirk that makes you want to join a monastery. An even more arch tagline ran underneath them. It looked like the death of culture as we know it. Halfway through the week, someone else clearly felt the same way. They went out in the middle of the night and sprayed on the hoarding in enormous letters the new logo: 'TV IS SHIT'. We couldn't have been more delighted if Father Christmas had appeared, bearing a sleighload of drugs.

It's hard to remember there was a time when TV wasn't the embarrassing forage for the lowest common denominator it has become but indeed there was. It's not only hard to remember, it's hard to imagine a time when the BBC would conceive an idea to record over a three- or four-year period the complete works of Shakespeare, do them with no lack of expense and transmit them, gulp, in primetime. It sounds like the product of a Lewis Carroll topsy-turvy fantasy world. But it actually happened. Elegantly designed in Elizabethan through to Romantic settings, they gathered together top-notch casts to perform them – actors, not celebrities on a scary day trip to Cultureland. They filmed them in a studio. And, most amazingly, they presented them full length. Occasionally with intervals, when the British nation could potter off and top up their sherries. It was the same cultural moment that my mother's family enjoyed around the radio, yet with the new technology. A family drawn together in their home to witness mythic stories; the whole of Britain (or a significant minority to be more accurate) gathered in household units to share in the same moment.

The results were creaky, a little stagey, somewhat stiff, but they were an education, and a great one to tap into. Over several years, on a more than occasional Sunday, we would settle *en famille* and watch the latest offering. The idea was conceived by a chap with a suitably Elizabethan name – Cedric Messina – and finished off by the famous egghead Jonathan Miller. The memories are scattered but strong: a highly romantic *Hamlet* with Derek Jacobi; a muddy *Troilus and Cressida*; an eccentric romp of a *Taming of the Shrew* with a mid-Fawlty John Cleese as Petruchio; an austere *King Lear* with Michael Hordern; a series of history plays conceived imaginatively in a children's playground with everyone playing 'Who's the king of the castle?'; and a past-its-sell-by-date *Othello* with a blacked-up Anthony Hopkins as the Moor and a Sergeant-Major Bob Hoskins as Iago. There were many others, but they have all dissolved into the great Shakespearean mush of shows seen and dropped into the blancmange of cultural memory. Though we coughed and sneered at these, saying they weren't Brechtian or hip enough, and do we have to watch them, and why can't we watch something really happening like *The Dukes of Hazzard*, we did watch them and not only out of duty. Experiences that are free and educational and let your mind shift or expand a little inside your cranium don't exactly fall off trees.

The climax of this prolonged state-subsidized education came courtesy not of the BBC but of ITV. As the last throw of various sorts of dice, they presented a deluxe edition of *King Lear* starring Laurence Olivier and, seemingly, everybody else in British theatre who could show up: John Hurt as the Fool, Leo McKern as Gloucester, Dorothy Tutin and Diana Rigg as the ugly sisters, Colin Blakely as Kent, Robert Lindsay as Edmund, David Threlfall as Edgar, Robert Lang as Albany. It was Olivier's last chance at getting through it without dying. It was the last time you could get an ensemble of that calibre together. It was close to the end of the life of its visionary director Michael Elliott. And it was most definitely the end of a whole era of pretentious, cultured television. A last hurl and a glorious one.

We all sat and lay down together to watch it. My father was in a state of nervous excitement. He had seen Olivier play Lear in the late forties just after the war and he couldn't forget an instant. He was terrified that Olivier wouldn't be able to repeat it, and that his failure would be a staging post on the slow march towards death that scares us all. If Olivier couldn't do it, if the years had laid waste to him as well as the colour of my father's hair, then time was truly marching on. Indeed, for the first quarter, though the cast were wonderful, the execution precise and the storytelling clear, Olivier was contained. My father, in between telling us to shut up if we so much as breathed while this was going on, kept muttering, 'He can't do it, he can't do it, oh fuck he can't do it,' as a slow deadness spread through him. Then, in the middle of the 'O, reason not the need . . .' speech, Olivier stops, turns away, draws breath, returns, stops, turns away again, draws a massive gulp of breath, then explodes like a tiger, roaring from the depths of some energy from sixty years before, bellowing like a raging wind. It makes your hair stand on end. The memory of it still does. I couldn't take my eyes off the screen throughout this, nor as the half life ebbed away from the event afterwards. A full five minutes later I turned to look at my father. He was as rigid as a rock, and tears were streaming down his cheeks.

A year ago, I found a video of the production in one of those dodgy Soho stores that use tapes of old theatrical productions as cover for the hardcore porn that lurks behind. I took it back to my office and watched it a couple of days later. I survived the 'O, reason not the need . . .' moment, but by the time I got to Lear and Gloucester meeting I was unpinned, when Edgar walked his father off the imaginary cliff I was sobbing, and, from the moment Olivier woke delicately to music and struggled to believe that his daughter Cordelia was looking him in the eye, I was shaking. A powerful sense of end, of frailty, of the skull beneath the skin, is shot through every inch of the production. It's a constant tale of fragility finding strength, before being cut down again. Olivier being in such a decimated and delicate state himself, and somehow finding the muscular authority for one last hurrah, the whole production becomes an essay in the absurd achievement of the human spirit in the face of desperate odds. And, like all the BBC productions, all for free on the great national theatre of the television.

O'Toole, actor managers and skinheads

'Speak the speech I pray you, as I pronounc'd it to you . . .' is the paradigm of every speech from an author to his company of actors. It is fresh, funny, self-mocking and alive. It quicksteps with the light, mental speed of a director giving last-minute notes before a first night.

If I have one golden hour from my adolescence, it would be in the kitchen of our farmhouse, after a big, rough meal, and a bottle of wine each, and Peter O'Toole at one end of the table, tearing in to that speech, waving an emphatic hand in the air with an impossibly chic cigarette holder clutched between his fingers. We were all sitting around wearing something ludicrous like kaftans (don't ask), and there was some riproaring row going on about whether Gertrude was a lesbian or not, and he suddenly launched into 'Speak the speech . . .' It had moral force and humour and lived at a dazzling height of wit and clarity I've never heard matched. Each word was crunched hard, spun fast and moved through at breakneck pace. To hit each detail of vowel and consonant, to do it hard and light, and at the speed of sound, was like hearing Glenn Gould in private, or seeing Jack Hobbs in the nets. Beauty on a precipice.

Peter was hiding away in our house, recovering from his rough-house reception for *Macbeth*. The play had had a legendarily appalling opening at the Old Vic. There was booing, and there were savage reviews, and there were long think pieces about whether this was the greatest disaster of all time. The very floppiness of it turned it into a hit, and it became one of the hottest tickets of the time. After the first night, with all the front of house giggly and aglow with the smell of a disaster, and all the shitty vultures who cluster at first nights swapping gleeful notes, my mother and father slipped round to see Peter. He was alone in his large dressing room. No one had bothered to come round. He knew a storm was coming and he knew he was going to have to front up to it. He also knew his mother was terribly ill in hospital. My mother and father smuggled him out of the back exit and drove him there.

Soon after, in the lull before the play went on tour, he came and stayed with us. His partner in a new company at the Old Vic, the actor Tim West, had disowned Peter's show and he spent much of his time composing letters in fruity legalese describing Tim West's intimate relationship with Satan. He brought with him his girlfriend, whom he gleefully called his 'fucking machine'. He sat at one end of our kitchen table and talked. And talked and talked. We sat entranced, as a gathering group of friends came to listen. After a late breakfast, he would start his peroration for the day somewhere like Sumeria in the eighth century BC, then talk his way slowly through the history of civilization, elucidating the threads that drew it all together. Javanese rudders, Greek pots, Roman stoic philosophy, Christian martyrs, Confucian sexual positions, German wood cuttings, Byronic travel routes, would all get hurled into the pot. Even at our young age, I think we had a fair idea that he was making a healthy sixty per cent of it up, but we didn't mind. His invention was far better than most people's facts. In addition he would tell filthy jokes, and desperate stories that would still a room. It was an actor at rest in excelsis.

All the time he returned to Shakespeare. Not to extend some thin thesis, or to prove a point, but as if returning to take slices out of a great soulful fruitcake he wanted us to enjoy with him. He quoted liberally, spoke of past productions, and remembered other performances. He raged against the appropriation of Shakespeare by the directorial mafia. How the river of honesty which had flowed for centuries between the actors and their audience had been poisoned and diverted by the thin neurosis of directors. 'Speak the speech . . .' was all the direction he needed, and he did not want others who had no idea about 'the modesty of nature' to screw that up. It broke his heart how no one saw the thing itself any more.

It was a great blast by the last of the Wolfits, the long line of actor managers running back to the sixteenth century. For three centuries Shakespeare was owned by companies formed around actors like

O'Toole, who toured the country with productions formed and staged like pyramids to allow their stars to sit regally on the top. There was a long line from Richard Burbage, the leading man Shakespeare wrote for, through Garrick, his great celebrant in the eighteenth century, through Kean, the early nineteenth-century tragedian who famously acted like 'flashes of lightning', through Henry Irving, the late Victorian actor and businessman, down to Donald Wolfit, the mad old buffer who toured England in the thirties and forties, dressed and made up like an alien from a different epoch. O'Toole saw himself as part of that line, and saw the end of that line as a tragedy in itself. He saw acting as a mystic art, as an achievement of grace, rather than as fitting into the intellectual construct of their director. The directors came in with all the artillery of the modern and killed off the wildebeest actor.

A few weeks later, the famous production of *Macbeth* came to Bristol. As a production, even to all of us who were smitten with Peter, it was hard to avoid the fact that it was unmitigated rubbish. The set was crude and ugly; the pace was turgid; and when Brian Blessed appeared as the ghost of Banquo wearing a bright red rubber body suit covered in waving flappy bits, like a lurid alien from a cheap fifties sci-fi movie, it was hard to maintain one's reverence. But when Peter stood there and belted it – too old, badly lit and wearing a silly dress – your heart raced. He didn't want to live on the sad plains of deconstruction, he wanted to be up on the mountains. He got there rarely, but you admired the attempt, and when he did, it allowed you some of what Byron called 'the greatest pleasure the soul is allowed': to see an actor fully match a Shakespearean line.

Two different instances of bullying followed the show, and soured the event. Immediately after, we waited outside the stage door, as my father nipped in to say hello, before driving home. Skinheads strode the West Country in those days like colossi. They were everywhere, and I'd already been given a couple of merry kickings closer to my home. A twenty-strong maul of them was strutting down the other side of the street in Bristol. I was terrified of them but, like all brands of bogeymen, drawn to them, and given to staring out of fear. Two of them noticed me staring, stopped, stared back and then started slowly moving over. All the while they spewed out a sort of daft,

Bristolian, De Niro monologue: 'What you fucking looking at? What you looking at, cunt? You fucking want some? Do you? Do you fucking want some?' I was too terrified to do anything but stand there, trussed up like the world's biggest ninny in a too tight, cheap, middle-class-boy-goes-to-the-theatre suit. I looked to my mother, my brother and my sister. They gave me that 'your problem, pal' look that you can always rely on in a crisis. A small crowd gathered to see what was about to kick off. A large majority of them seemed keen to see me get a good kicking. All of the puffed-up, I-know-a-famous-person pomposity of me drained in an instant through my feet into the pavement. I could do nothing but stare feebly back. Until a larger skinhead walked up and pulled the two smaller ones away, saving them for bigger fish to fry. I think I tried to look insouciant for about fifteen seconds and then burst into tears.

The second was an instance of the more insidious bullying of middle-class English opinion. The papers had pronounced *Macbeth* crap, and that was that. A week after I had seen it, an English teacher who had also been there started giving out about it. He had amassed a collection of stock phrases from the papers, which he archly intoned as if they were penetratingly original thoughts. He adopted a sort of ersatz sneery tone, full of weariness about the foolishness of these metropolitan types, as he gave himself a hard-on telling us how terrible it was. There was that then rare, now more familiar, delight in seeing something grand crash and burn. I attempted a muted defence and got drawn into an argument. I was already losing the argument fairly comprehensively when the teacher abandoned the pretence of originality and announced that anyway I was wrong because all the papers had said it was rubbish. This was enough for him and the class. I withdrew into my shell, but with a growing distaste for the discreet violence of the middle-class consensus. At least the skinhead had been straight about what he was doing.

subtext with my sister on a summer's evening

My sister and I always had a taste for quick verbal sallies. Small wonder that 'egg the Dromgooles' was a popular local battle cry. There is a lightning-fast exchange from a Danny Kaye film – *The Court Jester*, I think. He delivers a barrage of commands to a subordinate, then turns to another and, fleet as foot, says, 'Get it?' Before he's even finished those two words, an aggressive 'Got it' is fired back at him. Before that can even finish Kaye clips back a 'Good', and lets it taper away slowly. We used to lie in wait for each other within bushes or behind cupboard doors, then leap out, like Kato in the Pink Panther films, with a sharp 'Get it?' If we failed to get a quick response, we scored a point in some unobserved long game.

One late summer afternoon, we got hold of a passage from *Othello* and started playing around with that. It's the scene where Iago starts dicking around with Othello's brain. He does it deftly and with a wickedly quick discretion. The exchanges fly by:

IAGO Ha! I like not that.
OTHELLO What dost thou say?
IAGO Nothing my lord; or if – I know not what.

And then later:

IAGO ... your pardon for too much loving you.
OTHELLO I'm bound to thee for ever.
IAGO I see this has a little dashed your spirits.
OTHELLO Not a jot, not a jot.
IAGO I'faith, I fear it has.

And soon after:

IAGO . . . cannot choose but they must blab –
OTHELLO Hath he said any thing?
IAGO He hath my lord; but be you well assured,
    No more than he'll unswear.
OTHELLO What hath he said?
IAGO Faith, that he did – I know not what he did.
OTHELLO What? What?
IAGO Lie –
OTHELLO With her?
IAGO With her, on her; what you will.

Soon after, Othello falls to pieces, babbling spurts of nonsense before he lapses into a trance.

We liked the look of this dialogue and raced at it with our usual quick-fire repartee. Imagine Rosalind Russell and Cary Grant in *His Girl Friday*, and you've got the pace of it, if not exactly the look. As we did, funny things started happening. There was delight at the deft annotation of synapse-fast mental speed. It was all comprehensible and made perfect sense, which was a big plus. There was pleasure to be taken in Iago's rapier irony, and the finger-light touch with which he steers the great boat of Othello's heart. There was also a surprising sense that we were being controlled, that there was only one way to play this, and that it dictated its own rhythm. We could tinker about with it, but only within its own truth. If we didn't live within its music, it fell to pieces on us.

Murkier feelings started emerging as well, the longer we hurled the words between us. It was a summer evening, we were circling around among the apple trees, the light was failing, and as we ping-ponged this dialogue to and fro, meanings started percolating up we were too young to understand. A sexual frisson shivered in the intimacy of the exchange, the electricity of two minds trying to uncover each other's dark corners. Power games, ugly master and commander Pinteresque guff, floated around the language, staining the innocence with which we were offering it up. And as Othello crumbled, his soldier's bombast shrivelling down to a boy's fear, the fragility of his identity was exposed. His character was a frail mask. By the end of the scene, sanity itself was under strain, and the strength of language to retain a grip on sanity. All this floated up as we did nothing but toss the words into the air and let them conjure their own sour truth. There was no discussion, no 'goodness, isn't this interesting', just this demented high-speed repetition. And all this subterranean Pandora's box played itself out within this fizzing verbal joust.

I learned more in those two hours than in a year's teaching. About how to play Shakespeare, keeping it light, and fast, and not signposting intentions, just speaking. About the nature of subtext, the sewage system that runs underneath all great writing and gives it its own electric tension. About the clumsiness of great dialogue, its scrappy messiness, and how a smooth speech articulating its own meaning is often a terrible one. This is what separated Shakespeare off from his contemporaries. They all knew about stichomythia, the Greek term for rapid-fire dialogue, but nobody took it as far as Shakespeare. Nobody took it down to the level of words and breaths, with his accuracy and ostentation. He wrote speech, not speeches. He heard and reproduced the crackle and the spark, the myriad small tensions that make it alive. It was a lesson that stayed with me and earned me a living for a decade. All as the light closed in and we charged about.

Later we discovered the two equally fast exchanges between Othello and Desdemona, where the febrile, staccato rhythm of his dialogue with Iago falls like a shadow across their talk. Previously their conversation had been warm and easy, though a little stately. Now it is like this:

OTHELLO Fire and brimstone!
DESDEMONA My lord?
OTHELLO Are you wise?
DESDEMONA What, is he angry?

And a short while later:

DESDEMONA Trust me, I am glad on't.
OTHELLO Indeed!
DESDEMONA My lord?
OTHELLO I am glad to see you mad.
DESDEMONA Why, sweet Othello!
OTHELLO (*striking her*) Devil!

We tried out these exchanges, but there was little fun to be had with them. The build-up to tragedy, the set-up, is cruelly full of witty little games which sharpen the pulse. Tragedy, though, is tragedy, and you can't play with it, you can only watch it in fear. On our summer's evening, we finally got round to the climactic cry that is squeezed at the heart of the scene from all the tensions that surround it:

but yet the pity of it, Iago! O Iago, the pity of it, Iago!

The full pain of that cry eluded us, but the storm cloud that surrounded it steadily bore down on the sunny day of youth.

more Stratford, fast pints and chopsticks in church

Further experiences of Stratford in my youth were largely associated with my bladder. Other directors all seem to have had some epiphanic adolescent moment in Stratford. They are always writing of walking there from Manchester barefoot, of pitching their tent in a field and witnessing some cultish production of *King John*, which laid out their destiny before them. Not so with me, unfortunately. I principally remember Stratford for getting leglessly drunk, then floundering around looking for somewhere to have a slash.

The first occasion was by a country mile the worst. I had progressed from my comprehensive school to a very eccentric private school called Millfield. Part of the education programme there was a regular excursion on the ship-'em-in, ship-'em-out schools matinée trundle, which Stratford ran. This required a three-hour coach trip from my school in mid-Somerset. Usually the trip was reserved for older pupils, but because my enthusiasm for Shakespeare was noted, I was allowed to accompany my older brother on a first outing at the age of thirteen.

The trip up was fine, as was the show. It was Ian McKellen and Francesca Annis in *Romeo and Juliet*. He was, as he ever is, warm and glamorous and generous-spirited; she was elegant and attractive enough to sustain a prolonged 'corrr' from a row of big boys. The verse, as ever, flew by – most of it cheerfully incomprehensible – and we all stared stagewards in blithe ignorance. The proceedings were lost in a miasma of Shakespeare deadness – all fake spiritual health and rugby club vigour, though the occasional moment pierced. We crept back-stage afterwards to see Ian McKellen, who had stayed with us on our farm while making a television film with my father. He trooped us round back-stage. This was far from magical, largely because we were mired in adolescent dullness and professionally unimpressed by everything. 'Oh', 'uh', 'uhuh', 'yeah' was all that his charm could draw out of us, and he dumped us back at the stage-door as soon as he politely could.

The problems began after, as we began our timid search for alcohol. The teachers had allowed us an hour and a half to roam Stratford before returning to the coach. Full of a needless paranoia, and convinced there were teachers behind every corner, we crawled around, jumping walls and hiding behind dustbins, trying to elude our non-existent pursuers. Eventually we found a sad corner shop, so far out of the centre of town it was practically in London, and sent in the two eldest and gruffest amongst us to buy six cans of lager. Since I was the smallest, I hung around in terror outside, trying to look butch. The cans obtained, we strolled around with that guilt-filled feigned nonchalance that only the young and twattish can fully bring off, before finding a disabled toilet in a municipal car park and sneaking in there. Is there anything less fun in the world than drinking a can of warm Harp lager in a smelly toilet in a car park? No. Nevertheless we filled the silence with mutters of 'magic', and 'that's the stuff', and 'oh yeah'.

Because the buying and the drinking had taken so long we had to forgo the real function of our improvised cocktail lounge and rush back to the coach. We jumped on just as it was leaving. Excluded from the others by age, I sat by myself at the front, taking no pleasure in my guilty secret, just bemused by the flatness of beer. My bladder started to twinge after about half an hour and I knew I was in trouble. If I asked the coach to stop, all my crimes would immediately be discovered. I would be expelled. So would all the others. And I'd probably go to prison too. I would have to tough it out, but I knew that two and a half hours was impossible, and prayed that someone else would stop the coach. After a further half hour, I had a faraway look in my eyes as I stared out of the window at the motorway zooming by and tried to astral project myself into a different body.

A self-advertisingly sensitive teacher noticed me and thought he should come and help. This was a disaster. Knowing I liked my Shakespeare, he thought my glazed eyes and gritted teeth were a response to the tragedy we'd witnessed. He sat beside me and tried to elucidate what was wrong. I was incapable of more than a few muttered words before looking out of the window again. He understood this as me being crushed by emotion. He started a seemingly eternal monologue about *Romeo and Juliet*, the nature of tragedy and the pain of life. About twenty minutes in, I began to softly cry from a combination of shame, bladder pressure and cosmic despair. He took this to be a response to the bigness of his wisdom. Far from shutting him up, it spurred him on to further musing on the nature of existence. After a further twenty-odd minutes I could bear no more and let go. My mood immediately lightened, which the teacher couldn't at first understand, until his nose instructed him what had happened. He swiftly stopped his interminable blah about George Steiner and the relationship between Christianity and tragedy, muttered something like 'bloody child' and put a fair distance between us. I stewed.

Later trips were far more festive, and far less furtive. Confidence came with age and a greater knowledge of the general lack of punishment. As we pulled in to Stratford coach car park, our teachers would give a half-hearted but spirited speech about being ambassadors for the school. We would walk straight past them into the nearest pub. We had about an hour and we had to drink quickly. The juke box would be monopolized to produce incessant Jam; the mood was high and flirty and the pints would be despatched swiftly. One of our number, Mole, could open his gullet, so on these trips he came into his own. He could sink a pint in five seconds. We all managed about five pints, girls and boys, in the forty-five minutes we had before trucking up to the theatre, full of lunatic good cheer.

For the first twenty minutes we would laugh energetically at whatever humour came our way, before the troubles began. A silence would fall on our school party. At first light. And then heavy. A series of whispered 'when's the interval?'s would be asked, followed by a series of whispered 'fucking hell's, when we discovered it was two millennia away. We would start by twitching, then shortly after throwing our legs one over the other and squeezing. Soon after we'd be contorting ourselves, then finally trying to fold ourselves up into something you could put in a suitcase. It only took one to crack. It was usually my friend Crispin, who would blurt, 'Fuck this for a game of soldiers', stand up and shuffle his way out. The moment he did that, the rest of the school party would leap up and start bundling themselves out, stampeding and trampling over old folk and tourists as a large section of the audience charged for the exits. It was an exodus. Once fully relieved, but still completely pissed, we would crash our way back in. Actors would stop mid-soliloquy and observe the return of their lost flock. Heaven knows what they muttered at us under their breath. We little cared because we were soon all asleep, flattened by the steady Shakespearean line. Once Mole, the gullet man, got lost behind some fire doors, which led on to the stage, and tried to kick them open. This stopped the show entirely as security was sent to throw him out. Our teachers seethed. I remember, with some shame and no little glee, ruining one *Lear*, one *As You Like It* and two *Hamlet*s in this fashion.

It was, of course, yobbo activity, but there is something about Stratford that invites yobbo activity. One afternoon, after a show, we found ourselves in Holy Trinity church, where Shakespeare is buried. Another friend, Philip, sat at a concert piano and played Chopsticks, until we were chased out of there as well. It was an act of irreligion, of course, but directed not only at our stern old Christian god. It was also aimed at the whole kitschy, stuck-in-aspic, Shakespearean shtick. If we behaved in a punk manner, or as punk as well-fed middle-class kids could manage, the productions, with all their painfully studied 'relevance', deserved all that and a lot more. How else can you really react to the Shakespeare temple business than by kicking a little anarchy around the place? Punk was in the air at the time, and I was beginning to have an inkling of how close that spirit was to the heart of Shakespeare himself, and what a distortion of that spirit the Stratford shrine to him had turned out to be.

There is a central illogic in the relationship between a man who wrote believing his plays would be produced a few times and then evanesce into oblivion and an industry created to feed off his memory. Had he proudly presented his plays with a fulsome dedication like his friend Ben Jonson, had he shown any interest in their publication at all, had he left behind him any traces of himself, it would make a little sense. But he was never about self-memorializing. Shakespeare was all about becoming; Stratford seemed to be all about freezing.

The industry begun by Garrick, and institutionalized in the two centuries after his Jubilee, was never designed for troublesome auto-rebel teenagers. If we were going to receive the plays with the joy and the excitement they deserved, they would have had to have been presented with considerably more verve and freshness than anything we witnessed. There was never any hope of us buying into the merchandising.

in the wings, theatrical rivalries and nookie

In front of me is a tatty flat – black serge stretched over rudimentary carpentry – behind me another, equally shabby. Fourteen years old, I'm dressed in a fake sheepskin coat, a pork pie hat perched precariously on my excess of hair and a lit pipe in my mouth whose sickly sweet tobacco I'm sucking vigorously. The character I'm about to fail to portray is Uncle Les in *Zigger Zagger*, a play about football violence that's quite crude enough already before we all reduce its two dimensions to one. I've never looked a bigger tit in my life and I feel curiously at home. A peculiar sense of aptness sweeps through me. This feeling is not there in the dressing room with all its make-up and vanities and bleary camaraderie: nor is it present on stage, under the bright lights with all the shouting and the shining. I enjoy both, and feel free in both, but my greatest sense of being just and alive is in the nothing in between. It may be the effect of the pipe tobacco on a young brain (do pupils still do school plays so they can showily smoke in front of their peers?), but stuck between these two flats, in my ridiculous costume, where no one can see me, with hysterical excitement on either side, I feel at home.

The chance to act in a Shakespeare play didn't arrive until later, but I acted my socks off from an early age, partly as a way of getting close to him. In my head Shakespeare was theatre, and anything theatrical was a further approach towards the top of the mountain, where he sat Zeus-like. From the age of about five, I wrote, directed and took the leading part in plays at home. At first, these involved a tremendous amount of energy designing and building a box office, before writing out and colouring in tickets and programmes. At the end of all that creative effort, there was usually precious little left for the show. So we would settle for me or my brother donning a Batman cape, and then a noisy bout of wrestling. Usually ending in tears, as our parents broke the fourth wall to tell us off.

As we grew older, they gained in sophistication, with scripts written and sets built. Casting was the biggest problem, with my brother and sister using the ultimate sanction of 'I'm not doing your blummin' play' as a way of ensuring I was less of a pain in the arse. My sister would complain quite rightly about the feebleness of the women's parts, but her role model was Dee Dee from Pan's People, which made her quest for empowerment confusing. Rehearsals were turbulent, with frequent dramatic walk-outs, followed by me bawling to my mother, and her commanding the others to return to work. All in all, a grand preparation for the life to come. There were various other potty efforts before getting to big school. Leaping on to a rock as a pirate and shouting 'Avast ye!' in a sea of tomato ketchup that was supposed to be a Cub Scout tableau. Improvising a play during a summer holiday drama workshop which teetered wildly between the parent-loathing grumpiness of the adolescents and the Famous Five versus James Bond aesthetic of the younger members. The result was what the critics like to term 'uneven'.

Once I left the delinquent rough and tumble of my comprehensive school and graduated to the more sophisticated cruelties of Millfield, the amount of drama flourished. The school plays were conservative and cautious to a degree that deadened the imagination. We did *Zigger Zagger*, *She Stoops to Conquer*, *Under Milk Wood*, *A Man for All Seasons* and *Guys and Dolls*. Eat your heart out, Peter Brook. The productions were as dull as the choice of play.

A production of a Shakespeare play, *Hamlet*, was announced. I wandered around practising my downcast glance, my misty eye and my sword fighting. I gave my mother a little glamorous despising as well. The English library was given the benefit of a couple of soliloquies. Costumes were sorted out in some sort of butch, punk, romantic strain. Shirts both torn and frilly. The fact I hadn't been asked to audition worried me not a jot. Hamlet was mine, as if by right. When they put the cast list on the notice-board, I went into shock. Not only was I not Hamlet, nor was I Claudius, or Polonius or Laertes or even Rosencrantz or bogging Guildenstern. In fact I wasn't in it. I went into a profound depression, more acute and real than anything I could have mustered for the role.

One lesson I learned at school, the truth of which has lasted through all my working experience, is that people who are interested in being in the theatre make a small and self-enclosed village within the larger community they inhabit. The theatre community in Shakespeare's day, within a population of 200,000 in London, would probably have numbered about four or five hundred – taking in actors, theatre managers, musicians, technicians, patrons and hangers-on various. When academics muse over whether Shakespeare and Marlowe may have been close, and how well Shakespeare and Jonson may have known each other, it makes me want to giggle. In a community that small, they would probably have spent most of their time enumerating the number of sexual diseases they had caught off each other. With their toes as well as their fingers. The theatre community of today is much, much larger, yet almost everyone knows each other. As in any village, there is a huge amount of curtain twitching, a lot of bitching and much jumping from camp to camp. And as with any small village, there is always a low-level war going on between all the various small cliques – the church-goers, the drug takers, the parish council busy bodies, the labourers and the rich folk on the hill. Each forms a community within the community.

At school it was the same, and if I'd been anything other than deluded, I would have realized I hadn't a hope of nabbing Hamlet. The play was being directed by a teacher who had conceived a seemingly passionate loathing for my family. For some reason, he was determined not only to exclude us from his school plays, but also to have us expelled from the school. My father may have offered notes on his production of *Under Milk Wood*, which won't have helped. Nor did my brother pinning up a gynaecological study of his wife on a prominent window. He banned everyone in his school house from speaking to us and seemed to run his own security service trying to trap us in some compromising misdemeanour. He failed, just. Anyway, he probably hurt me worse by not letting me be in *Hamlet* than if I'd been expelled. He gave the part to my friend/rival Crispin, who had arrived at the school in the fifth form. Long battles had previously been fought to secure my status as resident literary, tortured, moody zany in my year, and it had cost blood. Then Crispin had arrived, more literate, more tortured, more moody and considerably zanier. All in all, conspicuously more interesting. And a much more suitable Hamlet.

So I swallowed my pride, and strolled around aiming at a sort of Prufrock chic; 'No, I am not Prince Hamlet, nor was meant to be . . .', while Crispin upped the stakes on the whole tortured shtick. Until his show opened. The other factor that distinguishes any theatre community, be it at school, university, am-dram or professional, is the burning desire to see your rival fail. It's best phrased by a fellow director, Max Stafford-Clark, who once said, 'Every time I read a good review for another director, my heart sinks.' The same would have pertained at any time over the last 3,000 years. Sophocles will have trashed that old fart Aeschylus, just as he will have been made nervous by that uppity young buck Euripides. Greene loathed and detested Shakespeare, who was jealous of Marlowe's glamour and was made nervous by the learning of Jonson, who worried that he wasn't as truthful and alive as Shakespeare or as dramatic as Webster, and on and on the Elizabethan daisy chain went, all revelling in each other's failures and depressed by each other's triumphs. The rictus-smiling camaraderie of theatre folk is a reality. They are solidly together defending their profession against the attacks of critics and nay-sayers. But amongst themselves they are savage.

As I was at school. Crispin opened in *Hamlet*. He was terrible. His zany had got the better of his moody, and he'd been too busy partying to bother with learning his lines. He got away with it until the last act, when he started taking cues so thick and fast that the prompt became a more prominent character than Claudius. Eventually, he said, 'Oh fuck it!' and wandered off, grabbed a copy and came back and read from it. Unfortunately the copy he brought back on didn't have all the right cuts, and the show was further held up by a series of arguments over who should be saying what. Did I gloat?

Later there was a production of *The Taming of the Shrew* mooted. Again to my astonishment I was not asked to play Petruchio. This cut even harder, since the nominated Katherine was my girlfriend. I moped and mooched. At the time this all seemed a sinister conspiracy to deny me my fame. Looking back, there was a simpler truth. I was rubbish. Self-conscious, graceless, awkward, posey and quiet. Through force of will, and being able to learn my lines, plum parts had been secured. Then I spoilt them by being vain, egotistical and crap. I was an explosive device waiting to wreck any show. The teachers had a point.

Aside from discovering the ugly pleasure of schadenfreude there were more healthy joys discovered in the theatre. In the house play competition we banded together with our fellow day pupils – very much the outsiders at Millfield, which largely comprised obscenely wealthy oil-rich international students – for a succession of festive productions. We came a nasty cropper with a First World War anthology I put together. This collection of songs, scenes and pro-war and anti-war poetry depended on a sophisticated system of opening and closing curtains to reveal magically assembled tableaux. Unfortunately, on the night in question both sets of curtains jammed, necessitating a lot of Morecambe and Wise activity as scene after scene was carried to and fro through the front cloth. I had given myself – surprise, surprise – the juicy anti-war poems of Sassoon and Owen. It was the first time I had ever spoken verse on stage. The evening was such a disaster I had a rush of who-gives-a-fuck energy, which I poured into a raging torrent of Wilfred Owen's 'Dulce et Decorum Est'. I'll never forget diving into a large blackness full of 500 arsey kids armed with that grenade of a poem and shutting them up to such a depth of silence it felt as if the world had gone quiet. Nor how I discovered in that moment – forced by the disaster of my own making all around me – that it's only when you're utterly without pride, and utterly without conceit, that you can start to offer anything up.

It's a discovery Shakespeare would have made over and over as an actor. Any sensitive actor knows the speed with which a moment of arrogance is followed by a moment of calamity. In one instant you think you're an elegant, intelligent sex-god; in the next you're failing to pull a cork out of a bottle and having to do some childish mime of drinks pouring in front of a thousand spectators. Yet, if you arrive in a moment alert, and sharp, and with low expectations, the speed of the trajectory upwards is equally swift. Shakespeare stitches this knowledge into many of his character's stories. There is a persistent movement from pride to bare-assed shame, and from humility to glory. It's the nightly transition of the actor.

The other pleasure that emerged from the theatre life, and which related backwards to Shakespeare, was the oldest one of all – drink and drugs and liberal amounts of snogging. There is a famous and rather arch Ye Olde Anecdotee of Shakespeare as a great swordsman tricking his way into the knickers of someone waiting for his leading man, Richard Burbage. He is also supposed to have fathered a child in Oxford under the nose of the cuckolded husband. There is another lobby that states he was, in some cold, dispassionate way, asexual. It's hard to know where the truth is pitched. But it is a theatrical truism that hardly anyone enters the profession who doesn't fancy a little bit of extra nookie. It would be hard to exempt Shakespeare from that. Indeed, as one of the greatest theatre animals of all time, and as a man whose plays exemplify the spirit of greed, and generosity, whether spiritual or experiential, it's hard to argue that he didn't fancy enormous helpings of extra nookie. What is equally certain is that he probably liked a glass or twelve. He writes beautifully of drunks in the tavern scenes of the Henry plays, Sir Toby in *Twelfth Night* and Barnardine in *Measure for Measure*, who declares with the glorious insouciance of the truly hammered that he does not want to die today. He writes too well for an abstemious man. There is a credible myth that his death followed a big night in a Warwickshire pub with his friends Ben Jonson and Michael Drayton.

We were hardly likely to drink ourselves to death after our school plays. They habitually ended with a glass of orange squash and, if we were all really letting our hair down, a sherry with the headmaster. But the house plays were different. We formed a gang and held regular Saturday-night parties at each other's homes. The rhythm of such occasions was set. We would arrive, be shunted into old farm barns and listen to punk rock. Boys and girls would club together on either side of the room. Cider and cooking sherry would be consumed at alarming speeds. Cigarettes would be smoked furiously, with a variety of affected ways of holding them. There would be some violent pogoing in the middle of the room. Two people would habitually turn green, lean heavily on vertical objects and then throw up to the general amusement of everyone else.

Then, at a certain moment, decided by who knows what, boys and girls would fall on each other, slobbering and drooling, tongues thrashing violently and hands flying up, down, in and around, like Donne's 'America'. If there was a surfeit of boys – which there almost always was – the boys would pair up anyway and set to. Somehow, through this violent courting ritual, I found my first love.

Yet, for all the drink and kisses, the rises and falls, and the ecstatic sensation that you are touching an audience's heart, for me the greatest thrill remained those moments in the wings. They afforded the greatest clue to Shakespeare's mind. Real life on one side with all its emotional freight of responsibility and care. The stage on the other side with its blaze of imagination and on-rushing story. A small, tatty space in between.

It's a funny space where someone not quite an actor, and not quite a human being, can feel at ease. There's a time-suspended nullity to it. Tom Stoppard explores it in *Rosencrantz and Guildenstern Are Dead*, with his two main characters who live almost permanently in the wings of life. It's a creative space, since its very emptiness demands its contrary, fullness, and pulls that out of the imagination. And a Shakespearean place. Not only in the biographical sense, since, as an actor of small parts, he would have spent half a lifetime there. Nor only in the sense of a revealing private place. Shakespeare often catches his characters in the wings as they leave a scene or as they approach one, and gets them to speak to us. This is the special quality of his soliloquies, the feeling that you are afforded a glimpse into the private recesses of a character's thinking. But also in the metaphysical sense. The twin poles of life in the wings – everything out there, nothing here – are the twin polarities of Shakespeare's universe. Where others pursue the great warfare between male and female, good and evil, right and wrong, or any number of smaller skirmishes, Shakespeare wraps all those lesser scraps into his comprehensive everything, which erupts into life in opposition to its great rival, nothing.

innuendo, O levels and Leavis

The standard of teaching of Shakespeare at my school was variable. For a couple of years we were subjected to the instruction of a horny little red-haired man with John Lennon spectacles. He could have found erotic innuendo in a Soviet document discussing trade relations with Finland. No work of literature was beyond his pornographic imagination. Every large object was phallic – practically everything that was upright in fact – and anything remotely circular just had to be a vulva. If the two things occurred in close proximity in a line of verse, he had to leave the room. Let loose on Shakespeare, he spontaneously combusted. On the day he took us through the filthiest of the sonnets he could hardly contain himself:

> The expense of spirit in a waste of shame
> Is lust in action; and till action, lust
> Is perjured, murderous, bloody, full of blame,
> Savage, extreme, rude, cruel, not to trust;
> Enjoy'd no sooner but despised straight;
> Past reason hunted; and no sooner had,
> Past reason hated, as a swallowed bait,
> On purpose laid to make the taker mad:
> Mad in pursuit, and in possession so;
> Had, having, and in quest to have, extreme;
> A bliss in proof, and proved, a very woe;
> Before, a joy proposed; behind, a dream.
> All this the world well knows; yet none knows well
> To shun the heaven that leads men to this hell.

Someone read it out innocently enough, and then he started in on it. He had that dreadful 'I know more than you do' manner, which really isn't the essence of education. 'So, class, what do you think the first line's about?' A few interpretations were timidly offered up. 'Nope,' he announced. A few more. 'Wrong!' Yet more. 'Miles off!' I don't think he fully understood what teaching was. Finally, he let us in on the secret. 'You see, in the Elizabethan world, spirit was another word for semen. For a man's semen! So if you're expending spirit, what do you think waste might be a pun for? Well, what for?' We were only about thirteen, and fresh out of sexual education lessons. We didn't need to be terrorized in this fashion. We all made it through his explanation of the choppy, brutal rhythm of lines three and four, 'perjured, murderous, bloody, full of blame,/Savage, extreme, rude, cruel, not to trust', and how that rhythm approximated to the jerky movements of rough sex. When he got to line ten, and started outlining how the three aspirant *h*s served as an aural approximation for the cry of a male orgasm, several people were trying to leave the room. As he climaxed on how 'to die' was a coded pun for 'to come', and how nothing was an analogous word for a vagina, his work was done. Any vague innocence we might ever have found in the work was lost in a slew of innuendo.

There was another teacher who had a passion for little but the sound of his own voice. At the beginning of term, he would announce which play we were going to read out loud, and then perform the same ritual. 'Ah, yes, *Hamlet*, what pleasure we're going to have. Now let's just skip through the dramatis personae. Horatio, the good and trusted friend. Lane, that's one for you. Laertes, the enraged brother. Dromgoole – you can have a go at that. Now Hamlet, a tricky part, requires an extraordinary vocal range. And great intellectual speed. I think I'll take that one. Let's see, Rosencrantz and Guildenstern, the two bumbling courtiers. Barton and Burrell, I think you could have fun with that. Ophelia . . . Tree. Gertrude . . . Joffe. Ah now, Claudius, yes, needs a lot of authority, and emotion . . . very difficult . . . I think I'd better take that one as well . . .' Each new term the same story, and each long lesson a willowy, impassioned rendition after the fashion of John Gielgud in the 1930s, with added tremolo.

And then as a huge and considerable saving grace there was Mr

Rosser. He was an extraordinary mix. A one-time rugby international who sometimes seemed passionate about nothing but the funny-shaped ball game, he could read a poem by George Herbert, and his eyes would well up. A Christian conservative, he had a sly, anarchic humour and a dislike of authority. And best of all he had an extraordinary nose for bullshit. He knew when a writer or a character was whistling in the wind. He could see the pomp and nonsense in Milton, and in Donne, and equally in Othello. It was a gift, and a great one to pass on. The knowledge of when a character or a writer is not telling the truth, when they're talking from an insecure base is invaluable. To know when a writer is walking steadily and with assurance, and when they are floundering and stumbling; to know when they are saying what they want to say, and when they are trying to impress; these are the first steps in getting to know them.

Mr Rosser had studied under F. R. Leavis and nigh-on worshipped him. I still to this day can't work out what Leavis was actually on about, even after reading two of his books. But what was passed down through Rosser was simple. The application of hard, cold, commonsensical thinking to a text. Just look at it. Look at it again. Start to make sense of it. Then look at it again. Start to relish it. Then look at it harder. It's so easy to go da-dum da-dum da-dum prettily through a line and fail to dig your mind into the soil. The harder you look, the more the texture appears. If it's beautifully made, the more solid the texture. The more solid the texture, the more resonances there are within it. And the more resonances, the greater the excitement. By equal measure, the harder you look, the easier and quicker it is to detect rubbish, since it cannot stand such inspection. Mr Rosser didn't teach us a single literary rule. He simply impressed on us the importance of looking.

There are few word paintings of any sort as rewarding to inspect as those created by Shakespeare. Once I had learned to see the patterns of imagery, the flecks of detail, the big garish colours, the cosmic backdrops, then Shakespeare became yet more alive. Our first big set text for O level was *Macbeth*, a play that should have been familiar. But, of course, I had only listened to its dark music before and sensed an accompanying mood. As I studied it properly for the first time, something that had been a two-dimensional entity in front of me, striking but flat, suddenly started to acquire depth. It stretched away from me, in all directions, as if mirrors coloured with *Macbeth*'s bruised and ugly shades had opened up before and behind. That thick texture, of rooks and witches and graves opening and stars in confusion and horses eating their own, surrounded me.

Revelations followed from the simple expedient of looking. The greatest gift in what Rosser taught us was that nothing was taken away. So many theories when applied to literature – if not all – seem designed to reduce it. The understanding is a way of flattening the landscape, of rearranging chaos, of explaining mystery. We were being taught simply to see clearly, and to relish. There were many more theories to come in the years ahead, some barmy, some persuasive. It soon became clear that their invention was in many ways the cement that held academic institutions together. Rosser gave us a suit of armour, with which we could always defend ourselves from the white noise of such deconstructive screeching, by simply looking at the text. And looking again.

first love, virtue and the last act
of *Hamlet*

It's a rare, and fine, pleasure for someone to plant in you a thought that later grows into an understanding. As we get older we grow resistant to learning. We evolve a complex series of grunts, facial tics and social mannerisms to let someone know 'Yes, I know that already actually.' In truth we're as clueless as the day at primary school when a teacher sets up a circuit with a battery, two wires and a bulb, and we all go 'wow'. We evolve a pointless reflex to contest facts and arguments, to let someone know 'Ha! Is that what you think?', when every cell in our brain is innocent of what they're on about. Life would remain a lot simpler if we continued going 'wow'.

One of the reasons we're always chasing Shakespeare is we're always seeing him disappear over the horizon, looking for more himself. His insatiable appetite for the new, his enthusiasm to go into unknown territory, keeps him way ahead of the game. If he had had the sort of mind that settled on what it knew, then lectured from a static position of certain knowledge, instead of chasing him, we'd be running in the other direction. Fast. Even as an old man, when countless writers from Wordsworth down forgo the radicalism and enthusiasms of their youth for a settled position from which they can sternly teach, Shakespeare went on experimenting and ferreting away for new content and new form. Many artists, as the dark approaches, build walls of certainty around themselves; Shakespeare, as with his protagonist Lear, sends himself out into the dark and wet night to see what life throws up. We don't buy into what he knows, we buy into his desire to know.

My first big love, one that evolved out of the cider, pogo, puke and snog social circuit of my teens, was one long learning experience. She was older by several years, better read and more intelligent. She was as passionate about literature as I was, but with her the passion ran deeper and with less affect. We were a comical couple in many ways, wandering soulfully around in heavy coats and long scarfs – even in midsummer. And how we burbled – D. H. Lawrence, Yeats, the *Four Quartets*, Hardy, Donne – all was grist to the mill of the adolescent rollercoaster we were on. We could hardly have an emotion without cross-referring it to a suitable literary text. This could have been painfully self-conscious – it was – but the heart and the canon lifted each other to fresh heights. Our joy at discovering each other, at paddling around within the potential in another human being, was elevated by the reading and quotation. And the poems and the prose were sent skyrocketing by that joy. We would sit and read poems to each other, look into each other's eyes, then well up. Not exactly butch, is it?

She was always ahead of me in literary knowledge – she had done her A levels before I had done my Os – and was constantly introducing me to new works. But that wasn't at the heart of what she taught me. She was a naturally good person, one of the few I've ever met. Goodness gurgled up in her like a spring. She had taken that virtue and applied it to *Hamlet* and understood it more completely than any text-book could make clear. Not in a wraparound, intertextual, aren't-I-clever, Harold Bloom sense, but in a personal, taking-possession sense. She had owned the wisdom of the last act, and was generous enough to pass it on to me.

The last act charts Hamlet's return to Denmark after the bit of dodgy plotting with the pirates. The frenzied neurotic of act IV, spattering his mother with abuse, raging ineffectually at the moon and scampering around the castle farcically with the corpse of Polonius, is replaced by a calm, serene, philosophic figure. He could be dead already, Jesus resurrected, so implacable is his serenity. He is briefly troubled by the challenge to a duel with Laertes, and the foreknowledge of what it will mean. He buries his troubles with a luminous sweetness of spirit:

Not a whit, we defy augury: there is a special providence in the fall of a sparrow. If it be now, 'tis not to come; if it be not to come, it will be now;

if it be not now, yet it will come – the readiness is all. Since no man owes of aught he leaves, what is't to leave betimes? Let be.

Sick with the turbulence of teenager rubbish as I was, with wanting and waste and rage, the idea of this new tone, this new approach, knocked my socks off. The rites of acceptance and transcendence are built into a religious education; within its structures there are ways of revealing 'the peace which passeth all understanding' in sufficient measure to calm any feverish breast. But without such education, that revelation is harder to come by. And without glimpsing a state so transcendental, it is very hard to be complete. I was a jigsaw with key pieces missing, flailing around, looking for a shape. My first love taught me that transcendental wasn't some mystic, hippy state, involving floaty white cheesecloth, it was a benign way of coping with the mess of life. That insight helped a shape to start forming.

Not in a Christian sense – why should it be Christian? Mention the word divinity, as in a further *Hamlet* line, 'There's a divinity that shapes our ends,/Rough-hew them how we will', and the sages assert that this is Shakespeare snuggling up to Christ. Balls. It seems almost certain that Shakespeare believed that Jesus Christ was one of the most beautiful humans who ever lived. The plays are rich with Christian imagery and language and symbolism. They could hardly not be: the world he grew up in was saturated in it. Shakespeare absorbed all of that with the same spongey inclusiveness as he absorbed the wit of a boatman, the arguments of Montaigne or the honeyed lightness of an Ovidian line. But, having absorbed, he didn't set out to defend it. He never wrote from a singular, propagandist position. In *Hamlet* he wasn't writing about Jesus, he was writing about Hamlet. Or more honestly Hamlet was writing himself. And he wasn't supporting the case of Jesus, despite the probable pressure, he was supporting the case of Hamlet, and every other scared and raging soul who lives in outraged terror at what the world may bring. Hamlet finds his own way to peace.

She took me through in a human sense. She had lost her father suddenly at the age of eight, an event whose echoes were still resounding within her ten years later. In all the time I was with her, she didn't once complain about the hand she'd been dealt. She hardly mentioned it. She had made it good somehow and had transcended the cruelty of her own history. It's small wonder that *Hamlet* meant so much to her. A journey from the loss of a father, through mess and confusion, to calm and balance can be lived with a Hamletian grandeur or in a small Somerset town. She showed me what that journey meant not through pained exegesis of her family history – nothing so vulgar – but through pointing me towards it in the play, explaining it in simple language and living it.

It's a strain that has never completely left me, the strain of acceptance. One can lose sight of it in an instant, when a milk carton won't open or in a long queue, and occasionally it can disappear for protracted periods. Yet every time I reread *Hamlet* or see it again, no matter how nutty the production, it recharges that battery.

academic fads, Bradley and clues to character

The whole idea of character in Shakespeare is scoffed at now. There was an explosion of interest in the nature of his characters at the dawn of the twentieth century, simultaneous with Freud's big moment, and during the infancy of the psychology industry. At the forefront was A. C. Bradley, who wrote a series of dense psychological studies analysing all of Shakespeare's great heroes. His books are shrewd, elegantly written and develop a strong narrative drive as he shoves his spade into the psyche of Othello or Lear or Hamlet. You share his gathering discovery as he gets to know his man. It has the allure of detective work.

Soon after his glory days, he crashed out of fashion quite spectacularly. Someone wrote an amusingly snidey essay titled 'How Many Children Had Lady Macbeth?', spoofing the whole idea of imagining back stories for any dramatic character. And soon after the great tide of modernism washed in and tugged every idea about psychological realism out to sea with it. The plays were now to be viewed as long lyrical poems, works of art, amalgamating themes and ideas and philosophies in complex patterns of language and rhythm. Anybody who mentioned character was deemed to be a relic from the Stone Age. A funny collection of men called Mr Knights and Mr Dover Wilson and Mr Wilson Knight all wrote with a ferociously excited prose about the grand play of imagery. Their names were suspiciously similar. It was hard not to conceive of them as a single man, sitting hysterically in a cupboard somewhere in Oxford, furiously churning out theorems and firing them out into the world under different disguises.

Later the airyfairyness of modernist criticism was coshed to death by the bootboys from the cultural materialist school and the structuralists. From the 1960s on, politics of every sort joined the battle with Shakespeare. Class politics, gender politics, race politics, town council politics, any old politics had to be applied to the understanding of the canon. If the word canon survived their assault. Shakespeare had to be judged according to the political realities of his own day. He had to be judged according to the realities of our day. He had to be judged according to constructs of reality that didn't even exist, they were merely collections of significations. Basically, he had to be judged and judged without humour. What did the plays mean? What were they transgressing, what reinforcing, what subverting? Who cares for silly bourgeois constructs like character, or precious flimflam about poetry, when we can get down to some good hard judging?

But however much the WilsonDoverKnight conspiracy took to bashing Bradley, and however much the political bootboys took to coshing them both, I never outgrew the joy I found in him. He opened my eyes to the work and the world. To a young man who was still confused by the difference between John and Jonathan, or Jane and Janie, and still trying to see what constituted a character, he was a godsend. Bradley led me to see Shakespeare more clearly, yet also showed how the work could help me translate all the scrappy humanity in my vicinity.

From childhood one uses stories to make sense of people. Fairy tales, Disney films, ancient myths, Bible stories all introduce you to a mush of figures, grand and small, mythic and realistic, who help to identify and colour in the world. At a certain age, you outgrow the strong colours and moral absolutes of your youth. The cranium expands, and the information fed into it becomes more blurred and accidental. Then you need a more sophisticated template of figures to translate that new information. It is hard to imagine a better template than the *Complete Works*. It gives you a collection of patterns for everyone around you. Where previously they have been existential blobs of life, soon you start to be more certain of their curves, and to understand the reason for some of their moves.

The earliest lessons in character were the crudest ones, the old saws that have walked through literary history from Aristotle to the present day. Hubris, the excessive pride of the hero leading to his downfall, is a child's delight. It's appealing when you're young, because it's simple, but also because it reassures you that that smart-arse who is captain of the football team and too intelligent *and* shagging the trophy blonde in the lower sixth is going to get the most God Almighty come-uppance. And they generally do. Nemesis, the revenge of justice on the over proud, is another great pillow of reassurance for the geek. And the Hollywood classic, the path through suffering to wisdom, offers a similar comfort package to any youth skanky with pimples, who has to take all the gip for having a collection of shirts his mother gave him covered in pictures of old naval heroes. These rules are crude, but they're also crudely true, and they offer a first psychological rubric.

The great tragic heroes, and Bradley's forensic analyses of them, opened the door to more complex organisms. Othello with his nervous bombast, his paranoia and his jitteriness glittered around my imagination. His language in its agonized and eventually successful attempts to be beautiful has all the strain and tension of a fellow auto-didact like Thomas Hardy, and all the blind force of Milton. His verse is an echo of every nervous outsider trying to prove himself better than every smug insider. Or any pompous ass, like myself, straining to impress with the tortured self-consciousness of youth. The excruciating dandyish circumlocutions of young men who think they're God's gift to wit were not a million miles from Othello's deliberate constructions of speech. His were just more successful and beautiful.

King Lear informed as an essay on the fragility of strength. His massive authority walks hand in hand with his ever-present knowledge that he is on a cliff path, and one wrong step plunges him into madness. His conversations with himself, shouting the black dogs of dementia out of his own head, were my first insights into the cerebral warfare that is any form of insanity, where the calm tussles with the eruptive. In a different key, his pathetic need for recognition mapped out the long beaches of loneliness that throw themselves open inside everyone.

Macbeth, with his ambition, and his fervour, and then his terrible deadness, was a stark warning about the dissolution of human contact. And then later his great barking laugh at death and fate, with his last lines welcoming the crushing hand of the inevitable, 'Lay on MacDuff!/ And damned be he that first cries Hold enough!', were my first true understanding of genuine heroism. Nobody had really replaced Geoff Hurst in my Olympian pecking order until I realized there are greater achievements than kicking a ball in a net. Macbeth's full realization of disaster, and his scream of defiance against fate, showed me that what you're dealt isn't heroism. How you deal with what you're dealt is what measures you.

Of course, at my school there were few black warriors misplaced in a strange society; no kings divesting themselves of authority to their daughters; and few rampant psychopaths. Thankfully. But the patterns described by these great stories chimed with events large and small within my life.

Beyond the heroes, there are a host of other muddied archetypes that correspond to people who walk through every life. There are the long line of Puritans, the negative forces, the nay-sayers to cakes and ale. Malvolio from *Twelfth Night*, the man more in need of a blow job than any character in literature. Angelo from *Measure for Measure*, the repressed rapist, who preaches bogus Christian values, the exemplar of Jack Nicholson's great phrase, 'Show me a business-man with a combination lock on his briefcase, and I'll show you a man who wants to piss in a prostitute's mouth.' And Octavius, the cold breeze of Arctic air who takes all the heat out of *Antony and Cleopatra*, and who on the return of his heartbroken sister to Rome hasn't the generosity to address her once by name. Life-deniers of this sort pop up everywhere from the school playground to the committee meeting.

There are the Osric and Oswald types, the first greasing his way through *Hamlet*, the second through *Lear*. The slicks, the greedy for position obsessives, the observers of form, the status junkies. The people who so often seem to run our world. There were the sad, discreet and silent gay men – Antonio from *Merchant of Venice* and from *Twelfth Night* – tending and nurturing their secret loves, crushed by the weight of their unspoken passion. There were the loyal friends, the loving patsies who follow the people they worship around and provide the safety, the castle that is true companionship – Horatio to Hamlet, Celia to Rosalind, Enobarbus to Antony, Charmian to

Cleopatra. They are studies of the benefits and the pains of platonic love, and warm service.

Then there are the malevolents, the psychopaths, the ones with a funny look in their eye – Iago and Edmund and Richard Crookback and Don John. From childhood on, it is easy to identify those characters in your immediate environment who can make your life worse. The trouble. They are not generally the combustibles. They will explode in your face, then calm down and befriend you. The trouble is the quiet ones, the beady ones, the watchful ones. You can smell the malignity reeking off them.

Shakespeare gives good solid motivation for his greatest villains. Iago has a racial motive (Othello is black), a career motive (Cassio has been preferred to him) and a *crime passionnel* motive (Othello has schtupped his wife). Edmund, from *King Lear*, has a rational motive (he is a modern rational thinker in a medieval superstitious world), a greed motive (he is clearing a path for his own power) and a revenge motive (his legitimate brother has always been preferred to him). Richard III has a bloody great hump on his back, which he and everybody else yabber on about, just in case you missed his motivation. But even with all these justifications, each of these figures has an extra gear of unadulterated sadistic cruelty which goes beyond any justification. And by a peculiar dynamic of the theatre, as these figures morally undergo a headlong fall in remorseless, imaginative destruction, the author and audience share an upward spiralling joy in their unfettered freedom.

We know these figures from childhood on. Shakespeare helps us to understand them, but only to a degree. He does not have the arrogance of the sociologist or psychologist who believes all criminality can be explained away. He knows that, after a certain amount of practice, evil develops an independent life separate from its creator. The two boys who took the small Bulger child for a deadly walk were scary. Their game was scarier. Shakespeare lets these people loose in his world. He offers no solution to the problems they create, but helps us respect the fact of their existence.

*

And then there are the flying consciousnesses, the rasping, rapping mouths exhilarated by the invention of their own minds – the Rosalinds, the Hamlets, the Falstaffs. Every school, every gang, throws up its own wild stars, livewires who can translate free thoughts into original expression. The people who begin monologues, usually on a trip of comic invention, and pull into their gathering stories any scraps of philosophy or pop culture or obscure detail or surreal spin they can pluck from the ether. They perform, and they explore as they perform, going to new places in their minds, and in their connections, stretching the limits of their own rhetoric, and learning, learning, as they go. Those two great adolescents Rosalind and Hamlet have this quality, and that other perpetual adolescent Falstaff shares it. On stage they are often orated by actors three decades too old. But they are kids, catherine-wheeling off the troubled fertility of their imaginations. Relishing language and reinventing it at the same time. They are thicker on the ground when young, before the inhibitions and self-censorship of maturity begin to crab and confine.

One of the heartbreaks of ageing is watching the verbal firework you knew and loved fizzle out, as tax and property and children rain down. It's a special ability – a radioactive force – that sort of star quality, and it has a predestined half life. The heartbreak is that the star who has lost his sheen often feels the lack most acutely. Each one is a one-off, unique and beautiful in their own way and at their own moment. Shakespeare's don't correspond to any other: they merely set the standard for others to aspire to. Hamlet is the greatest ever, Rosalind not far behind.

And beyond these there are a thousand other characters large and small; caricatures and complex figures; significant plot fulcra and small fragments of decoration. There are angry fathers, condemned men, cuckolded husbands, nagging wives, drunks, senators, true believers, nihilists, uncle tom bollocks and all the rest. Each fragmented life that Shakespeare holds up to view has a fierce independence all its own; each ferociously asserts its own I am.

Which belief system has a better pantheon of characters with which to interpret the world? If each age or era produces a shaman who can tell stories which help that time to understand itself, which shaman has come up with a better, broader and richer collection of figures?

Few religious prophets have told stories with any of the complexity or range or ugly humanity of the Stratford man. They tend to wrap their ultimate meanings up in themselves, and in their own journey through the world. They had their reasons. Shakespeare trod another path. His perceived world is too broad, too various.

There were and are too many stories, too many individuals, too much life, too many contradictions, too many corners, to be all held together in some streamlined theology. Shakespeare's world with its teaming swill of strange and contrary human beings, its loose ends and its tangents going nowhere, with its discreet moral lessons, its pervasive mildness and its silent respect for the darkness in the human soul, is the best universe any human has yet created to help us understand our own mess. The way into it remains through its extraordinary people.

a Glastonbury cabaret, apeshit sessions and the Falstaff pattern

Long before we appeared, we knew we were going to bomb. Big time. What hurt us was that the evening had originally been our idea. An all-night theatre cabaret, gathering together the weird and wild from Glastonbury. Old hippy performance artists, beat poets, singer-songwriters, anarchist magicians, political agitators, punk bands – all the fun of the psychedelic fair. In a rather safe middle-class way. And, as a centrepiece, the show from my company – a stripped-down experimental version of *All's Well That Ends Well*. We had rehearsed this a little too quickly. We thought it a fascinating deconstruction, with some interesting moments of mime, some primitive chanting and some freeform improvised movement. There wasn't much of a plan behind it, but we bristled with pride that it wasn't conventional in any way. The fact that it wasn't good in any way either bothered us less. Until we saw the audience.

The organizer and co-founder of our company was a great deal more democratic and inclusive than us. He had mentioned to a couple of local skinheads that we were putting together the evening. Mistake. Two skinhead bands got on to the bill. Three others showed up. Try telling a skinhead band they can't play. Two hundred of the West Country's finest skinheads crammed into a small room to listen to their heroes play thrash metal. When their bands played they were electrified, pogoing so hard that the floor bent and creaked and hurling each other against the walls. When their bands weren't playing they were either bored or pissed off. Bored was manageable. They either fought amongst themselves or competed to demonstrate acts of wilful destruction. One bit the top off a bottle of beer and massacred his own mouth. Another, who had a sizeable sense of fury but little idea of what to do with it, bottled himself. Both were carted off in ambulances. When they were hostile, that was more worrying. They were so verbally abusive to a Brechtian illusionist that he left in tears. And they had so little time for one long-haired hippy singing pained songs about his youth that they picked him up and carried him off the stage, chair, guitar and all, and dumped him outside. They were far from the ideal audience for a radical reworking of one of Shakespeare's problem plays.

We were bought a little time by the fact that the organizer of the evening was in our show, and he had asked the skinheads along. That gave us a crucial few minutes, while we demonstrated with a sort of brutal ballet how Helena cured the King of France. But things started slipping quickly downhill after the clown started trying to raise a laugh with his material. The director, who was also in it, started redirecting as we went along. He walked amongst us murmuring, 'Faster, faster.' Then, shortly after, 'Fast as fuck.' Then he told us to shout. For a while this calmed the audience down as we screamed the lines directly into the faces of the skinheads, trying to meet aggression with aggression. It may not have been what Shakespeare intended. But we knew that nothing would save us once the director started whispering to us, 'Cut the next scene, cut scene four,' then after a brief pause, 'Cut scene five as well'.

Once the first objects started flying towards us, we decided the sensible thing would be to cut and run. So we did, turning and bowing briefly as we scampered out to hide behind screens. Our organizer, who was so bombed out that little would deter him, decided that this would be the moment to go out and try and sell programmes for our show. He emerged, crying out, 'Programmes, programmes! Read about the lives behind the faces.' Funnily enough, they didn't sell, and he was soon drowned out by the next skinhead band. And it was back to the pogoing. By about five in the morning the event did achieve a sort of funny, attenuated beauty, after most had gone and the blood and the puke had been cleared away, as first a jazz singer, then a punk poet, performed mild sets for the bleary and bombed-out who remained. But it wasn't the most triumphant night for taking Shakespeare to the people.

A year or so before, a group of family and friends had started a theatre company with a name so clumsily right on it still makes my teeth ache. Cheapstreet Theatre Co. Even though our first production was in a town called Street, that still can't excuse it. Cheapstreet – we thought it an intoxicating mix of the butch and the left-wing. We were sick of the restrictions at school, so we mounted a production of *Little Malcolm and His Struggle against the Eunuchs* in a small art gallery above a café, the same art gallery that would eventually sway under the weight of 400 Doc Martens. It played to about thirty people a night, and was considered an event. Others soon wanted to join in, so that winter we succumbed to over-ambition and presented a triple bill – *Saved* by Edward Bond and two plays by Barrie Keeffe, *Barbarians* and *Gotcha*. These were the sort of productions which ambled along fairly aimlessly until one of the actors got the chance to say 'fuck' or 'cunt'. At that point they would pause before delivering, then spit the words out with unnatural relish, usually in the direction of their grandparents.

If the shows had any distinction, it came courtesy of a wonderfully benign local genius called Tom, the organizer of the all-night cabaret. He was the wildest scion of the local industrial family. About twenty years older than all of us, he was an inveterate hippy/punk/beat/any-old-counterculture figure, who floated around Glastonbury and Street in bizarre combinations of Somerset farmer and Indian clothing. He wore a permanently puzzled expression, and, though mostly incoherent, could be outrageously funny and brilliantly gnomic. The myth ran that he used to drop acid in his cornflakes. It's hard to know whether that's true or not, but he drank regularly in a murky cove called the Rifleman's Arms under Glastonbury Tor, where the cider was so long and strangely stewed that it often seemed to have hallucinogenic properties all of its own. A friend and I went back there recently and asked with the cheery condescension of the visiting Londoner for a pint of their strongest cider. We had to go to bed for a day afterwards. Tom would regularly sink several.

He didn't direct our shows, exactly, but he slowly took them over. Having helped us to find a venue for our first show, he started turning up more and more regularly at rehearsals. He wouldn't give notes as such, but unprompted he was capable of panoramic rambling monologues. They would travel from Lear to Lenin to Leonard Nimoy. It was hard for us to piece together their relevance to the work in hand, but they always expanded horizons and raised stakes. He started to grow our theatrical vocabulary and made us conscious of Brecht and Meyerhold and Artaud. But he was far from a drama teacher. His imagination flew far further. It was about approaching life in a fresh direction rather than simply stagecraft.

We started to hold weekly, what Tom called apeshit, sessions. We would all gather on a Thursday evening. Tom would name the ritual and place an appropriate object in the middle of the room. If it was the water ritual, there would be a jug of water; if bread, a loaf of sliced Hovis; if fire, a packet of Swan Vestas; if Tom had forgotten to buy any props at the Spar store across the road, he'd say it was the air ritual, and there would be nothing. We would then proceed to bugger about weirdly for three hours around this theme. This could involve hurling our arms around each other and harmonizing with choric voices; it could involve expressive dancing *à la* Isadora Duncan; making instant sets with sheets and planks; or monologuing about visiting spacemen and one's relationship with one's mother.

Beyond the props, there were always Shakespeare texts to pick from, passages on the relative element to shout and swirl around the room. There was no structure to the evenings apart from the occasional stern word if a moment of imagined aggression was about to spill over into a fight, or if someone was taking advantage of the freedom to stick their tongue down someone else's throat. By 10.30, amongst the fifteen of us, you'd have someone orating Ophelia in a corner, five people lying in a star shape, two sobbing, one trying to start a fire and two trying to stop them, two sitting in boredom and two running around stark bollock naked. At that point, our mothers would appear, and we'd all be driven home.

The evenings were astonishingly daft, but they were a tonic. Although there was a neat and tidy bourgeois conclusion to them, they were still subversive of everything we had been trained to think of as drama. They were the empty space credo formulated by Peter Brook, with punk mess added. Shakespeare flew in this context. The words were merrily ripped from their narrative and emotional home, and used as fragments, pictures, little bombs of sensation and meaning, shards of linguistic music. There is such weight in Shakespeare – who knows where from – such blood and thunder and flight in each phrase, such cohesion and such connection, that if you do explode him with the most amateur modernism and chuck him into an evening of adolescent arsing about, he still defines it. His voice remains the dominant one.

Inspired by our modest success in the South-west and by our own appetite for some elixir of adolescent glory, we took two shows to Edinburgh over successive summers, first *Little Malcolm* and then *Barbarians*. The first was not great, largely because I exercised my producer's privilege and gave myself the main part. And was rubbish. Our guru, Tom, steered me towards a course of talking as fast as I could. All the other actors worked out they had to bring on their own performance, plus a set of crayons to colour me in. The second, *Barbarians*, was a better show, largely because I had excluded myself, and chosen to direct, but it played only to the proverbial two Canadians in kagoules. But Edinburgh then was the most fantastic, spiritual dry Martini. Each day we would all fall in love – in love with that fierce nonsensical love of the over-young and over-alive. Each day a new possession with a pair of sad eyes. It felt like doors were opening all the way ahead.

They were for us as individuals, but not so much for our company. The core of our group were now ready to drift away to different universities, and to follow different paths. Others wanted to continue to make something of the company, and it felt shitty to go. But bourgeois ambition was driving us forward. Worst of all, Tom, our inspiration and unofficial leader, seemed to feel hurt by our departure, to feel a whisper of betrayal. He had taught and illuminated and entertained us and we were all disappearing. I'm sure he said 'fuck 'em' within half an hour of realizing we would not be playing with him any more, but the brief moment of hurt was an eye opener. He changed the name of the company and grew it. Its next manifestation was as a work scheme for unemployed teenagers, and then that mutated into an outlandish and marvellous outfit who travelled the world with companies of four or five doing deconstructed Shakespeare productions in Georgia and in Sierra Leone. Our contact with them dribbled quickly away to nothing.

Looking back, though there was no consciousness of this at the time, Tom was one of the first great Falstaff figures of my life. Falstaff is always celebrated as a character, a free-floating consciousness. He is the descendant of the old Vice figure from the Mystery plays, the ancient English figure of the Lord of Misrule. He is almost separate from the plays he appears in, a free life rampaging through the beautifully modulated world of the two *Henry IV* plays, and the domestic sitcom world of *The Merry Wives of Windsor*. He was one of those independent creations who ran away from his own author, then started to talk back with flagrant cheek. There is credible evidence that Falstaff was in large part based on a playwright who Shakespeare was adopted by and then superseded – Robert Greene. He felt sufficient bitterness to pen a vicious squib about young 'Shakescene'. Yet though Greene was quite probably an influence, Falstaff's lack of respect, his cruelty and his dishonesty must also have been drawn in some measure from Shakespeare himself. Yet once he was made, once all the separate influences had coalesced into something complete, it was never going to be possible to put them back in a box. He was too out of control for *Henry V*, too much 'fuck you' for a play of such singular purpose. So Shakespeare exercised his ultimate authorial control and killed him off.

But the Falstaff story is not just of a character, it is also of a relationship, the one with young Prince Hal. The reason the Falstaff paradigm has pertained so long is as much the relationship as the character. It is a story we all know, and many of us live through. We all seek and find out looser, loucher, wilder alternatives to our parents. We are all thrilled and entertained by them, finding truths and freedoms outside the box we've been in. Then at some moment we walk away from our play parents and back to our real ones. It's a classic rite of passage – hitching a lift on a free spirit, and then returning by train. I have had the same relationship three or four times since – it is a nasty by-product of being greedy.

We all wish that Falstaff, after the young, newly crowned Henry V has rejected him so clinically, after he has told him with the contempt of power, 'I know thee not, old man,' that Falstaff would pause for a moment, then murmur, 'Fuck him. Pompous cunt.' But he can't. All he can offer is the pathetic hope, 'I shall be sent for soon at night.' (And the hasty excuse, since his creditors are all standing around him breathing heavily). We recognize in that small delusion all the hurt of rejection, and all the sad chasm between youth and age. Especially now, with time having moved on, as I watch with amused despair as others do the same to me.

unlearning, A levels and opening up to *Lear*

In a history lesson, during the run up to A levels, a rather obvious thought struck me. I put it to the teacher with all the hesitancy attached to an insight that had probably occurred to everyone else years before. 'So, really, what we're doing here . . . er . . . is not so much learning new stuff as . . . er . . . unlearning everything we thought was true before.' 'That's right,' came the reply with a weary brio, 'and when you get to university, you'll unlearn all this old twaddle too.' At the time we were going through our second stage of revisionism on King John. Having been bad King John at primary school – the noncey weakling beside his superhero brother Lionheart – he then morphed into good King John at the O-level stage – the diligent moderator beside his reckless and pathological brother. Now he was veering back to the bad as a conniving autocrat. It was dizzying. The degree of relativity, and the lack of assurance, unsettled me. If all this was so easily reunderstood, then teachers, parents and the whole structure of authority was only provisional. That was great. But then also I would and could never be right. That was disappointing.

Of course, the reinvention spread across all subjects. The promises that were made in childhood of a secure, ordered and logical world kept blowing up in your face. Mathematics, which had begun as such a musical and harmonious doddle, grew up into the twisted perversity of calculus and worse. Latin, whose bright morning had been the crystalline simplicity of 'amo/amas/amat/amamus/amatis/amant' was now clouded over with the enervating weirdness of strange moods and irregular verbs. Biology, which had been all cheerful mantras about 'birth, reproduction and death', descended quite speedily into baffled incomprehension. And worst of all was physics. A friend who had already travelled to the faraway lands of university delivered the news about quantum physics as we sat in the pub one evening. This seemed to basically boil down to the proposition that half of reality wasn't there. All the old crunchy solidity of Newtonian apples falling and bopping people on the head had slipped into this queasy and nauseous world of absence and presence, of matter as a strange equation.

(There is a weird equivalence to this in a passage in *Troilus and Cressida*. Troilus, under the most intense fissile pressure, having seen his new-found love Cressida consorting with another man, finds the dissonance between last night's love and tonight's betrayer unbearable. He cracks up and in the process seems to discover quantum physics:

> This she? No; this is Diomed's Cressida.
> If beauty have a soul, this is not she . . .
> This is not she. O madness of discourse,
> That cause sets up with and against itself!
> > . . . this is, and is not, Cressid.
> Within my soul there doth conduce a fight
> Of this strange nature, that a thing inseparate
> Divides more wider than the sky and earth;
> And yet the spacious breadth of this division
> Admits no orifice for a point as subtle
> As Ariachne's broken woof to enter.
> Instance, O instance! strong as Pluto's gates:
> Cressid is mine, tied with the bonds of heaven.
> Instance, O instance! strong as heaven itself:
> The bonds of heaven are slipp'd, dissolv'd, and loos'd

Reality, which had been whole, has suddenly become contingent, and all this 300 years before Einstein.)

English literature seemed for a short while a haven from all this stormy promise breaking. Since it was so obviously subjective, and interpretative, there was never any promise of certainty to be later exposed as a lie. Yet in truth the same simplifications had taken place, and the same former reductions had to be exploded at each new stage of education. We were studying *Lear* for A level, and the organizing themes which Examining Boards used to turn a monster into a pussy-cat are still clear in my mind. The exam questions walked you down familiar paths. 'It is only through an intensity of suffering that Lear achieves a purity of wisdom.' Discuss. 'I stumbled when I saw': discuss the relationship between blindness, vision and true sight in *King Lear*. 'As flies to wanton boys are we to the gods / They kill us for their sport.' Is *King Lear* an atheist or a Christian play? 'Thou, Nature, art my goddess . . .' Is Edmund's idea of nature the only one expressed within the play? And on. Many familiar polarities, order and chaos, nihilism and religion; and many familiar journeys, suffering to wis-dom, blindness to sight. As pathfinders through the murk of the forest, these were a help. It made it easier to get from one side to the other, hacking your way through, platitudes in hand. As stimulants they were useful, helping you to recognize some of the patterns within the forest, some of the trees for what they were. But finally, a forest is a forest, and you've got to accept the fact. If you want to enjoy it, you have to roam around within it for a while, sit down occasion-ally, inspect some bits, smell others, eat your sandwiches, then go home. To be driven through a preordained path like a pack of Cub Scouts, with a scoutmaster pushing up the rear, doesn't give the same pleasure.

Of course, no play resists such simplification as magnificently as *King Lear*. It's an exploded play. Shakespeare himself fails so com-pletely and so deliberately to wrap it up, it's hard to see why acne-ridden sixth-formers should be encouraged to do so on his behalf. There's an exhausted indifference to the way Shakespeare ties up his own loose ends. The killing off of Goneril and Regan – Whoops! What was that? Poison! Aarrgghh. Dead! – is as perfunctory as a child's play. It is as if Shakespeare is infected by the casual cruelty which marks out the world of the play. 'What shall I do with Regan?' flits into his head. 'Oh, I don't know, kill the silly cow.' There is no tidiness, and there is no intention of tidiness.

Ditto with the guff about the gods. I read essay after essay trying to find some sort of shape for the various references to God or the gods or the elsewhere that permeate the play. They all had a slant, pushing the play towards a positive Christian message or a bleak nihilist one or a celebration of old English pantheism or who knows what. I cheerfully agreed with whatever I'd read most recently. And would argue it forcefully, blithe to the contradiction with what I'd been arguing the week before. Yet now it seems clearer than ever that there is no shape, nor any pattern. There is just a story with some characters in. They blather about the gods; they chuck out invocations, curses, prayers and pleas with all the liberal abandon of any human in a state of crisis. Albany is constantly reaching for a theological maxim with all the pompous complacency of the profound Rotarian he is; Gloucester is all over the place, veering wildly from rage at the gods to calm acceptance, then back to self-pity; Edgar is on a peculiar emblematic journey of his own or, in modern parlance, working out his shit; and Lear is far too monomaniacal to work out any consistent theological position. They are all creatures with needs, and particular fields of reference to express those needs. They have all the thought-through consistency of a lashed-together raft in the middle of a big storm in the Atlantic.

We all lurch insanely from praying to some mystic force to knowing the finality of our death; we celebrate our own free will and we blame our failures on fate. *Lear* is true to that confusion. I learned a lot about religion from *Lear*, about the thirst for it, its dishonesty, its consolations and its cruelties. But I didn't learn a viewpoint or a single understanding. Shakespeare puts religion in the context of life, within the greater totality. He doesn't try to make it the one and only context.

School is often the place where geometry meets life and holds it down for a while. In some areas it can pertain – geography always seemed a zone of pleasing certainty, though that may be unfair to the wild and groovy world of geographers. In others it can't. Even then, *Lear* was too big a noise of life to be contained. It bust the straitjacket of its own teaching. The sound track to A levels was the sharp and sweet violence of punk rock. Nights spent reading Dover Wilson on *King Lear* would be underscored by the catholic choices of John Peel's exotic taste. The rawness and the wit of punk rock defied any analysis. You've just got to let it into your ear, and then give it the room to fuck you up. It was only when I gave that room to *Lear*, and stopped trying to control it through pat understandings, that it could start to happen.

touring Europe, giggles and cultural übermen

How do you communicate bliss? Children dance and grin to bursting, but once you pass a certain age that sort of behaviour will just get you carted away. As we mature, we are left with a whole range of modes of communicating our depressions and our fears, but with very little vocabulary to convey euphoria. We don't believe any such state will occur, so have not bothered to develop a language to match it. This is my problem as I approach a telephone box under a mountain in a Swiss town. I'm eighteen, calling home to speak to my parents and insanely happy. There are great drifts of snow about, a cold, whipping wind, and I am lit up. I am acting Benvolio in a university production of *Romeo and Juliet*, which is on a three-week tour of Europe. Nobody in the world could be having a better time. It's a Sunday afternoon at home, my parents are sleepy. The words to match my feeling won't come, but I babble and beam down the line, and something of my delight is carried electronically from Switzerland back to Somerset.

Why so happy? Well, it's the end of my first term at university, and freedom and independence are changing the shape of my body and the confidence of my moves. It's an adventure, steaming along every day in a coach from one bourgeois town to another; travelling, working and partying with a relentlessness that leaves no fragment of time for the wasted hours of adolescent introspection. It's a new set of peers, who to my amazement seem to enjoy my company and to find something vaguely interesting in me. I'm acting at last in a Shakespeare play. Not very well, admittedly – but the swells of energy that surge beneath the text are keeping my mood buoyant. There is a constant fizz of intellectual wit and bite around the bus I am on. Juliet fancies me. Or so I have been informed by Romeo. And, best of all, I'm on tour.

Touring Shakespeare was part of the mythology of my youth. My father had done it round the London parks and on occasion the pubs of northern England. He had also toured Shakespeare twice round Europe with university companies. Beyond him were acres of sentimental shtick about the whole concept of strolling players. Unfortunately the feyness of this image – the whole ghastly actor-chappy 'let's put on a play' archness – obscures two central truths. First, in England theatre was born out of touring. For several centuries theatre was not about bricks and mortar. Nor, essentially, was it about theatres. Aside from the monumental pageants of the Mystery plays presented in cathedrals, the principal source of theatre was small companies who toured around smaller versions of those Mystery plays, or more contemporary Tudor plays. These ensembles would truck along, night by night, from large country house to small market town, very like the company that wanders into Hamlet's court. When Shakespeare writes about those actors in *Hamlet*, it's not a whimsical portrait of a medieval fantasy, it's documentary reportage.

He himself was probably first mouse-trapped into a love of the theatre by the Earl of Leicester's men. They were a touring company which his father booked in for a show in Stratford. The young Shakespeare would have been hustled by his father with a fair degree of self-importance to the best seats at the front. The room would have been bristling with a vigorous sense of status. He would no doubt have seen the comedy in the manoeuvring of the burghers of Stratford. He may well have been disappointed by the crudeness in the acting. But at some point something happened – an actor caught a moment of grace, or some line forged something new in his imagination – and his heart was stopped for a few brief seconds. When it started beating again, it would have been hungry for more. Just as with my father in a Welsh village, or any number of others before or since, who have had their fantasies redefined by a group of drink- and vanity-soused renegades passing through. Though in Stratford the players may have worked in a grand room, more often they worked on makeshift stages in the yards of pubs. The action needed to be vigorous, sharp and urgent to keep people away from their pints, or to keep those who had delved deep in their pints from losing interest. Pub theatre and touring theatre – now offshoots of our drama industry – were its birthplace. It is only later during the life of Shakespeare himself that theatre becomes about theatres.

The second truth about touring is that it is top fun. There is an outlaw whiff to it still. Companies are thrown together in places they have never visited before, far from family and responsibilities, and they move through towns at such speed that the whole concept of accountability takes wing. It is a child's dream of irresponsibility written in fluent adult. 'It doesn't count on tour' is a mantra in the theatre profession applying to everything from smoking crack to committing adultery to thieving. The company polices itself but follows nobody else's rule. The ongoing social archetype of 'rogues, vagabonds and sturdy beggars', the itinerants separate from the rules of the central state who exercised the paranoia of the Elizabethan state, has always carried a whiff of outlaw glamour. Although much of that glamour has been calcified, there are still enough knee tremblers going on in dark alleys, enough cocaine flying up twitching nostrils and enough hearts being casually broken to justify some of that old, dark glamour still attaching itself to the travelling actor.

At eighteen I was too young for coke, and far too nervous for knee tremblers, but hugely ready for excitement. Our *Romeo and Juliet* tour delivered a breadth of experience I hadn't imagined possible. The rhythm of each day was a constant. Wake up in a strange house. Make faltering conversation with strangers in English / Flemish / German / Italian / French as you eat ham and eggs in some new and alarming combination. Make way to bus, where you meet all your fellow company. Speed off gossiping about what happened night before. Fall asleep. Arrive in new town at theatre. Empty the show out of the bus. Fit it up. Have an hour off. Return to theatre. Rehearse. Perform. Go to reception. Get drunk. Go to party somewhere. Get very drunk. Crash out in a new strange bed. Wake up somewhere new and strange.

Within that set and breathless rhythm there was constant surprise. We travelled slowly down through Belgium, then through north Germany, zigzagging down to Bavaria, a couple of dates in Austria, several in Switzerland, then back up to Paris and home. The hosts we billeted with could be anything. In Belgium, we were with wealthy diplomats, who gave us a midnight tour of Brussels, which stretched our polite ability to be interested to its utmost. In Germany, there were students who wanted to stay up all night singing or banging; American military families who wanted you to pray to Jesus with them; earnest intellectuals who wanted to discuss Shakespeare and his existential identity; Swiss banking squillionaries in vast mansions who wanted you to discuss the finer points of the La Tour grape; and families who wanted you to go to bed and go fast. Whoever we were with we found strange and odd with the imaginative exuberance of the young on a new release programme from their parents. Perfectly dull couples in banking would be transformed into psychotic weirdos as we related our adventures of the night before.

Within the constant whirl of work, we would get an hour of rest each day. We would all gravitate in the same direction, towards the nearest cathedral. Sleep was impossible – too much of nature's caffeine in the system, and nowhere to go – so peace was the next-best thing. A high-vaulted, cool-aired monumental slab of stone peace was what each cathedral offered. Just a half-hour, sitting silently, letting the stillness of centuries calm down the jazzy jumping of your internal organs, was as good as two hours' sleep. The contrast between the cathedrals provided a wonderful psycho-portrait of the different characters of Europe. The great squat stone fortresses of the north – outposts for militant Christianity against pagan hordes further north – became slowly more camp and more baroque as we travelled south, piling themselves up into larger and larger wedding cakes. A similar journey happened with the crucifixes. In the north, especially in Trier, Christ was a Schwarzenegger lookylikey, straining with all his muscles and strength to tear himself off the cross and thump the onlooker. As we travelled south he slowly softened and feminized, sinking backwards into a passive and beautiful suffering. The great bi-polar tension of Europe – Protestant and Catholic, Christ the warrior and Christ the victim, rage and acceptance – was played out in architecture and sculpture.

The show itself was a mixed bag. Crowds streamed in to see it because it was a Shakespeare play presented by a Cambridge company at Christmas. It touched all the right buttons. It was an enormously sombre, po-faced production, in Victorian costumes, with long bits of slow physical theatre played out to the music of Prokofiev and Shostakovich. The director thought it was like Pina Bausch; we thought it more a slow-motion Pan's People. Those passages may have been quite captivating: we found them irresistibly silly to perform. The problem was greater with what came out of our mouths. We were none of us trained actors and found it hard to make ourselves audible, let alone comprehensible, to a foreign audience.

The reaction was always extraordinary, seven or eight curtain calls each night. The first time we received the full Teutonic ovation we were amazed. We were already back in the dressing rooms, getting changed back into mufti, when we realized the clapping would never stop. We went back out half-dressed and received our acclaim. We spilled joyfully out into the foyer for the reception. Confidently we bounced up to our hosts. 'So, you liked it, then?' we expected. 'No', we were told by sour faces, 'we thought it was shallow, childish and poorly executed.' 'Oh . . . um . . . OK', we gulped, and moved on to ask someone else. 'We thought it was intellectually poor. And you are all bad actors.' The response was uniform. They all thought it was rubbish. And yet everywhere we went, they clapped and clapped. This was European culture. Savagely polite and savagely unforgiving.

In Innsbruck we were booked into an absurdly large hall which Pavarotti would have had trouble being heard in. There were 2,000 people there – a thousand of them schoolchildren stuck at the back. Within twenty minutes they realized they weren't going to hear a word. A healthy 500 of them had left by the interval. The other 500 transformed their programmes into paper aeroplanes, which came winging their way towards us on warm drafts of air from the gallery. By the last scene, as Romeo married Juliet, they were acting in a paper D-Day. People continued to leave all through the second half. When the show finally ended the first two rows suddenly got up and an embassy of what appeared to be angry-looking burghers walked on to the stage. We thought we were going to be told off for being crap, but instead discovered we were part of a local council re-election campaign. Each of the dignitaries walked down the line of our curtain call placing a medal round our necks and shaking our hands, like the queen at the FA Cup final. This procession was followed by a long series of speeches exhorting the small crowd that had remained to vote Nazi or whatever in the next local election. It was only when we got off stage that we had a good look at our medals – large, gold-coloured, chunky, plastic things reading 'I Love The Tyrol'.

Around the time we got to Heidelberg, a sense of the absurd began to creep in. The production was so sombre and humourless, our passages of physical theatre were so long-faced and gloomy and the reaction from the crowd was so serious and grim that the natural humour of a group of undergraduates started to bubble dangerously. Giggles set in early when we all had to stare in a menacing manner at each other – Montagues and Capulets – across the stage. I, as Benvolio, was deputed to stare out Tybalt in a butch manner. This would have been fine, but he was very camp and very twinkly, and he kept pouting at me. Within seconds I was giggling, and others would join in.

By the time we got to Basle, the problems had become acute. With all the references in the play to 'Light to my chamber, Ho', 'Peace ho for shame', and 'What ho!', we had developed a theory that the Capulet household employed a Chinese manservant called Ho. It only took Capulet to stride on and call out 'Peace Wang!' in an authoritative manner, and we were all in deep trouble. Later in the same show, the actor playing Tybalt and I decided to swap our small ancillary parts in the second half. I, at least, had the decency to learn my lines as the Apothecary, though I couldn't get through without a lot of inappropriate laughter. The other actor came on as Balthasar, my usual part, with little idea of the plot let alone his lines. When Romeo asked him the way to Juliet's tomb, he said, 'Ermm . . . left past that mausoleum, then . . . oh, I don't know . . . ask the chemist,' and walked off. By the end we were all in tears.

The next morning we were in big trouble. The director had a long shout at us on the bus. It started as a scoutmaster-type rant about being ambassadors for the university, and later it took on a more peculiar edge. The only actor who wasn't behaving badly was the director's best friend. He got hold of the tour log, a large book which was filled up with any old nonsense which people chose to insert. The director's friend wrote out a long Nietzschean essay about Shakespeare. Shakespeare, he explained, lived, wrote and imagined at a height of existence which we should all aspire to. In acting his plays, there were those who could live and create at that height, and there were those who couldn't. Those with big souls, large minds and strong hearts, the überman director and his überman friend, two spiritual Schwarzeneggers, could live there; those with small, trivial, banal spirits couldn't. These untermensch, the rest of us, were thus destined to live small, trivial and banal lives. Thus spake the undergraduate.

This was offensive on an infinite number of different levels. Aside from the fact that the man writing it was playing Old Montague, a part of two lines, which was all his big soul could work its way around, it was the sort of high-handed, anti-democratic, culturally esoteric nonsense which is red rag to a bull to a group of students. The director chose to take up his friend's points in his next scoutmaster speech to us, and was cheerily shouted down. The group separated into the über-Shakespeare brigade, the director and his friend, and the rest of us. Arguments raged. Much was at stake. They had behind them the whole piss-elegant, Stratford-worshipping, relentlessly bourgeois, quietly racist, deeply English orthodoxy about Shakespeare the holy and the wonderful. We had our punk sensibility, an instinctive distaste for all that nonsense and an overwhelming desire to laugh.

Never the twain would meet, but it was an early taste of that automatic cultural arrogance which poisons Shakespeare and so much classical theatre. Much of my revulsion to what they were saying was because they were expressing the same sort of horrible, elitist crap which had run through my head from childhood. I had felt superior because I was on to Shakespeare. Growing up surrounded by farmers' children, unable to ride a bicycle, fairly rubbish at sports, useless at swearing, hopeless at conkers, gauche with girls, I thought that Shakespeare was something that gave me an edge. I had fallen in love with him for all the right reasons – it's hard not to – but, having fallen, I thought my lifetime companion marked me out, made me special. It was a vile and redundant brand of arrogance, but I hadn't realized it was in me until I saw it exemplified by the two übermen on the bus.

It was a turning point. The warmth and the humour and the grace was with the gigglers and the dissenters. You couldn't help but feel that there was a loud raspberry within the heart of Shakespeare as well, a big farting noise that separates him cleanly from the Olympian sternness of the great Germans, Goethe and Schiller, and the poised perfection of the French, Racine and Corneille. (There are also issues of quality control which separate him from the Spanish, Lope de Vega and Calderón, but that's another story.) The same rude humour takes him away from those of his acolytes who want him to be as humourless and po-faced as themselves. I followed the fun.

Beyond the giggles and the arguments, other fun was also to be had. I was being set up with Juliet. After our last night in Paris, we scored some dope off a twelve-year-old called Serge, who went round in a Belmondo overcoat – he promised us five kilos and returned with a thin joint. We smoked that, and after I had topped it with an end-of-tour bottle of cherry brandy, I was heartily sick in Juliet's lap. Love blossomed.

Richard III, schism and three old ladies in hats

Six months later, for my next working encounter with Shakespeare, the love affair with Juliet had turned mighty sour. She was Queen Elizabeth now in my production of *Richard III*, and the tender follies of the winter had turned into the stewed savagery of the summer. She was older and cleverer than me, I had behaved in various stupid ways, and she took her revenge on me with all the scientific precision of a child dismembering an insect. I deserved everything I got. Partly for what I'd done and partly for being so pathetically eager for punishment. I was medievally in thrall to her. The greater the glee with which she performed her slow daily kneecappings, the greater the slavish appetite with which I'd roll up to receive them. If I'd had any strength, it would have been laughable, but I had none. It was a low ebb emotionally. Yet it was a high tide by comparison with my development as an artist as expressed by *Richard III*.

A school friend, who had worked on one of our productions, was born and bred in a Yorkshire town called Middleham. A picturesque town set in the Dales, it is topped by a Gothic ruin of a medieval castle, whose one great claim to fame is as the place where Richard III was born. It is a mixed blessing – it brings a whiff of monarchy, but also a connection with one of history's most enduring villains. Flying in the face of opprobrium, they decided to present a festival to celebrate the quincentennial anniversary of Richard III's coronation in 1483. They were determined to record how their boy had done good, even if their boy had murdered a morgue full of relations, and disappeared two young nephews for good measure.

Through our connection we were asked to present Shakespeare's play as the centrepiece of the festival. However, as with all things

Richard III, the festival soon descended into schism. There was a powerful lobby on the committee, arguing that Shakespeare had given Richard an unnecessarily hard time, that Richard was a good king and that the only voice heard shouldn't be a negative one. This lobby was led by an actor who had made his name in *Doctor Who*. His line in historical revisionism didn't go down well with the other town burghers, who threw him off the committee. Not to be undone, he set up a fringe festival, whose centrepiece was to be his own riposte to Tudor propaganda, a play titled, with little subtlety, *Shakespeare Was a Hunchback*. A piece from the nyah nyah nyah school of dramaturgy. So Middleham, a town of about 500 souls, now had a festival in a large cattle auction barn, and a fringe in a smaller one. To our great confusion, we were asked to appear on the fringe as well. For various reasons we were told this would be politically expedient, so we booked in for both.

We were due to rehearse and perform in early summer at the end of my first year at university. I flailed around Cambridge trying to raise a cast. Friends smelled a rat and demurred. So we ended up with the usual homegrown components. My brother, my sister and me, each of our respective partners, and one extra, who must have felt a gooseberry on a variety of levels. The style would be a loose reflection of Brechtian ideas. This didn't reveal any deep understanding of Brecht, but rather a vague second-guess at what everyone seemed to think Brecht meant. The aspiration was less profound alienation, more acute pre-emptive defensiveness. This meant factory trousers to trumpet our proletarian credentials, white T-shirts, a clothes rail at the back for accessories to define each different character, two benches which we sat on throughout and the occasional iconic prop. Lights would be up throughout, and all the great pageants, state events and historic battles would be summoned up through theatre magic. That was the idea. Since there were only seven of us, and there were forty-nine parts, and the play was as long as fuck, and we only had two weeks to rehearse it, we chopped the play to bits to make it manageable. This left enormous holes in the plot. Not to be deterred we composed a series of Brechtian ditties, which my brother's girl-friend, an apprentice opera singer, warbled prettily to move the plot along.

Rehearsals foundered on various rocks. We all drank a lot at night, and found it hard to set to in the morning. I had cast my brother as Queen Margaret, and he subverted all the women's long keening scenes by playing her in the style of Hattie Jacques. I was permanently worried about what my girlfriend was doing when she wasn't in rehearsals, so tended to rehearse as little as possible and, when not rehearsing, spent a fair amount of time hiding in bushes spying on her. Plus most of us couldn't act.

One evening, outside in the dark, there was an electrifying grace note. The actor playing Richard was gifted, prodigiously so, and we tended to organize our productions around him. We were rehearsing his soliloquy on the night before the battle of Bosworth. Richard wakes after a dream full of visions of his old victims and burbles in fluent, terrified, paranoid dementia. In a play full of stately, stylized, Senecan complaint (dull) or mad action plotting (nonsense), this is a sudden explosion of Shakespeare's most distinctive voice. It is the mind – ruptured, ugly, lost – speaking without prettiness or decoration or dishonesty. The actor hit the rhythm, fast and jerky, and was momentarily possessed by it. It was hair-raising and beautiful. Each word was just and perfect, each action the same. He wasn't acting the part, he was it. He wasn't being naturalistic and truthful, he was poised at the height of excess of spirit and exemplary imagination that Shakespeare wrote at. He wasn't being human, he was a poem of humanity. While he was in it, we both floated up above the ground, disconnected from our immediate here and now. He finished, we descended and were quiet for a while. It was an experience built on shaky foundations, so it didn't reappear. But that moment redeemed all the surrounding dross.

We attempted to do a dry run of the play to friends and relations before setting off for Yorkshire. I had read a Peter Brook book about his *Midsummer Night's Dream*, and how they'd done an ad hoc showing of the work in a community hall before moving into the big theatre in Stratford. I was aiming for the same sort of low-key magic. Our showing ground to a halt after various clumsy stutters, when two of the parents became so incapacitated by laughter that we had to go out and tell them that if they were going to behave like that we weren't going to carry on. They couldn't stop behaving like that, so we terminated the run in a huff. Nobody emerged with a lot of dignity intact. Afterwards they wiped away their tears and made muted noises about how we'd made very interesting choices, before exploding into laughter again. It wasn't auspicious.

Our first performance in Yorkshire was to a school audience. Four hundred boisterous young tykes crowded into a gym on the hottest day of the year to watch us try to remember the plot. Within minutes they'd lost interest. Soon after, they started embarking on hazardous and imaginative schemes to try and escape through the windows or the various doors. The four teachers who were on patrol kept catching them and dragging them back in. Three couples in the front row held a snogging competition, seeing who could maintain the longest tongue lock. Since we were all on stage throughout, when not acting we became curiously fascinated by what the audience were up to and often missed our moments to join in. At the end we were told off by a teacher – not because we were awful, which we were, but because one of our actresses had referred to her breasts. We left chastened.

Amazingly, things got worse. Our next performance was on the fringe. Tickets for the festival were steaming along: tickets for the fringe distinctly less so. We had to make a radical adjustment from 400 schoolkids to three old ladies. All of whom were wearing hats. At some point the sheer absurdity of the whole endeavour gripped us. After the small-town politics, the frantic casting, the silly re-hearsals, the giggling parents, the fugitive schoolchildren, here we were giving our all to three old ladies parked stiffly under their large floral hats. When the actor playing Richard and I, as Richmond, stood back to back, giving our inspirational battle cries, it all became a bit too much, and giggles crept in. As we did the battle of Bosworth, frantically running to and fro shouting a lot, giggles expanded into laughter. When it came to my coronation as Henry VII, and my sister dropped my crown, and we all watched it roll off the edge of the stage, and listened to her saying a muted 'sorry' before shuffling off to get it, we all became helpless. And when the one and only lighting cue – lights down – came twenty lines early in my final speech before rapidly returning again, we could none of us remain vertical. Six of us were on our knees or lying on the ground, unable to continue. We crawled off, howling like dogs. Only my girlfriend, considerably better and more serious than the rest of us, remained seated on her bench. As I fell off the side of the stage, I saw her through the mist of my tears, sitting po-faced and white with fury. The friend, who had invited us to come up, shouted at us, demanding that we apologized to the audience. So we shuffled round to the front and formed a rather bizarre receiving line to mutter apologies to the three old ladies as they left. It was hard after that to consider going on.

Yet then, as is ever the case in any Shakespearean story, a corner was turned. Mired as we were in shame and feelings of inadequacy, we were properly scared into attuning ourselves for our next attempt, our first performance on the festival. It was in an enormous cattle auction barn, with a temporary wooden stage, and a grandstand built for a couple of hundred. Birds swooped and soared between their nests in the roof. The smell and the stains of cattle spattered the place. The audience, all local, bounced in and moved during the show between their seats and the bar. The fact it was so large dictated to us that we had to give it welly. We did, and something in the language and the story responded to our energy and quadrupled it. The fact the space was so open and clean and full of air demanded honesty from us. We gave it, and the lines came out clean and muscular and hard. The warmth and the delight of the audience – realizing we were daft southern buggers but not minding – helped us share our gathering momentum in the story. Something in Shakespeare arrives when the conditions are right. The underground energy, the wide music in the language, the strength in the people, they all kick in and inflate what you are doing, making it bolder and brighter than you would have thought possible. It's a surge that singers must feel when the orchestra swells during an opera, yet here it all emanates from the spirit of a single man. By the time we finished, we were astonished, and refreshed.

It was the end of the theatre company. The second performances on the fringe and the festival fell a little flat. Overall the venture had been a conspicuous failure. But our one glad afternoon had wiped a fair amount of shame away.

the Cold War, academic attrition and a brick

At seven o'clock on a spring morning in 1997, I'm standing on Trinity Bridge surrounded by students, all ten years younger than myself. It's the end of a long night of partying. I've just returned to Cambridge (always a bad idea to return anywhere) to direct a student cast in a half-hearted production of a Lope de Vega play, *Peribáñez*. The show, which required throbbing Spanish passion, was largely cast with nice middle-class English kids and went off with about as much *duende* as a bottle of Babycham. But the party has been splendid, with many young ones rushing in and out bursting into tears because A had left B for C who fancied D who was really gay and fancied B. All in all a good night.

And there in a heartbreaking spring Cambridge marbly dawn, all bleary-eyed and thin-brained, I start berating my ex-cast. What's wrong with us, they protest. I'll tell you what's wrong. You've no politics, no substance. When did you ever stand outside King's College with a bucket collecting for miners' wives? Eh? How many leaflets have you ever handed out outside McDonald's? Eh? What do you know about Bomb Consciousness? What do you all bloody know with your ecstasy tablets and your *End of History* books and your Starbucks and your bloody lifestyle choices? Where's the beef? Eh? Where's the fucking beef? I rise to a rhetorical climax, then just to prove to them and the world what an all-round top fellow I am, I stride off to the train station to travel back to London. I pass out on the train and am rudely awoken by a conductor several hours later, as the train pulls into . . . Cambridge. I have clearly been to London and back and no one has dared wake me. With all the dignity I can muster I cross the platform to get on a different London train.

Thankfully the students I berated were savvy enough to know one thing – that the main thing I'm expressing is envy. They don't rise to my 'you haven't lived if you didn't live through the Cold War' shtick. They can see I'm simply trying to exorcize the ghosts of my own misery, having been rudderless in that great fog. And deal with my jealousy at the fact their generation in particular, the Naomi Kleinites, are incubating a far more complex and rigorous oppositional politics than anything we ever came up with.

I could have gone on for hours about what they missed out on in the great deadness of the early eighties. Joan Baez appearing on an episode of *Fame* to join the students for a Ban the Bomb sit-in and singing 'Blowing in the Wind'. That still brings me out in a sweat. Trying to disguise one's accent while shaking a bucket for the miners. Reading *The Fate of the Earth* by Jonathan Schell and earnestly discussing it. Looking into the eyes of a friend and saying meaningfully, 'Only the cockroaches will survive.' God, it was miserable – flat, rational, earnest, grave and serious. The art as dull as the politics. The plays reasonable and deadly, the music whiney and monotonous, one victim eternally trying to out-victim another. You would have said there was a tall poppy syndrome. But they wouldn't even have allowed poppies then, let alone tall ones. They'd be far too colourful.

At the very moment when we suffered most acutely from a need for imagination – when we couldn't even muster the primary school insight that everyone east of Berlin was probably pretty much the same as everyone west of Berlin – just at that moment, cultural functionaries of left and right ploughed in to destroy anyone who had any. We are stumbling into the same idiocy now, with two camps of two-dimensional villains, the neo-cons and the jihadists, both shutting down the capacity for imaginative compassion, for themselves and their followers, so they can crush the humans in the middle. It's at just these moments when we most need art, real bold imaginative art, that the oxygen supply for such art is most drastically reduced.

It was at just such a moment in an entirely different context that Shakespeare appeared and dazzled his audience with the complexity of the human. The tension that stretched the solar plexus of his world tight was the rift straining Europe to breaking point between Catholic and Protestant. Each country was split, each village, each family. Shakespeare's father, as a Stratford alderman, had to enthusiastically toe the authority line and assist in the destruction of Catholic icons; at home he was hiding Catholic documents in the tiling of his roof. Shakespeare's cousins were executed for Catholic conspiracy, and their heads would have adorned poles affixed to London Bridge when he first arrived in town. Which side are you on? Where is your allegiance? What is your history? All these questions would flicker through each brain on meeting any stranger. All of them would be asked out loud by the forces of either side, followed by the statement of today's stupidity, 'If you're not with us, you're against us.' It is a horrible reduction of the human capability, an insult to the human potential.

All the every-action-is-political baloney which we lived through in a minor key, Shakespeare and his time had to live through as if under a magnifying glass. Small wonder the Stratford man kept his cloak of privacy so tightly wrapped round himself. And great wonder that he reacted to this state with the most wilfully perverse response imaginable. He decimated the stupidity within the distinction between Catholic and Protestant, within any grotesque distinction between people, by presenting in the display case of his work all the infinite variety of human nature. He didn't retreat into taking sides, or into some defeatist despair. He banged out year after year, with the energy of a zealot, art that said here, here is the human, and here is the world, here, here and here. It is infinite, and none of you can shut it into any of your vicious little boxes.

The Cold War was a nebulous historical moment. It was as internalized as it was real. It was as much about a failure of thought as it was about a long wall with towers. It's presumptuous, of course, to claim to have been in a war, when there was so little fighting, so little death, so little blood and mess. But it would be equally fatuous to deny that we were shaped by the air we grew up in. If the capacity of the mind is formed in infancy and early youth, the direction of it is shaped when you come to intellectual maturity between fifteen and twenty-two. That's when you read the books which will influence you, hear the ideas that will steer you, absorb the insights which will shape you. You can change and accept new ones. But it's danged hard. Mine was the last, the fag-end, of the boring old left–right, communism–capitalism political generations.

Literature studies and Shakespeare himself were rife with it. You'd expect the groves of academe to be gentle places, withdrawn from the engagement of politics. But Cambridge was seething. A year before I arrived, there had been an enormous conflagration, when a young teacher, Colin MacCabe, had failed to obtain tenure (basically was sacked) because he had been indulging in the occult arts of structuralism. One faction believed that he had been poisoning the minds of the young with a lot of new-fangled communistic nonsense. The other faction believed that his right to teach what he wanted had been brutally repressed by a jaded junta of ageing conservatives. They snarled at each other a lot. When I arrived in 1982, the battle was still fresh and ongoing.

At first our sympathies were with the junta, since that was how we'd been taught at school, and changing our mode of understanding looked like an awful lot of hard work. This was only confirmed when a couple of us looked into the whole structuralist thing and found it rather intimidatingly mathematical, and rather gravely serious. However, once it became clear that the reactionary brigade were largely drooling old men in ageing three-piece suits, it became imperative to try and engage with the revolutionaries. Two of my friends entered into this enthusiastically. They were told to write essays on a rather dull Victorian novel by Mrs Gaskell by a lecturer at the cutting edge of the structuralists. They could hardly manage to read it let alone write about it. So they turned up at their tutorial with a carrier bag. When they were invited to read out their essays, they declined. They told their young professor that they had tried and tried and tried to write an essay but nothing would do justice to the complexity or the depth of their thoughts on the subject. They had discussed it amongst themselves and resolved that there was only one way to express those feelings. With enormous solemnity they then reached into their bag and took out a large brick. They placed it on the table between them with an air of quiet triumph. Somewhere inside themselves they had hoped that their professor would see the joke and they could all have a laugh. But they underestimated him. He was fascinated by their submission and engaged them in an hour and a half of brow-knitted analysis of their brick. After this magnificent display of humourlessness, it became harder to side wholeheartedly with the revolutionaries. We resolved prudently to agree enthusiastically with whoever we were with at the time.

Nowhere did this argument thrash around more violently than over the corpus of Shakespeare. On one side, there were those still worshipping at the literary flame, seeing the plays as long poems, full of imagistic connections and linguistic echoes. They saw his work as living eternal and outside time. On the other side was a loose affiliation of different street-fighters – structuralists, post-structuralists, cultural materialists and new historicists. The first two were always rather hard to fathom, but the second two repaid considerable attention. They held that Shakespeare must be seen in his historical moment, and the plays should be seen as living responses to that moment. That their strength and their power and their universality depended on their specificity, and that it was impossible to understand them without understanding the slew of forces, small and large, that swilled around them. This is hard to deny.

The cultural materialists won a big round, just as I was trying to sort this out in my head, by publishing a collection of essays starkly entitled *Political Shakespeare*. Its cover is a fantastic example of lumpen, early 1980s anti-chic. It is all red and white and black, and the lettering is aggressively cheerless. Don't even think about smiling when you open this book, is the message sent out. But once you did get inside it, a lot of what it was saying was unanswerably true. There are a few predictable essays within it, exploring the colonial patterns within *The Tempest*, and a bit of unfair slagging-off of Shakespeare for being an evil old patriarch and not giving the women enough of a look-in.

What was exhilarating about the essays was their dynamiting of the old preconceptions about the Elizabethan world order. This had been drummed into us at an early age, and was later reinforced by reading an antiquated cultural historian called Tillyard. The basic thesis was that a stable world and cosmological order had existed since the middle ages. God was at the top, above various ranks of cherubim and seraphim, descending on down to first kings, then barons, then peasants, who scraped in just above the animals, who had a merry little hierarchy of their own. A complex cosmology was worked out to suit. The presumption had always been that this order had pertained through to Shakespeare's time, and that he was a profound believer in its maintenance and viewed any disturbance of its delicate calibrations in a very dim light. Ulysses, the dishonest and scheming little politician from *Troilus and Cressida*, is usually cited as evidence:

> O, when degree is shaked,
> Which is the ladder to all high designs,
> Then enterprise is sick! How could communities,
> Degrees in schools and brotherhoods in cities,
> Peaceful commerce from dividable shores,
> The primogenitive and due of birth,
> Prerogative of age, crowns, sceptres, laurels,
> But by degree, stand in authentic place?
> Take but degree away, untune that string,
> And, hark, what discord follows! each thing meets
> In mere oppugnancy: the bounded waters
> Should lift their bosoms higher than the shores
> And make a sop of all this solid globe:
> Strength should be lord of imbecility,
> And the rude son should strike his father dead:
> Force should be right; or rather, right and wrong,
> Between whose endless jar justice resides,
> Should lose their names, and so should justice too.
> Then every thing includes itself in power,
> Power into will, will into appetite;
> And appetite, an universal wolf,
> So doubly seconded with will and power,
> Must make perforce an universal prey,
> And last eat up himself.

It's a speech that's regularly trotted out at Conservative conferences.

This whole theory smelled a bit fishy even at school. The idea that everyone knows their place and is happy there doesn't bear an enormous amount of historical analysis. But you tend to let these things go by, on the anything-for-a-quiet-life principle. What the new historicists revealed, through extensive research, was that

Shakespeare's society was far from stable. In fact it was convulsively dynamic. There was an overpowering sense all around of a world where one form of ruling power – ancient, dynastic and largely Catholic – was giving way to a new and more vigorous one – mercantile, newly wealthy, meritocratic and largely Protestant. Tectonic plates at all levels of this world were shifting. The Catholic/Protestant dialectic was its costume, but what filled that costume was a variety of different energies. With all this change swirling around, the calls for calm and for order were frequent. They were the sign of a nervous society. As the book has it:

In the late sixteenth and early seventeenth centuries . . . this almost hysterical demand for order at all costs was caused by a collapse of most of the props of the medieval world picture. The unified dogma and organisation of the Catholic Church found itself challenged by a number of rival creeds and institutional structures . . . the reliance upon the intellectual authority of the Ancients was threatened by new scientific discoveries. Moreover in England there occurred a phase of unprecedented social and geographical mobility which at the higher levels transformed the composition and size of the gentry and professional classes, and at the lower levels tore hundreds of thousands of individuals loose from their traditional kinship and neighbourhood backgrounds.

The old order fought to maintain their dying culture, the new powers sought to enforce with violence their new dominant culture, and various wildcats scurried around fermenting new subversive cultures. Within this fluidity of cultural movement, the opportunity suddenly arose for Renaissance man to forge himself anew. Operating on the pick and mix principle, men and to a lesser degree women could fashion new identities for themselves within and without different ideologies. And at the heart of this broil of opposing historical and cultural forces was the theatre, and Shakespeare himself. Rioting dockers, strident sex-workers, old Catholic gentry, puritan maniacs, merchant millionaires, spies and minor royalty all attended his theatre. He watched them, listened to them and took them all into himself. He reflected what he saw and what he heard back on to the stage, in front of the people who had created it. He was the still eye at the centre of a storm. I find this a more persuasive understanding than the old one of the conservative gentleman giving loudmouths a ticking-off.

The ideas of *Political Shakespeare* were excellent. Their only problem was the language they were expressed in. Each of the authors often strained to write with the most painfully tortured prose. There was a bullying pride in using esoteric language and in coldly shutting out the less educated. It felt like the attitude of the masters, exercising a Stalinist repression of the stupid. Instant migraines followed on from trying to draw out its meaning. As a for instance: 'If we only talk of power producing the discourse of subversion we not only hypostatise power but also efface the cultural differences – and context – which the very process of containment presupposes.' That sentence should be shot for cruelty to the English language. But that was the sickness of the age. A desire for power was expressed even by those who were trying to subvert it. Everything was about control. To write about subversion in a language that was available to all, and that had a little flair, would have been too bold, too anarchic, too free. It would have been giving too much away, in a time which relished giving nothing away. Miserable days.

Hopefully the next generation yet, the ones born in the eighties, whose minds were opening up just as the world's started shutting after 9/11, will listen to the E generation, to the generation I was berating at dawn on that bridge over the Cam. They'll get a lot more sense from them than those whose minds were blighted by the blinkers of the Cold War. Hopefully they too will pay attention to Shakespeare, and how he took the divisions of his own day and used them to catapult him to a new imaginative place, at one and the same time within his own world and free from it.

sick jokes, heartlessness and playing Pandarus

Where are my tears? Rain, to lay this wind, or my heart will be blown up by the root.

It's a peculiar moment when you discover your own capacity for emotional deadness. It's not one you've looked forward to. One hopes that time will reveal heroic reserves of passion, reservoirs of rage and love and compassion. To look inside and find nothing is a rude surprise.

The first time you discover the depth of your own heartlessness is probably allied to the growth of sick humour. When I was about twelve, a spate of grisly sick jokes mushroomed up about a woman called Lesley Whittle. She had been strung up and left to die down a drain. The incident had festered in my imagination as news items can in young minds. Fretful hours were spent before sleep picturing the pendent body in the darkness, screaming unheard cries. When I heard the first cruel joke about it I was appalled by the heartlessness of the world. When I heard the third cruel joke, I laughed, and appalled myself.

Later, you get to an age where you measure a tragic event by the time lapse before the first gags appear. The fiery evaporation of the Space Shuttle *Discovery* was swamped in a barrage of irreverent gags almost before the debris had hit the ground. As an adult, you come to understand the necessity of humour as a release mechanism. It's a way of countering the confusion generated by God's great mess. As a child, one can be alarmed by one's own capacity for cruel humour. Later, mired in the self-consciousness of adolescence, one finds it impossible to deal with any weight of emotion. When family members weep, one sniggers; when death occurs, one smirks.

Then you read *The Waste Land*. This comes as something of a relief. There's something so modish about Eliot's despair, so etiolated and elegant, you feel your heartlessness is an entrée to an exclusive club, full of the emotionally dyslexic. Other poets, especially twentieth-century ones, gather you into the same Club Anomie. Stir in some novelists and philosophers, and your lack of connect starts to become an almost heroic thing, an existential rejection of bourgeois ties of sympathy. It's a slippery slope from the moment anyone opens *The Outsider* by Albert Camus and reads its coolly calm opening line: 'Mother died today. Or maybe yesterday; I can't be sure . . .'

Yet, when you enter these dreamy anaesthetized lands of emotional disconnect, it's only a way of avoiding looking at who you are. Joining an army of any sort is more often than not a way of avoiding responsibility for one's actions. A kid who joins the regular army is hiding his loss of identity and his need for violence beneath a disguise, a uniform embroidered with baloney about adventure and honour. A kid who joins the far more wussy army of miserabilists, putting on the uniform of great coats and lingering stares, veiling faces beneath long hair and dancing jerkily to Joy Division, is hiding from the cost of failing to connect emotionally.

This moment in Shakespeare's life, the moment when youth picks a personality for adulthood, is the one most shrouded in darkness. From the age of eighteen through to the age of about twenty-eight, we have precious little information about him. Yet no shortage of conjecture. Scholars have variously imagined him as a lawyer; a tutor in Catholic Lancashire; a soldier in the Low Countries; an aristocrat's amanuensis in Northern Italy; and whatever else takes their fancy. The profligacy of the options is a compliment to the Protean expanse of his later imagination. It is also a clue to the probable truth. Far from choosing a single, stiff uniform at that moment, to defend his vulnerable identity, he did the opposite, and chose whatever attracted him on any passing whim. He chose the shape-shifting, malleable identity of the actor.

This is borne out within the plays by the freedom with which his characters reinvent themselves: dukes disguise themselves as friars, princes as common men, lusty girls as strapping boys, Antony and Cleopatra, with cross-dressing delight, as each other. Throughout the plays, characters save themselves or improve their situations by taking on the role of another – most obviously Viola and Rosalind, but the trope continues elsewhere. It is hard not to imagine that this liminal fluidity of personality had also liberated Shakespeare within his own life. At the moment when many decide to fix themselves with a personality, he decided, within a gently watchful curiosity, to float free.

Yet, when I took on the role of Pandarus in a university production of *Troilus and Cressida*, I discovered that, whatever the uniform of stylized disaffection, it could not conceal the absence within.

My ego was mildly peeved that I hadn't been offered any more leading roles at university than I had at school. I was even more disconcerted that I felt so at home in the role of Pandarus. He is a diseased, cynical, gossipy, sentimental go-between, who shuttles between Troilus and Cressida, bringing their infatuation to sexual fruition. He does it all with a seedy lubricious delight. It was a little out of kilter with my self-image. The director had placed it cleverly. It was a modern-dress production with Greeks and Trojans as vagabond modern gangs full of a disaffected lust for violence. Pandarus was an elder figure with a sentimental nostalgia for good suits, Sinatra records, and everyone knowing their place.

Yet what looked like a gift of a comedy part with some cheap laughs, a fair amount of stage time, the closing words and a song fairly quickly morphed into something else. It was when I tripped up over the words 'Where are my tears? Rain, to lay this wind, or my heart will be blown up by the root' that I fell into the chasm of Pandarus' problem, and by extension my own. He stands there watching Troilus and Cressida, at the moment when they are forced to separate, and when they are in the full fiery flush of their grieving. He is unable to feel a thing. Two young bloods trapped in the writhing of their own passion, and he can't cry. He asks the question, 'Where are my tears?' and he realizes the silence that follows. There are none. He begs, 'Rain,' for he knows that otherwise the wind of events is going to tear the heart out of him, its roots long desiccated by his own lack of feeling. It's a hair-raising moment. This wasn't the smooth étranger elegance of a Gauloises-smoking rebel, this was a shabby man in despair who can't find his own pulse.

Standing there hitting that moment in rehearsals and on stage, there was no hiding from its application to me. I was stuck in that particular student moment – away from the weave of connections of family and home, and before I had woven my own new carpet of connection. It's an empty moment, and it uncovers a hole that's always been there and is hard to close up again. It's a nihilism whose release valve is great surges of sentimentality. I could still cry for an uninterrupted forty-five minutes at *ET*. I could still shake with sobs while watching Michael Buerk's reports from the Sudan, and I was still happy to grandstand politically about the suffering of the miners' wives (they never did thank me). But a tragedy up close and personal – *Troilus and Cressida* on stage – or any of the smaller tragedies that stalk a student life – abortions, overdoses, heartbreaks and breakdowns – all left me perfectly cold. Playing Pandarus brought this up close.

Connecting with him, a man who could report great emotions but couldn't generate them, a man who could look but not feel, was dreadful. It came from a place particular to Shakespeare – his understanding of the pervading squalor of human response. His heroes are, of course, grand and are there to grandstand, which they do with the required magnificence. They trace paradigms to show what happens at a subterranean level through our lives. Macbeth's fall from an opportunity into a well of nothingness; Lear's progress from a closed autocrat in a tank to a wide-open baby screaming in a field; Hamlet's ascent from a roil of confusion to an arrow of flight. These are journeys the arc and curve of which we all follow for brief and extended periods of our own messy narratives. We understand those subcurrents through the stories these heroes have lived through before. They also describe how at moments of deep connection – through passionate love, or great grief, or insane jealousy – we do rise above ourselves and live in a state of clean simplicity.

But they are not all of Shakespeare. His speciality is the non-heroes, the confused, the human, the scrappy and the messy. The rest, who don't charge about tracing grand patterns. They are there to show how we are ninety-five per cent of the time. When we're awkward and self-conscious; when we stumble and fall; when we're gossipy and small. They are the people who love to hover close to action but are frightened to join in. They are amongst Shakespeare's sharpest creations, and they are us. At that time at university, I was too close to all of them. The only consolation was that through understanding Pandarus, I realized that I was understood. He was a man in the wings of life. Previously, I had found this detached loneliness desirable. It was calm, and it was separate. Shakespeare taught me that it was also inadequate.

Squalor abounded. The show was a huge hit, and very influential, spawning a huge number of copycat productions, at university and in the professional theatre. On the last night, we had an enormous splash of a do. There was a warm and wonderful smoky girl whom I had met during the show. She told me she was up for a night of pure passion. I took her home, but a disastrous night ensued, and after it an abrupt and sour affair. A couple of years later she died on a boat which was rammed on the Thames, taking down much of a twenty-first-birthday party with it. I opened a newspaper and found an obituary for her. A shiver of mortality ran through me, but not enough sadness. It felt like a universe of heartlessness spread out from that show.

Where are my tears? Rain, to lay this wind, or my heart will be blown up by the root.

cultish concepts and *Timon of Athens*

Two contrary, but equally poisonous, orthodoxies came together in my first production of a Shakespeare play at university. I had chosen to direct the rarely produced *Timon of Athens*, a savage scream of rage at the iniquities of money. It ticked several boxes for me, being set in Athens, which dovetailed with my classical studies; being full of political fire, which suited the anti-Thatcher moment; and being largely devoid of human relationships, which suited my own naivety.

The first orthodoxy was drawn from a book called *Free Shakespeare* by John Russell Brown. This book, which made little impact on the world before or since, generated a cult following at Cambridge. Ardent young theatricos would sit and read it to each other. Directors could quote it. Its high priest at university was a director called Stephen Unwin; his devotees a highly gifted generation of actors, including a young Tilda Swinton and Simon Russell Beale. They produced an iconic *Measure for Measure*, and a beautifully lucid *Comedy of Errors* according to the principles of this book. The second production was deemed to be a masterpiece, and if you were interested in theatre, you had to troop along and see it two or three times and engage in long discussions of its merits. Elegantly designed, it was a peculiar and effective hybrid of gauche clowning, proletarian chic and subversive wit. The evening was partly ruined by Tilda Swinton, who sat at the back of the stage throughout by a piano, chainsmoking with a diffident relaxation, which doomed whatever took place in front of her to penumbra.

As, I imagine, with all cults, no one had any real idea what it was about. At the heart of the principles was a return to an ideal of honest Shakespeare. Stripped-down was the predominant aesthetic. No naturalistic or excessive design; no detailed characterization in acting; no excessive emotional empathy; no emotionally manipulative music; no use of narrative suspense. Basically, no, no, no, just stop it. All this made a lot of common sense for students. We didn't have the money for any design, nobody could compose music, few understood any characters beyond our own middle-class student archetype, and twelve of us could hardly have raised an emotion if we'd been stuck in a burning building.

The second poisonous orthodoxy was an almost directly contradictory one, that of the concept production. This is a small word to cover an enormous amount of theatrical rubbish. The PR version of a concept production is that a director produces an idea which liberates the energies and realities of a play and helps an audience to see them anew. The truth is that a director who has only half or quarter understood a play wrenches it towards him, by imposing an idea which will bring it within the realm of his own understanding. So you set *Hamlet* in a loony bin; or *Romeo and Juliet* in a mafia-controlled little Italy; or *Lear* in an abstract nowhere; or *Twelfth Night* on the moon; or whatever. One of the worst Cambridge aberrations was a *Midsummer Night's Dream* in which all the characters were disabled: Oberon was blind; Titania deaf; Puck had no legs; the fairies were all on crutches. One actor was late to join rehearsals, and when he arrived, he realized that everyone else had already claimed the major disabilities. Approaching the director and asking what he should do, he was told with little sensitivity, 'Oh, I don't know. You're ugly, try that!'

Now a concept production was the first great sin to the Free Shakespeare mob, but my arrogance got the better of my obeisance to the cult. I couldn't resist a bit of showing off. So I conceived a production in a studio theatre, with two very distinct halves. The first half was a promenade production, with the actors and the audience milling around a festive and jolly Athens full of champagne and party poppers. The walls were all painted bright white and covered with bright golden cartoonish decorations denoting Athens. My lodestar, artistically, was *Asterix at the Olympic Games*, though I would never have admitted as much. For the second half, when Timon retreats from the city to his cave by the sea, we transformed the theatre into a black room, sweeping curtains along the walls, building a stage in the middle and surrounding it with chairs. From promenade theatre to theatre in the round. Astonishing. Brilliant. What more did I have to do? Why bother rehearsing?

Rehearsals were a bit of a bother, actually. We enjoyed a very exciting first weekend playing theatre games and doing extended improvisations, where I wandered round magus-like, pulling strings, and orchestrating dramatic moments. This was great but unfortunately had nothing to do with *Timon of Athens*. When we got down to the play, I quickly got bored by the actors asking questions about language. Why fuss with all that, when they should just be thrilled by my brilliant idea? But they persisted, and I learned, as I had to learn before, and as I would have to learn over and over again. With Shakespeare, just as with a new play, you had to work out who you were, your relationships with the others, and moment by moment, word by word, how you were developing the tapestry of the evening. Having seen so much Shakespeare on stage, before and since, where people just come on and boom it out at you, I had thought, with my natural laziness, that I could get away with that. But thankfully my aesthetic standards are louder in my head than my desire for a quiet life, and they demanded the work.

Once we did settle into exploring it, various exciting things started happening. There is one bleak scene in the second half between Apemantus the professional cynic and the fallen Timon. It's a sort of nihilist version of *Gladiators*. Each character competes to express the bleakest and most savage vision of humanity and the universe. We fooled around with it one morning in a room where Erasmus used to teach. The mood was light and playful. The content was despair. The results from that morning were delightful, tracing patterns of despair in a void with a forensic accuracy and a resigned cheerfulness. They made the connections between Shakespeare and Beckett made by Jan Kott, a revered Polish academic, come to life. Having begun as insubstantial and inane, the idea developed muscles and became theatrically quite striking.

Unfortunately, when it opened, there was hardly anyone there to see it. Much of my second year at Cambridge, when I wasn't acting Pandarus or directing *Timon*, was a blur. There was a lot of speed, a lot of Special Brew and long afternoons in the bookies, making five and ten pence bets on the dogs. My small claque of friends were all, like me, rather unenamoured of Cambridge and retreated into a sort of half-cock Martin Amis world. Two of that claque were in *Timon of Athens*. One had designed it. Foolishly I asked another to produce it. A charming fellow with a great political sense, he had managed to raise a huge sum of money to mount the show. A large proportion of this, I think a third, went on our favourite budget item, Hammers and Nails. This basically meant speed and Special Brew. So with budgets he was a master, but with publicity he was a disaster. The show opened to a trickle and closed to a flood, but when no one comes at the beginning of an experience it's hard to surmount that initial disappointment and make it joyous.

It finished as a tight and clever and artful evening, but a small-hearted one. *Timon* is one of Shakespeare's meanest plays, rippling with rage and bitterness and envy. The language is choppy and lurid. The story is stunted. But the fault wasn't the play, it was a production that was too pleased with its own ideas. Shakespeare demands a big heart, and a big lung. If you don't bring either, you will be found out. There is little that's beautiful or important in proving to the world how small or vicious people are. It's easy and it's glib. A great swathe of modern drama is shot through with little but visions of self-loathing and misanthropy. Shakespeare condensed most of it into one play and packed so much into such a tight space that it became a spectacle within itself. A black hole of hatred. Everybody has a Timon moment at some point in their lives. It's good to get it out of the way.

One funny off-shoot of the production was helping in the birth of a feminist theatre company. With a regrettable paternalism, I had changed the gender of the three servants in the play to female. These three servants carry the moral weight of the first half and are the first to warn Timon of the dangers of excess. I thought making them female would be a brilliant political point and earn me lots of brownie points with the girls. Unfortunately my ideological credentials were vitiated by asking the same girls to dress up in skimpy costumes as dancing girls earlier on. Fierce discussions ensued about the exact deconstructed meaning of them wearing bikinis and rolling around on top of the chaps. I didn't so much join the discussions as look companionable and intense. The resulting compromise was a little tame. Later, the three actresses were part of the formation of a feminist company called Trouble and Strife. Two other ex-girlfriends had formed a women's comedy act called the Millies. In my blithe egomania, I actually thought of myself as a sort of sympathetic father figure to the feminist movement. I hadn't the wit to realize that I was the enemy in the first case. And the joke in the second.

skiving, a surprise discovery and tragic splendour

The standard of education at Cambridge was poor, the standard of its application calamitous. Most of the dons seemed too involved in their own publications, or their turf wars, to notice we existed. Students could go missing for whole terms without anyone noticing. That was fine by us. Education was seen as a negligible add-on to a social life, or a theatre life, or a drug life, or a political life, if you did any of those things. If you didn't, it was an add-on to not much. At the end of my second year, with exams in classics looming, my director of studies, having identified who I was, further identified the notion that I needed to have something to write about. He gave me some subjects to investigate and instructed me to meet him at a certain address. I made my way there, and we marched through a large building looking for a room to work in. 'This is a big place,' I said looking about me, 'what goes on here?' 'Lectures, Dominic, lectures.'

Classics was enjoyably exotic, but altogether too much like hard work, and, having scraped through my Part I exams, I announced that I now wanted to change and return to my first love, English literature. Once the classics department worked out who I was, they announced that they couldn't be more delighted to get rid of me – they practically threw a party – but the only problem was that the English department didn't want me, nor did any other department in the university. I panicked at the thought of another year staring at irregular Greek verbs, begged the English department and eventually cut a deal with them. If I did about three-quarters of my work for the third year in the summer holidays that preceded it, they would let me in. I pottered off to Morocco, spent the summer nose-deep in a text-book and was finally admitted.

This left a third year free for the most part for plays, including as an eccentric choice Sophocles' three Theban plays, which I translated, thus becoming a Greek adept, six months too late. There was a panic late in the year when I realized I had to write a dissertation in two days and do all the relevant reading. I installed a good and kind girlfriend at the other end of my room with a typewriter. I wrote whatever bollocks came into my head out in hand, folded the sheets into paper aeroplanes and sent them sailing down the room to her, where she would turn them into a nice, crisply typed dissertation. We worked flat out for thirty-six hours and only just got 7,500 words in on time. Halfway through writing it, I realized that the title I had submitted – 'Bringing It All Back Home, Literature from the Vietnam War, The Creation of New Journalism' – wasn't only an embarrassing attempt to be groovy, it was also nonsense, since Tom Wolfe had invented New Journalism five years before the Vietnam war hit its height and several thousand miles away. I skirted round this by adding a question mark to the title and spending a couple of thousand words vigorously trashing a thesis no one had held in the first place.

This was all enjoyably idle, but also a daft waste of time, opportunity and resources. I still kick myself two or three times a year for wasting one of the only times in my life available for the development of my mind and nothing else. It wasn't me, it was a general culture. The presumption was that if you'd got into Cambridge, that was all you needed to do. There was also a presumption in the early eighties that all we were preparing ourselves for was long years of drawing unemployment benefit, so why shouldn't we start practising doing nothing early on? I hope that nowadays they wake them up with a bucket of cold water and whip them along to lectures and the rest. I understand that paying for your education has had something of that effect already. The shame was when I forced myself or was forced on to a subject, the intellectual excitement of it thrilled me.

While working on *Timon of Athens* as a director, simultaneously I was looking at Aristophanes for my classics course. It wouldn't take Einstein to see the connection. Shakespeare set out to write a satire based in fourth-century BC Athens. Consciously or unconsciously, and it's hard to tell with his extraordinary magpie tendencies, the structure he adopted for the telling of his story is very close to the model invented by the man who wrote a series of satires of fourth-century Athens from a more contemporaneous viewpoint, Aristophanes. The shape of *Timon* is completely unlike any other structure Shakespeare uses in his work. The first two acts are like the fourth and fifth acts of a preceding play, rising to a swift and troubling climax. As a resolution of the crisis that ensues, one man has to leave his community and journey elsewhere alone. Once he is installed elsewhere, a series of people from his previous community come to meet him for a series of dialectical dialogues. It is stunningly similar to the model for Aristophanes' *Akharnians*, and *The Frogs*, and *The Clouds*. It was so obvious that I thought it must be a commonplace, but, on looking through all the academic discussions of *Timon*, it soon became clear that no one had spotted it before. It was a discovery.

I thought I was Hercule Poirot, Stephen Hawking and F. R. Leavis wrapped into one. I didn't tell anyone for a while, wondering whether I should get a patent for such an important bit of research, and to whom I should apply for the big money. When eventually the pressure to reveal became too great, and, with a tremulous voice, I revealed to my friends my amazing discovery, that, yes, Shakespeare had based his structure for *Timon of Athens* on an Aristophanic model, I was half expecting them all to burst into tears, or strike their foreheads, crying out Hallelujah! In fact, two of them went off to play bar billiards, and a third went to buy another round. It was deflating. When I went to see my tutor for this dissertation, I thought I was assured of a more exclamatory reception. Far from it. He simply poured a bottle of wine down my throat and asked if he could give me a kiss. I stumbled quickly out, adjusting to the fact that my discovery wasn't destined to rock the world of academe.

I wrote it up, and the case remained fairly watertight, but the invitation to lecture at the Royal Society of Literature never came. The insight for me was into Shakespeare's extraordinary ability to absorb sources and make them disappear. Ben Jonson's tag for him of 'little Latin and less Greek' has stuck for centuries, but has never been fully understood. For a Stratford grammar-school boy, who crammed classical literature in from dawn until dusk, 'little' and 'less' was a gargantuan amount by comparison with our standards today.

The plays are drenched in classical references, primarily Ovid, but a diverse collection of others saturate the work. What Shakespeare didn't do as much as his contemporaries was display his learning. There's very little of the look-how-learned-I-am writing that Jonson for one excels in. It wasn't Shakespeare's way. He read, absorbed, understood and then forgot. It got into his marrow rather than sat on his sleeve. With Aristophanes he displayed his model so discreetly no one could be interested when the connection was pointed out. So it goes.

The other great joy was in my frantic last-minute studies for the sonorously titled Tragedy paper. This was one of the few compulsory exams that everyone studying English had to sit. Why do we attach such extraordinary value to tragedy? It's still thought of as a moral cold shower that all young things need. Get some tragedy in them, that'll sort them out. Everyone emerges from Cambridge pretty fucked up, so it can't be all that successful. Wouldn't we all have been better off with a compulsory Frivolity paper? We could have spent all year studying the plays of Noel Coward, the lyrics of Captain Sensible and the Flake adverts. This Victorian idea that tragedy cleanses pertains and won't disappear in a hurry. But my preparations for this paper revealed one great source of joy to me, the endless, non-stop, turbo-charged, headlong sublimity that is *Antony and Cleopatra*.

No other play starts at such a ludicrous height. By line fourteen, as Antony and Cleopatra whirl on, we're on to:

CLEOPATRA If it be love, indeed, tell me how much.
ANTONY There's beggary in the love that can be reckon'd.
CLEOPATRA I'll set a bourn how far to be belov'd.
ANTONY Then must thou needs find out new heaven, new earth.

It's not a bad entrance. Only eighteen lines later, we cascade into Antony's:

> Let Rome in Tiber melt, and the wide arch
> Of the rang'd empire fall! Here is my space.
> Kingdoms are clay; our dungy earth alike
> Feeds beast as man. The nobleness of life

Is to do thus; when such a mutual pair
And such a twain can do't, in which I bind,
On pain of punishment, the world to weet
We stand up peerless.

It's poetry at a height of richness and wit and passion that you imagine is unsustainable, but Shakespeare keeps churning it out. Of course, poetry is everywhere in the canon, but the verse of *Antony and Cleopatra* is burnished and wrought with a deliberate beauty that takes it closer to the rarefied fineness of the Romantic achievement than anything else. There is the stand-alone, breath-defying beauty of Enobarbus' description of Cleopatra's arrival in town – 'The chair she sat in . . .' – and throughout the lovers drive themselves to fresh and new heights of refinement. The first few times you read it, it has a steamrollering effect, flattening you with its excess. It's amyl nitrate writing.

It's only after a few readings that you start to notice its fundamental comedy. The poetry is wonderful, but it is effortful. Mr Rosser's old training in how to spot writing that is easy from writing that is forced came good again. Excluding Enobarbus' word painting, which comes from the centre of himself and is spoken quietly to his friends, the rest of the poetry is the most extraordinary performance. At every moment throughout the play Antony and Cleopatra are in company. There are always crowds or soldiers or slaves or attendants or messengers. There is always someone else there. For one brief moment in act III they are left alone together, and it's a disaster. Their love can only fly when there's someone watching. They are also permanently saying goodbye to one another. They need the sweet sorrow of parting to jack them up to the height they want to motor at. All must be public, all must be painful. They need the pressure to bring themselves off. They need it to be Antony and Cleopatra. There is simply no way they could sit in front of the telly alone together for the night, with tea and biscuits. Companionable silence just isn't their thing.

Shakespeare knew celebrities and he knew legends and he knew the price of maintaining an aura. He had watched Elizabeth, a shrivelled, wrinkled, exhausted old lady, at close quarters and seen how she put on her charisma and seen the effort in it. He had watched Essex and

Ralegh and Southampton cruising up and down the Thames on sunny days in dolled-out poops, playing to the crowds on the shores. He had watched his best friend Burbage giving it a bit of the old actor charm to pull the ladies. He knew about the frightened child in the public hero. He pitches Antony and Cleopatra far beyond even them. This glorious, scabby, decrepit old couple, both raddled by time and fights and fucks, keep raising the odds against themselves and keep pulling it off, coming out smelling of myth and eternity. They are not just playing to the crowds of their day, they are pitching themselves against the sniggering giggle of time as well. Their efforts are constantly being thwarted by the comedy of reality. Antony can't find anyone to kill him and botches his own effort. The asps take a devil of a time to finish madam off. But finally their effort pays off, and they rise above place and time. Antony dies exhausted with the effort, on the breath, 'I can no more'. Cleopatra takes his spirit and hurls it up to the stars with the benediction:

> The crown of the earth doth melt. My lord!
> O! wither'd is the garland of the war,
> The soldier's pole is fall'n; young boys and girls
> Are level now with men; the odds is gone,
> And there is nothing left remarkable
> Beneath the visiting moon.

This is endlessly loving, but it's also her job. She has to do this for Antony, just as she has to take a breather and gather her resources before her own final assault on the title. Throughout the play sublimity rubs up against comic and grubby life. Having dispatched Antony, Cleopatra needs to immerse herself in the sublunary for a while before regaining her stride for her own departure. The glory cannot live without its opposite, the tawdry. So she prevaricates messily with Caesar and almost loses the sympathy of the audience before triumphantly reclaiming her own fake magnificence:

> Give me my robe, put on my crown; I have
> Immortal longings in me; now no more
> The juice of Egypt's grape shall moist this lip.
> Yare, yare, good Iras; quick. Methinks I hear

Antony call; I see him rouse himself
To praise my noble act . . .
                              . . . Husband, I come:
Now to that name my courage prove my title!
I am fire, and air; my other elements
I give to baser life.

She gets there. Against all the odds, against her own nature, against
the spite of others – in the first seven lines before she gets on she's
called 'tawny' and a 'gypsy' – and against the cruelty of time, she
achieves her apotheosis. It's an extraordinary achievement by her
and by Shakespeare. He gives an autonomous creation, mired in the
obstacles of buffoon reality, the chance to write her own story, and
she takes it. Without all the comic cruelty, it would be a Disney fairy
tale, but with the cruelty, it's a true beatification. The saint of the
dirty old beautiful slappers.

But, of course, it's not just a celebration of the celebrity spirit, or a
can-do kit for those who want to deify themselves. The reason we
watch *Antony and Cleopatra* with appalled fascination is because
Shakespeare is, as ever, saying something about us. We may not want
all that these two want, we may not want any of it. We may fancy
mowing the lawn and reading the *Daily Express*. But what they are
doing, excessively and stupidly and heroically, is what all of us are
doing every day. Making an effort. This is what struck me like a
baseball bat as I studied this play. Being human is not a given. It is
an effort. Each day we try to be human, each day we succeed a little,
and fail a little. But each new day we try again. Antony and Cleopatra
try further, they try to be hugely human, living out our potential for
us. We don't want their excess, but we celebrate them for taking so
far what all of us do in a minor key. And just as they work against
the odds, so do we. Every day is a minefield of knocks and blows and
comic falls that could break us and leave us crumpled on the floor.
Yet every day we make the effort to get ourselves upright. Two of
Shakespeare's most comically silly and tragically glorious creations
show us how.

Loki and the steal parts

One day after university, from pure and impure motives, I bought a collection of Penguin digests of different world mythologies. The pure intention was to understand a little about what fed the spirits of different cultures. The impure intention was to look like someone who wanted to understand a little about what fed the spirits of different cultures. So the Bhagavad Gita sat beside the Qu'ran which nestled up to a book on African myth beside a Bible and so on. One or other would be chosen to protrude from my jacket pocket at dingy post-student parties. Joseph Campbell's comparative studies of different myth systems were all the rage at the time. So was Duran Duran. I chose to go for the spiritual ticket, rather than the big hair and turned-back sleeves.

For some reason, the belief system that momentarily entranced was not a fashionably exotic one from a hot country. No, with my unerring instinct for missing the moment, I was drawn to Norse myth. Thankfully it wasn't the camp end of their mythology that drew me, with all its Viking short-skirted chic; nor was it the Nazi end, with all the Aryan gladiator figures smoting and smiting, and going about their Wagnerian shenanigans. Come to think of it, there's precious little distance between the camp end and the Nazi end. Nor was it the humour that must be inherent in a belief system that organizes itself around a woman called Frigg.

No, what excited my interest was the central symbol of the great tree of life, Yggdrasill. A monster tree, Yggdrasill is an ash, at the centre of all worlds. According to your everyday Norse, it is the World Tree of life and knowledge, and of time and space. On the top of the highest branch sits a huge eagle; at the bottom, twisted round its roots, is coiled a monster snake. The eagle and the snake hate each other, and are destined to spend eternity in a perpetual state of loathing. It is a great image for the infinite number of different bi-polar tensions which serve to create the world and the society we have engineered within it. What makes it magical, however, is an extra element. Between the eagle and the snake, there lives a squirrel, Loki. His mission in life is essentially twofold: mischief and survival. To that end, he spends much of his time scurrying between the eagle and the snake, telling each in turn what terrible slanders each is saying about the other. He goes off on adventures of his own. Indeed, having begun as a subsidiary deity, he rapidly became one of the most popular, quickly upstaging all of the other lumbering, monolithic figures with his wit, his intelligence and his sense of fun. At the top and the bottom are the eagle and the snake being all powerful and ostentatious and heroic, and frankly rather fucking dull, and there's this squirrel motoring in between, keeping the conversation lively.

Loki immediately helped me get a lock on three of the figures who fascinate me most in Shakespeare, the unholy trinity of Pandarus (from *Troilus and Cressida*), Lucio (from *Measure for Measure*) and Parolles (from *All's Well That Ends Well*). In these three troubled and confused plays, traditionally named the Problem Plays (which seems a bit of a cop-out as far as nomenclature goes – why not the Oh Fuck It, We Can't Think of a Name Plays), these three operate within the plot and without. They are far from the heroic centre, but, with their exquisite self-awareness, they are a delight to watch. Actors call them 'steal' parts, characters who can slip in after the leads have done all their gurning and grunting and steal the attention and the hearts of the audience with a well-turned joke. It is tempting to guess, because of both the honesty and the upstaging, that these are the parts Shakespeare wrote both about and for himself.

They're not flattering self-portraits, but they are all undeniably human. All three like to pretend they're closer to the action than they in fact are; they delude themselves and others that they are forthright military men, when in fact they're replete with cowardice; and all three are cruelly exposed. When the going gets tough, they start crying and screaming. Their journeys through each play are human and various. When Lucio is found out for all his bragging about his close relationship with the duke, he is married off to a whore. He begs the prince for mercy from this fate. When Parolles is sadistically exposed by a gang of soldiers for the coward and traitor he is, he resolves to stop pretending to be a captain, but to carry on bearing his shame with him.

> ... Captain I'll be no more;
> But I will eat and drink, and sleep as soft
> As captain shall: simply the thing I am
> Shall make me live ...
> Rust sword! Cool blushes! And Parolles, live
> Safest in shame! Being fool'd by foolery thrive!
> There's place and means for every man alive.

It's a gently immoral resolution. If everyone thinks I'm a dick, I'll carry on being a dick. Much is written about Shakespeare's heroes and their relation to the society they live in, about the dynamic of individuation and the tribe. But there are more non-heroes, and there is something affirming about the process by which they don't change. They don't go through some great transforming catharsis. They just resolve to go on being who they are and fold themselves back into the tribe they emerged from. The glory of Shakespearean society is its capacity to accommodate everyone.

Pandarus' resolution lacks the same humanist warmth. The dark heart of a dark play, or another smudged mirror in a hall of smudged mirrors, at the end of *Troilus and Cressida* he is left alone and abandoned on the stage, having been thrown to the ground by Troilus. In a repulsive conclusion he addresses the audience as if they are all pimps like himself. He tells them that he is near death with the venereal diseases he has picked up. A man who speaks prose throughout, for the last few lines he launches into deliberate doggerel.

> As many as be here of pander's hall,
> Your eyes, half out, weep out at Pandar's fall;
> Or, if you cannot weep, yet give some groans,
> Though not for me, yet for your aching bones.
> Brethren and sisters of the hold-door trade,
> Some two months hence my will shall here be made;
> ... Till then I'll sweat, and seek about for eases;
> And at that time bequeath you my diseases.

This is the most astonishing gob in the eye for an audience. Faced with an audience of 2,000, many of whom will have scratched their way through various infections, with whorehouses on all sides, he coolly tells them he's going to die of the same and bequeath what he picked up to all 2,000. It lacks charm, to put it mildly. This is not someone who has been made transcendentally wise by his suffering. This is a failed man, whose failure in love and life has done nothing but ossify the bitterness in his spirit. It's the silent old sod in the pub, stretched thin with contained rage, nursing his pint and muttering about foreigners.

All three, Lucio, Parolles and Pandarus, set their plays alight with their wit and their self-knowledge. When Shakespeare's more epic moments strain our sympathy or our credulity, they pop up and reassure us, because we know them. We know them from the pub or the garage or the office, their boasting and their self-deceptions and their horror of being found out. They live in this sublunary world with us, and their presence helps us to understand that the Angelos and the Isabellas and the Cressidas and the Bertrams and the Helenas are not too far away either. And that we all make the best of this grubby little world, and can't help but try and make a little trouble along the way.

post-university fug and Michael Bryant

If I had to define two of my happiest experiences watching Shake-speare (in English), they would both come from the same period, mid-1980s, and from the same place, the National. One was *King Lear*, directed by David Hare, the other *Antony and Cleopatra*, directed by Peter Hall. Both were large public events presented in the Olivier Theatre.

We were wandering around in that dreadful post-university fug. We used to call the parties that happened then 'What's-your-alibi?' parties. Gatherings of graduates full of hysterical noise as everyone frantically tried to make their existence more exciting than everyone else's. And less empty than it was. All looking for an alibi to excuse themselves from the failure of their own life. Dreams of immediate world conquest had dissolved into temping and signing on and tele-phone sales. I had drifted from cheese packing to telemarketing to waiting on tables to being a night watchman. It was not the destiny I'd envisaged.

Twice I snuck into the National alone, twice I was left with a weight of experience I had not expected. There were fault lines running through both. Anthony Hopkins was fitful. As Lear, he spent a lot of time still being Lambert le Roux, a part he'd recently played. As Antony he spent a lot of time still being Lear. He also had that wonderful casualness of giving up on a scene if it wasn't going well. If he wasn't happy, he just mumbled fast then walked off smirking. But if he liked his material and if another actor sparked him up, he could fire into life. There was some support playing that was disparate and corny.

But there were glories. In *Antony and Cleopatra* there was Judi Dench. By a sheer effort of will and imagination she transformed herself from an unprepossessing figure into the most beautiful woman in the history of the world. Every atom of her was alive with a smoky sexual danger; every particle had a deep-seated hunger for self-magnification. Cleopatra is often played as a histrionic figure, a drama queen, shrilly confecting mini-dramas. This reduces her and the play irreparably. What she has, and what Dench played, is a real human need for importance. It's not just Cleopatra who wants to be celebrated, it's any Kathy or Colleen who wants respect and beauty and specialness. Dench played it from a base of truth and persuaded you all the way to her self-destruction.

And in both, there was the great Michael Bryant, first as Gloucester and then as Enobarbus. Entirely unknown outside Britain, and rarely spotted outside the National Theatre, this extraordinary actor appeared in almost everything emanating from the National for over twenty years. Rarely the star, though perfectly capable of carrying a show, he gave an unbroken sequence of peerless character studies. He was a prime example of that great Shakespearean virtue, modesty, always bringing the appropriate energy, discreet when he had to be and stepping in when necessary; always deftly cleaning up other people's mess. He accumulated detail unobtrusively – no big noses, limps or speech defects – presenting himself transformed, rather than some showy reinvention. He could share a stage with a truckload of stars all waving their arms and pulling focus and shouting their heads off and upstage them with a small, quizzical expression. And he could break your heart.

Never more so than with Gloucester and Enobarbus. Both characters lead the sub-plot, both live within the scope and the shadows of their masters. Both are essentially passive, adoring their old masters, betraying them, then reunited with them in spirit. Gloucester has three killer moments, all passive. He meets Lear, lost in the labyrinth of his own madness, and falls before him. Through the love within his own grieving, he pulls Lear back into the world:

LEAR I know thee well enough; thy name is Gloucester:
　　Thou must be patient; we came crying hither:
　　Thou know'st the first time that we smell the air
　　We wawl and cry. I will preach to thee: mark.

GLOUCESTER Alack! Alack the day!
LEAR When we are born, we cry that we are come
  To this great stage of fools.

Later, when he hears of the loss of the battle, he provokes his son Edgar to come up with some of the finest words of comfort ever spoken.

GLOUCESTER No further, sir; a man may rot even here.
EDGAR What! In ill thoughts again? Men must endure
  Their going hence, even as their coming hither:
  Ripeness is all.

And the last moment is so passive he's not even on the stage. Edgar relates how, after all his various concealments, he finally revealed who he was to his father.

EDGAR I asked his blessing, and from first to last
  Told him my pilgrimage: but his flaw'd heart, –
  Alack! Too weak the conflict to support;
  'Twixt two extremes of passion, joy and grief,
  Burst smilingly.

It takes something for an actor to stay at the heart of a moment when he has none of the lines, none of the wisdom, none of the action. It takes more to inspire in others the feelings that deserve that rhetoric. Michael Bryant deserved it. He presented, at the beginning of the play, a meticulous picture of unsure, compromised human goodness. And, as the play progressed, he showed in Gloucester a vacuum of human need, the terrified aloneness of a man betrayed by those closest to him, in a world slipped free from all its usual human bonds. It was this vacuum that demanded to be filled by the love supplied by Lear and Edgar. Actors can say wonderful lines wonderfully, but for a scene to make sense, they need a receptor, a listener, a provoker, a justifier. Bryant as Gloucester served that purpose.

Enobarbus similarly dies of a broken heart and, what is worse, he knows he will. There are no bounds to his love for Antony and Cleopatra and, having betrayed them both, there are no limits to his self-loathing. When Antony treats him graciously and returns all his goods, he cannot bear the kindness:

> I am alone the villain of the earth,
> And feel I am so most . . .
> . . . This blows my heart.

He seeks out a ditch to die in, and soon after returns to kill himself with grief:

> . . . throw my heart
> Against the flint and hardness of my fault,
> Which, being dried with grief, will break to powder
> And finish all foul thoughts.

It's a viciously specific image, saturated with self-loathing, though he dies on a breath of love, crying, 'O Antony! O Antony'. Bryant approached it with dignity, as he approached everything. There was no wailing, no screaming, no empty demonstration of his own capacity to feel. He spoke it with the clear-eyed, intellectual certainty of the certain suicide; the cool desiccation of the hollow man. And then, when you thought he had tipped it too far into heartlessness, he showed with a caught breath the frozen reservoir of feeling that lurked out of sight.

As with the Problem Plays, where Pandarus, Parolles and Lucio upstage the heroes all around, it was these performances I took away from these two shows. It's the human trapped in the large event, the smaller figure in the corner of the canvas, whose heart is not big enough to sustain the pressure of the moment. For me, as ever a self-conscious outsider living in the wings of the world, they felt like two self-portraits. Swirling around in the meaninglessness of early adulthood, trying to work out who I was, I felt it was time to jump into life.

an excess of life, a nervous collapse, a bad play and a democratic personality

I did jump in, way out of my depth, and almost drowned. It took a Shakespearean project and a Shakespearean insight to swim me back to the shore. Life, which drifts around you for so long, inevitably invades. The great umbrella and protective clothing of family and structure and institutions, which pertains from nursery school through to university, is suddenly taken away. Their disappearance is a blow. Not on the scale of Lear, not sodden and raging on the blasted heath, but still, for well-insulated, middle-class youth, the sudden exposure to the wind and the rain of the world is something of a shock.

My singularly eccentric school left me with many of my best lifelong friendships. One of those friendships took me to a Greek island, and introduced me to a passion that lasted long beyond the holiday. It was a tumultuous mess of a passion. It was on, it was off; it was open, it was possessive; it was raging, it was dead in the water. It introduced me to worlds I had had no connection with before: the aristocracy, the underworld, the green movement, royalty, Buddhists, AIDS victims, heroin. Worlds full of paradigmatic stories – the urban myths that float up from the underclass and down from the upper class were all lived out in front of me. I was at dinner with royalty, I was helping a man inject Methadone in his willy. I was planning a big party to raise environmental funds; I was talking to a young man in a coma. I was surrounded by the eternal chanting of Buddhists; I was disputing the future of the planet with intellectuals. I was being betrayed; I was betraying. I was bringing up a child, not my own; I was watching his father slowly die. Life had invaded. In existential terms, it was an extension of the Victorian image of the hungry poor man looking through the restaurant windows at the rich men feasting within. Suddenly I had been invited in and served a thirty-course glutton's delight. The lazy nihilism of adolescent ennui, cultivated at university and ossified by the fug afterwards, was exploded by the challenge of love, and by the depth and the dazzle of life. The disaffection and disconnect of early adulthood ebbs away for everyone but the hardiest gloomyboots. Some lose it in the grind of life and habit; some lose it in new families, new love and new necessities; some lose it in booze. I lost it in a firework display.

Then, in the middle of this whirligig, my father phoned. He told me that all was not well between my mother and him, and they were separating for a while. I affected a diffident insouciance, and tried to sound grown-up and understanding. We had all seen this coming for at least a decade. We had watched my mother and father drift further and further apart. We knew there were dalliances. We knew my father spent an inordinate amount of time in London. It had even been mentioned as a possibility. Yet, however much it could be foretold, and however much we determined to be grown-up about it, it was still a hammer blow. It felt like a destruction of the happiness of youth. Like all betrayals, the greatest damage is the damage done to one's own history book. When betrayal happens in a relationship, one's tenderest feelings are for the past, and all the promises and joyful moments, which now appear as shams. So, with the separation of parents, the most threatening black cloud is the one thrown over the memory of childhood.

A ludicrous nonchalance was the act I chose for a month or so, until I was back at our farm for a weekend. My girlfriend chose the moment to end our relationship for the third, fourth or fifth time. She drove away with her child, whom I had come to love. My father and my sister were jittering around the house, fractured and alone. I went to bed with a light fever. The temperature soon went, but I found I couldn't get up. I stood up and fell back down again. I walked a couple of paces and retired exhausted, as if I'd crossed the Kalahari. I tried reading, and the words swam before my eyes. Eventually I struggled myself into a television-watching position and lay there, for a week. Cricket and cookery and current affairs swam before my eyes.

My mother and father, who were using the house alternately, checked in with food and concern. Fears ranged from AIDS to glandular fever to the fashionable disease of the time, ME (a psychologically telling acronym). Tests were done and fears wiped away. Looking back, it is clear it was in part the desperate focus pull of a puling child, a flailing look at me, when the true drama was elsewhere. But, most of all, it was an old-fashioned nervous collapse, or breakdown. My nervous system simply shut down my body. It took a long look at the amount going on – love, excitement, experience, familial breakdown – and decided to shut the lot out. I was like a stage manager, suddenly plucked out of the neutral greyness of the wings and hurled into the Day-Glo luridness of a West End musical. Playing the lead. After floundering around for a while trying to sing and dance, my nervous system pulled me back offstage.

Recovery was slow and took an oblique path. Once walking was possible, I took to following a circular path I had traipsed since I was small. A two-mile circuit around a moor of the Somerset levels, it had always had a restorative effect. With the Mendip hills curving around the horizon in the distance, small and large earth mounds protruding like earth's sleeping breasts near and far, and Glastonbury Tor presiding regally over the flatness all around, it is a balmy landscape. The peaty earth, the spiky trees and the rhines, cut through to let the water flow, are far from beautiful. Yet it's where I feel most at home. This particular walk I had taken at a run before my O levels and A levels; I had stumbled round it at dawn with bottles of whisky at the end of long parties; I had clutched the hand of my first love and cried tears of connectedness as we floated round it, talking pretentious bollocks about D. H. Lawrence. Every changing detail in the hedgerows, and every fixed curl of landscape far away, was written on my inner eye. It put me back together again.

The other path was a new venture. And yet another homage to Shakespeare. I wrote a play. Having learned his speeches as a child, having drawn pictures of his scenes, learned about people and the world through studying him, directed his plays to elucidate his meanings, acted his scenes in theatres, I felt now was the time to try and do what he did. The story I conceived was nauseatingly close to my own experience – a house in Balham full of young people going through various emotional and existential flaps during the 1987 general election. On the night of the election reality intervenes in brutal ways, and soon after they have to put their broken pieces back together. While writing it, I thought it was a masterpiece. It poured out over a few weeks in a fury of creation, with a supercharged rhetoric I thought was Shakespearean in its scope. My mind and body were swept out of their torpor into a state of high agitated excitement. At one moment, writing a scene of terror and violence, I felt possessed by creative forces, as if the floors and walls and ceiling were all bending in towards me to assist in this creation. My goodness, I thought, there are powerful forces at work here. This is Shakespeare and his witches. This must be good.

It wasn't, it was bad. What it had in rhetoric and force, it lacked in talent. I revised and revised it, trying to make it something it could never be without the gift of playwriting. The dialogue was deliberate, rather than heard; the characters were illustrative rather than real; the story was forced, rather than organic. I was reading Shakespeare at the time, as an inspiration, and a source of comfort. But in truth he served more as a judge of technical failure. The *Complete Works* sat there silently disapproving.

The play served its purpose. It worked as a ladder to help me climb out of the well of my own depression. The wisdom in it was sparse, and varied from the trite to the true. But the act of creation helped bring a little harmony to the jangle. Two insights pertain. Both Shakespearean. The first was an old one dressed in new clothes. At the end the main character – one of the most thinly disguised autobiographical figures in the history of rubbish plays – tries to clean up the mess of his life, walking round his room with a bin bag, dumping the detritus of his previous life. He resolves to walk forward with calm into his new life, whatever it brings. 'Whatever?' his friend asks. 'Whatever,' he resolves as the lights go down. (Thank the lord I trashed every copy.) However badly rephrased, it's the old lesson: the providence and the sparrow, the ripeness and the readiness. The lesson that is always learned, and always forgotten.

The second insight came from one character, a nurse and football fan. When justifying an act of sexual betrayal, she compares her personality to the crowd at an Arsenal match. It is as various, as complex, as democratic, as exploded. One moment it all joins together to react in one way; another moment it is at war with itself; at another it is simply a fractured collection of individuals. It is not a dictatorship, it is a democracy. It is an understanding gifted by Shakespeare.

The separate, individual, aliveness of each of his characters, from Hamlet to Barnardine, from Cleopatra to Pistol, is one of the most particular achievements of his work. It is one of the foundation stones of our internal and external democracy. Shakespeare could grow all these people inside himself, he pulled them out and carved them into minutely detailed puppets, then his creative magic was generous enough to set them free on the stage as real humans, independent of their creator. With such a shining example of rich and creative complexity before us, how can we not attempt to be as human? How can we allow our lives to be coarse or brutish or stupid? How can we allow ourselves to be manipulated or manufactured by religious or political or lifestyle zealots? If all his creations are as rich and as messy and as jangly as their creator, as they are, then how can we insult that achievement by living lives more stupid, more ordered and less democratic? We are a mess inside, a shifting mob of different influences, as at a football ground, swirling, changing and growing. That is why freedom and democracy still remain the best way of expressing us. A mess of a society is the best way of reflecting our own contrariness. We take that for granted too often. Every time we meet a fundamentalist, of whatever hue, we should spit in their eye. For Shakespeare. Or maybe offer them some cakes and ale.

fathers and sons, three plays in a day and plenty of sack

Event Shakespeare used to be a rarity, now it's a commonplace. The company that first brought it to prominence was the English Shakespeare Company, a blaze of fire through the rather dour 1980s. While much theatre at the time was consumed with sombre, diagnostic tracts analysing the failure of something or other, and the all-round awfulness of Thatcher, ESC charged around doing mammoth tours and mounting ludicrously over-ambitious projects. They led a rock star international life, meeting girls they had picked up in Japan at an airport in Sydney shortly after they'd waved goodbye to their girlfriend from Buenos Aires. They caroused and they argued and they offended and they seduced. It was an extension of the old rogues and vagabonds style, except in 747s shooting through the air, rather than rickety carts cutting through the mud of old drove roads.

Their grandest project was the entire history cycle, the two tetralogies, starting with *Richard II* and seeing it right through both *Henry IV* plays, *Henry V*, all three *Henry VIs*, and rounding it off with *Richard III*. They put the productions together over a couple of years, and at one point played all eight shows at the Old Vic, presenting the whole lot over the weekend. It was a grand fuck-you of a project, brimming with chutzpah. The signature note of the productions was their post-Falklands look at *Henry V*, with their football hooligan take on institutionalized English violence. When the troops set off for France, they began chanting, 'Here we go, Here we go, Here we go . . .', and waved banners with 'Fuck the Frogs' splashed on them. It was blunt.

Presenting all of the plays has been attempted before and since. It always pulls an audience lured in by the sense of ambition and spectacle. But this was special, marked out by its cheek, its emotional directness and by the truth of much of its updating. It was a Marxist version, strong on power struggles, and on the violence that underpins all class relations. Not thin ascetic Marxism, more the pot-bellied variety.

We gathered to see the second half of it on a Saturday morning at about ten. My father, my brother, my sister and I. My parents had only recently split, and we were all in that delicate territory, renegotiating relationships. Old ties of authority and submission had broken down and had to be reconstituted as adult friendships. We were all dreading the day, partly because of that uneasy emotionalism, and partly because a whole day of history plays isn't automatically a cause for rejoicing. But the first half of the *Henry VI* trilogy is so plainly daft, with the English and the French taking, losing and retaking castles with the frequency of children in a revolving door, that we were soon disarmed. It's written in unambitious demotic language, it's full of battles, and if you lose track of what's going on there's usually a breathless messenger who storms on every five minutes to give you a recap. The gusto of it, and the brutality, appealed mightily.

At lunchtime, we reeled out into the street. My father was emphatic. 'This is going to be a long day. The best way to get through it is with a flagon of sack inside us.' We were unsure as to exactly what sack was, or whether you could find it in late twentieth-century Southwark. When my father explained that it was as near to sherry as damn it, we concurred. I had developed a taste for cooking sherry as the fastest and cheapest route to euphoria at school. (Actually a bag of glue was both faster and cheaper, but lacked the heady glamour.) So we quickstepped down to the nearest tapas bar and glugged a bottle or two of sherry each, together with some chilled potatoes and some charred chorizo. I can think of few better ways to set yourself up for a matinée. As the middle of the Henry VI story swept on, with all the anarchic class war of the Jack Cade episodes, the savage infanticide of the children and the torture of the old soldiers, we were laughing and cheering and booing and transported. The sherry sweetened our spirits and opened our ears to the language. As the *Henry VI* trilogy drew to a close and the young Richard III began his scheming, we were breathless.

At dinnertime, we emerged into the world again, lightly hung-over by our lunchtime excess and starting gently to flag. My father's instincts were sound again. 'It's going to be a long evening. I say a lot more sack.' 'And some Class A drugs,' added another. Resistance was futile. There is nothing like sharing narcotics to ease the passage from one way of seeing your parents to another. Needless to say, by the time we returned for *Richard III*, the last show of the day, we were uproarious. Though I remember it as a slightly lacklustre show, with the cast tiring and lacking the fury that had propelled the first two sessions, I think we more than compensated as audience members. We simply gulped it all down, large drafts of Shakespeare to go with all the other excess.

In a day we travelled the distance from a father and son to a friendship. The relationships between fathers and sons underpin the history plays. In fact, they underpin much of the canon. In the first part of *Henry VI*, one of the first complete plays he wrote, most of the writing is cheerfully barmy, more Hollywood action movie than political history, as English biff French and then get biffed back. The stage is a dizzying revolve of battle after battle, pageant after pageant. It only really sparks into greatness towards the end, when, in the midst of battle, there is played out the ferocious love and mutual protection of the warrior Talbot and his son. With blood and thunder swirling all around, they save each other and find a moment to declare, within the code of martial masculinity, their love for each other. Within that love is a fierce sense of pride in their name. Shortly after, they both die, but their death is redeemed by the solace they found shortly before. This moment prefigures many others elsewhere in the canon, where father and son unite to save the honour of a family name.

It was clearly an issue with a heavy emotional investment from Shakespeare. He had watched his father, the upwardly mobile peacock of Stratford in his childhood, fall into disgrace when he was fifteen. Plagued by debts, and struck off the town council, his father became incapable of supporting the family, a mantle which passed to William. He was determined through his early life to bring honour back to the family name. This was not so easily done, since the name itself, Shake Spear, or any of the innuendo attached to it, doesn't lend itself to much more than a dirty laugh down the pub. Nevertheless a powerful motor throughout the author's life was to regain the respect for that name that had resounded around Stratford in his childhood. Hence the weird paradox of a man who saw so penetratingly through all pomp and ceremony, who did so little to be anything other than anonymous through most of his life, working so assiduously and successfully to gain a coat of arms in the late 1590s. This was his last gift to his father. The old man would have had no truck with his son's plays; his authority would have been threatened by the money which his son so ardently acquired; he would have been challenged by his sophistication and fame. They would probably have had little left to talk of. But to bring back from London a coat of arms, and the status of a gentleman, was to set certain things to rights.

Of course, the greatest bond between father and son expressed in the canon is the one between Hamlet and his dead father. As far as we know, Shakespeare wrote *Hamlet* shortly before his father died, and it was first performed shortly after his passing. The author himself took the role of the father's ghost, thus providing enough material to keep a room full of psychoanalysts in furious debate for a decade, or finger-entwined silence. This relationship is the paradigm of all the others – a father betrayed and a son who has to restore his honour. It is an imperative so fully expressed in the plays, it is easy to imagine that there were no words for it at home. The silence between William and his father, John – the son who consorted with earls and queens (various), the smalltown alderman who had lost even that position – must have been a profound one. It would have been a silence only deepened by the death of the young Hamnet, Shakespeare's only son, when the male inheritor for both father and grandfather disappeared. All the proper lines of inheritance were tangled and wrong: an enfeebled head of the family, an absent and up-himself son, a dead grandchild. William and John would have felt that keenly, but not found the words to express it. But on stage, Shakespeare was able to set that all to rights, declaring the right bond between father and son with a passion he could not match in life.

poetry, passing away and funerals

Stumbling through a Scottish valley in the inkiest black, towards an old Scots baronial pile, I mutter a poem to myself, to stop the wind in the trees from whistling up a terror. It's a sonnet I'd been stumbling across a lot recently: 'Like as the waves make towards the pebbled shore . . .' There's nothing like a muttered poem to release angers, celebrate joys or settle fears. I have lilted Dylan Thomas' 'Time held me green and dying / Though I sang in my chains like the sea' in front of various waves, Atlantic and Mediterranean and Irish. I have strode into many a new crush, barking Betjeman's haiku-like ditty: 'I think what most of all I'd like / Is to be the saddle of your bike'. And there's no shortage of rivers I've walked beside and rendered Auden's 'As I walked out one evening'. I shouted it once walking down the Willesden High Road, drunk and frustrated. A policeman walked up and told me gently to shut up. But in Scotland I speak softly, using the steady ebb of the lines to comb my brain. The old castle I was approaching in the dark held the end of a glorious but tumultuous relationship. Time was about to be called on it. And, again, I was much preoccupied with death.

It was the middle of the British AIDS crisis, and mortality had suddenly become vivid in a way none of us had expected. This was a long way beyond the trips to hospitals with cellophane-wrapped garage flowers for ailing grandparents we had all anticipated. This was staring into the eyes of young men, panic screaming from their pupils, and having nothing to say, nothing to offer, beyond the strength in an answering stare. This was smearing cream on purple, yellow and green sarcomas which parodied the beauty of the skin. It was enjoying the wild good humour of laughing at the gates of death, and the transforming grace that overcomes the body and spirit, hours before passing.

I went to a New Year party in one hospice that was camper and wilder than the seediest Berlin dive. I sat at Christmas lunch with a friend who had only a week to live. An oxygen tank sat between us, a mask clamped over his face, which he removed for a few crumbs of plum pudding. We had design meetings in another AIDS ward, where the nurses would sit, scalpels in hand, helping us with the modelbox.

A peculiar culture of dying sprung up with its own icons, its own rituals and its own myths. One of the most persistent of these was that of the beautiful death. 'He died beautifully,' people would murmur afterwards. 'He looked like a saint, like Jesus, he was released, at peace.' I couldn't agree. No death is beautiful. It's always an ugly crime, and I can never get over the grand cheat of it. But one of the achievements of the community which suffered most at that time – the gay community – was how they managed to decorate so many deaths with beauty and significance. Notwithstanding the scale of the tragedy, each passage was distinct and personal. It never became about statistics and remained about individual stories.

There's something strangely liberating about death when you're close to it. One of the best examples of this in literature is the wild over-excitement of the conspirators immediately after they have killed Caesar. Rather than express regret or grief for what they have just done they cackle manically:

CINNA Liberty! Freedom! Tyranny is dead!
   Run hence, proclaim, cry it about the streets.
CASSIUS Some to the common pulpits, and cry out
   'Liberty, freedom and enfranchisement!'
BRUTUS People and senators, be not affrighted.
   Fly not; stand still. Ambition's debt is paid . . .

This is a brutally unsentimental piece of writing. Instead of the 'Oh my God, what have I done?' of Hollywood cliché, it's a group of people bouncing around with delight. It captures precisely the wild exhilaration which fills the air briefly, the teary and giggly explosion, as death passes through a room. There is a freedom when something so often imagined is suddenly so real. The anxiety evaporates. It's no compensation for loss, but it serves as a momentary wild distraction.

With the deaths came the funerals, and with the funerals came the Shakespeare. Peter O'Toole said once that he was worried he was turning into a cuckoo clock, he appeared with such sickening regularity in pulpits spouting:

> Fear no more the heat of the sun
> Nor the furious winter's rages;
> Thou thy worldly task has done,
> Home art gone, and ta'en thy wages.
> Golden lads and girls all must,
> As chimney sweepers, come to dust.
>
> Fear no more the frown o'th' great;
> Thou art past the tyrant's stroke.
> Care no more to clothe and eat;
> To thee the reed is as the oak.
> The sceptre, learning, physic, must
> All follow this and come to dust.
>
> Fear no more the lightning flash,
> Nor all the dreaded thunder-stone;
> Fear not slander, censure rash;
> Thou hast finished joy and moan.
> All lovers young, all lovers must
> Consign to thee and come to dust.
>
> No exorcizer harm thee!
> Nor no witchcraft charm thee!
> Ghost unlaid forbear thee!
> Nothing ill come near thee!
> Quiet consummation have,
> And renowned be thy grave!

This passage from *Cymbeline* is a wonderful meeting point for various of Shakespeare's concerns. It includes his yearning for privacy after death, for time to conceal him, the longing echoed over his grave. There is the hunger of a busy animal who has lived too much and created too much and loved too much and danced attendance on tyrants too much and feared the shifting weather too much, his hunger for a nice long eternity of kip. And there is a loving and human benediction for the many loved ones – his father, his son, his brothers who have predeceased him. It's not surprising it's so often intoned over coffins.

Against my wishes, and certainly my expectations, I ended up as something of a professional at funerals, arranging three and acting as MC at a further two. Most were AIDS funerals. I wasn't particularly good at it. But if you're a director, there's a sort of weird transfer of authority towards you, like the captain of a ship or a justice of the peace. People expect you to be able to stand up and make things better. There was some inspiring behaviour at these events. A child, with the glorious carefree gravity of innocence, mocked the collapse of the congregation, by standing stiffly tall and reciting cleanly:

> Full fathom five thy Father lies,
> Of his bones are Corrall made:
> Those are pearles that were his eies,
> Nothing of him that doth fade,
> But doth suffer a Sea-change
> Into something rich & strange
> Sea-Nymphs hourly ring his knell.
> Harke now I heare them, ding-dong, bell.

There was a Buddhist service where the persistent, mesmerizing chanting (Nam-myoho-renge-kyo) and the hot glow from the electric heaters round the walls induced a sort of hysteria. A beautiful human-ist do, where a boy's choir tumbled into James Fenton ranting angrily at death, which rolled into 'I'm Going Home' from the *Rocky Horror Show*, and spilled into *Romeo and Juliet*:

> Take him and cut him out in little stars
> And he will make the face of heaven so fine
> That all the world will be in love with night
> And pay no worship to the garish sun.

That extract also did service at John Kennedy's funeral. When the world is reassembling its broken heart, you can't reach for a Hallmark card.

There was small behaviour beside glorious. With all the absurdity that humanity is capable of, several of the early AIDS funerals became society events. The heavy knell of mortality hardly sounded through the strong walls of celebrity neurosis. At one memorial service I remember a famous model arriving in a flash-storm of popping bulbs an hour late, looking like she'd been in make-up and costume for a month. She made one nervous and existentially confused tour round the room, then bolted for the exit. At another I had to do a seating plan of Byzantine complexity, observing the niceties of English social gradation, with a princess at the front, and each step of English class emanating one by one away from her. For this same one, I had to coach an old friend in delivery of the consoling Shakespeare chosen for this occasion:

> Like as the waves make towards the pebbled shore,
> So do our minutes hasten to their end;
> Each changing place with that which goes before,
> In sequent toil all forwards do contend.
> Nativity, once in the main of light,
> Crawls to maturity, wherewith being crown'd,
> Crooked eclipses 'gainst his glory fight,
> And Time that gave doth now his gift confound.
> Time doth transfix the flourish set on youth
> And delves the parallels in beauty's brow,
> Feeds on the rarities of nature's truth,
> And nothing stands but for his scythe to mow:
> And yet to times in hope my verse shall stand,
> Praising thy worth, despite his cruel hand.

It was a cruel and emotive choice for the death of a young and beautiful man, whose flourish had been thoroughly transfixed by all the sarcomaed viciousness of AIDS' great laugh at vanity. The young woman who was to deliver it was his oldest friend. A glorious mess of a girl, who had been in and out of rehab and prison, she was entirely resistant to the poem for ages. But when she stood up, she straightened her back, the wind ran through her, and she sang it clear and straight. There's a mode of Shakespeare delivery that only the English can do. We don't take a dishonest short-cut to purity or beauty. We bring all our baggage with us – our irony, our shame and our raggedy misdemeanours – then somehow rise above that to a rough purity, a clumsy beauty.

The continual presence of Shakespeare at funerals in solid English Christian churches never stops bemusing me. It always seems rather like inviting a naked man to run around the altar screaming 'God is dead!', 'God is dead!' 'Rien de afterlife, suckers!' Though controversy rages about whether Shakespeare was a Catholic or a Protestant, with the Catholic faction running away with it at the moment, and though Christian ideas of providence and mercy and tolerance and forgiveness infuse all his writing, there's precious little consolation for those searching for the big white beardy spirit in the sky. And there's even less for those who are hoping to be wafted up to clouds on high. The theme of 'Fear no more . . .', 'Full fathom five . . .' and 'Like as the waves . . .' is pretty unequivocal. You live and then you die. And though you may turn into something rich and strange, what is certain is that the scythe will mow, and you will turn to dust. What mention there is of heaven is pretty muted compared to the toughness of all the finality.

Yet, though Shakespeare offers little in the way of conventional religious comfort, he does put you to sleep gently. His proposition is simple: the movement of time is inevitable, and death and decay walk behind it. Knowing that, accepting that and seeing the natural order inherent in it is at the centre of the most consoling passages of the Bible and of Shakespeare. Achieving that knowledge is approaching a sort of liberation. History was more than the study of facts and figures and dates for Shakespeare. It was the demonstration of time, and as such it was to be worshipped. The rise and fall of a king or a character was as ineluctable and as strange as the growth of a blade of grass for the scythe to mow. To see that history – what has gone, what exists and what is still to come – and to find one's home somewhere within it, is to break free from it. To accept the end of the story with the same excitement as the beginning and the same delirious pleasure as the middle was, if anything, what Shakespeare was trying to help us towards.

too much Stratford and falling out of love

No faith can be tested without a temporary loss of faith. Just as any love has only shallow roots until hard questions are asked of it, so faith, belief and respect can only grow once the possibility of their absence has been explored. Everything can only be seen once nothing has been understood. The devotional poet George Herbert wrote verse which frequently busts wide open with rage at God. He is wonderfully declarative with his defiance:

> I Struck the board, and cry'd, No more,
>   I will abroad
> What? Shall I ever sigh and pine?

Here and elsewhere, he tells God royally to go and get stuffed. He charts the journey of revolt, its freedom and excitement as he plunges into the world and seeks out its delights. But then freedom is chased down hard by emptiness, and excitement rings a loud but hollow bell. Always by the end of his poems, and the end of his journeys, he is called home by the voice he ran from:

> But as I rav'd and grew more fierce and wilde
>   At every word,
> Me thoughts I heard one calling, *Child*:
> And I reply'd, *My Lord*.

One of my good friends had to leave the church recently, driven out by the happy, smiling dictatorship of the new evangelicals. The church accepted his departure. There is an inbuilt mechanism within the career structure for an Anglican priest. They can have a moment away, to explore the alternative of a life without God. They know a life of service is gruelling, and everyone needs freedom from it. They trust they will return.

So with Shakespeare, at some point I was going to get disenchanted. That moment duly arrived. Yet, as with my friend the priest, it was not Shakespeare himself who drove me away, so much as the industry that had grown around him. The Christian church is a peculiar political, cultural, traditional and social construct thrown up around the inspired philosophical imagination of a beautiful subversive 2,000 years ago. It often bears little or no resemblance to what that subversive said. So the Shakespeare industry is a peculiar repository for various political, academic and social costumes that people want to hang on the worlds imagined by a troubled and ambitious country boy 400 years ago. Those costumes often bear little relation to what was originally meant.

The pinnacle of this Bardic construct is of course the reinvented Stratford, and it was a couple of visits there that turned me right off Shakespeare for a while. I had started as an assistant at the Bush Theatre, a small theatre devoted to new writing. It is a magical place which packed 110 people into a tiny ex-dining room above a pub. Extraordinary plays had been launched there, and extraordinary acting careers. It was an alchemical little crucible, regularly turning metal into gold. The passion of the people working there, their pride in their craftsmanship, and their joy in throwing up new stories were all a revelation. Everything I had learned at university, all the Brecht and Stanislavsky and Artaud, I had to throw overboard. The Bush traded on instinct and common sense and a just sense of truth. That was the new lesson. It was a hundred light years closer in spirit to the theatre of Shakespeare's day – a relentless, remorseless factory of new plays – than the Shakespeare Industry. While I was assisting at the Bush, and having my head rearranged, I made two trips to Stratford to see friends in plays.

Both productions I saw were hugely successful and highly respected. There was much to admire in both. One was set in the 1920s, the other in a sort of slick post-modern nowheredom. They were both cleverly achieved, and at the same time absolutely ghastly. Some dreadful patina of middle-class respectability was smeared over them both – a choking hold of well-mannered charm. The passion was all fake, nice young men shouting angrily, nice young girls crying prettily. The sexuality was spookily ersatz, lots of third-rate smouldering, and Michael-Jackson-like crotch-grabbing. The humour was tired and desperate, with the comics doing everything short of paying people to laugh.

And behind it all there was a terrifyingly banal assumption. We are literate, well-educated and posh; you are literate, well-educated and posh. We will all enjoy this experience together. And we promise not to do anything to upset you. There was no danger, no unpredictability, no freshness and little honesty. Nothing seemed to matter, nothing seemed to connect. I wasn't looking for experimental rearrangement. I just would have liked a sense of excitement in telling the story. It wasn't there.

I fell back into a rather stupid default auto-rebel position. The robo-whine of half-wit avant-gardistas. 'What's the use of Shakespeare? He's so, like, old. We've got to make art for now.' I joined bandwagons decrying how we spent too much money on Shakespeare. I sat late at night talking of the curse of the heritage instinct within British culture. I disputed what the plays had to say to us now that couldn't be said more vitally by a character on *EastEnders*. I questioned the value of all this fusty, dusty, musty old language.

> But as I rav'd and grew more fierce and wilde
> At every word,
> Me thoughts I heard one calling, *Child*:
> And I reply'd, *My Lord*.

cultural détente, Shakespeare abroad and a *Twelfth Night* from heaven

'I wish someone would put that fucking Iron Curtain back up,' was the rather tart remark ascribed to a senior manager at the National Theatre. It was 1993, and the 'great bliss in that dawn to be alive' of 1989 was entering its hangover period. After the velvet revolutions and the crumbling walls and the dispatched dictators of the late eighties there was a huge effusion of cultural détente. Actors and artists rushed towards each other with arms outstretched, trading the suffering of the East for the dollars of the West. Hardly a week went by at the Bush without a Bulgarian or a Ukrainian delegation marching solemnly in. Much of the traffic went the other way – writers, actors and directors dispatched to the outer reaches of Mongolia to give and take. It was a relationship full of passion, but no amount of passion could make up for the financial inequity. Like any rich landlord dicking around with a girl from the village, it was destined to end in tears. Once the West had gobbled as much suffering as it wanted and fully indulged itself in stolen spirituality, it went home to its supermarkets and its television and its air travel. And as the East kept clamouring for more contact and more co-production and more connection, the West behaved rather as with a jilted lover, changing the locks and altering the phone numbers.

At the Bush we developed an ongoing relationship with a collection of Romanian writers, touring Romania, commissioning a series of plays and producing one in Bucharest. For about three years, Bucharest was my second home, hopping to and from probably the least glamorous location in the world. And before that relationship began, I spent two months on a disastrous bursary to the old Soviet Union in 1990, together with another director. To our bemusement, we were sent there in August and September, the very time when all the theatres shut up shop to take their holidays. We traipsed around the streets from one meaningless meeting to another, with whichever antique drone our hosts could dredge up from under the dust sheets to talk about her time with Stanislavsky. It was also a time of extreme austerity, before the black economy had kicked in, and for protracted periods there was literally nothing to eat. To add a surreal flavour, we were billeted in Moscow in a large lump of cement with holes in, surrounded by nothing but North Korean scientists. Thankfully soon we escaped south and found more warmth, more honesty and more food in Georgia.

Wherever I went in the old Eastern Europe, the prime cultural currency was always the same: Shakespeare. In Poland, in Romania, Hungary, Russia, wherever, Shakespeare was at the centre of their culture, and the centre of the way they understood themselves. Every meal would be followed by a six-hour round of toasts. These would habitually begin with a welcome, followed by one for world peace, then one for the children of the world, then one for Princess Diana and, coming in a hot fifth, one for Shakespeare. Throughout the communist experiment, productions of Shakespeare had been constant. For practitioners, academics and audiences, they were one of their prime ways of facing up to the tyranny of ideas, and of imagining new solutions.

No one could ban Shakespeare. It would be like banning music. So, whoever the totalitarian dictator, they would have to tolerate subversive productions of *Julius Caesar*, a play essentially sympathetic to assassination, or *Richard II*, an essay in the occasional necessity of regime change. These plays were pitched astutely by Shakespeare in his own day, who had to cope with both the paranoid repression of Elizabeth and the perverse repression of James. They have inbuilt mechanisms to bamboozle dictators. Long speeches about order and continuity and the idiocy of the mob are there to appease the controllers, while small and large acts of rebellion fizz around them to delight the subversives. For the dissidents of the old Iron Curtain countries, Shakespeare productions were often their only way of sending coded messages about the resistance to that tyranny. Famous versions of *Lear* and *Richard III* from Georgia, and of *Hamlet* from Romania, had toured the West before the great thaw. The ferocity of their visual imagery and the weight of their passion were a wake-up call to the lazy corpulence of so many Western productions.

Every town I went to was producing Shakespeare, and in every university there were professors and students hungry to talk about him. The authority they invested in us, as directors from the land of Shakespeare, settled like stardust. It was embarrassing because it was so patently unmerited. They often knew more about him than we did, and in many cases understood him better. Their feel for the muscular mechanisms of power that run through his plays was sharp. Ours was flabby. When we play at repression, it's feeble – RADA graduates getting butch and Nazi. When they did it, it was real. They knew about corruption. They knew about forced silence. They knew about people disappearing in the night. *Richard III* for us is something of a panto, however we dress it up; for them it was a chilling parable about the power grab of a dysfunctional human being.

My favourite single production of a Shakespeare play anywhere, ever, was in Bucharest. I operate a no-favourites policy in all things, from children to meals to productions of my own. But this was so head and shoulders above all else that it lives in a separate universe. It was Andrei Serban's production of *Twelfth Night* at the National Theatre of Bucharest. Three of my trips to Romania were arranged around dates when this show would be on. It's hard to explain the strength of its draw. Gone was the elegiac, wistful melancholia of so many English productions: this was the opposite. It was dangerous, funny, hugely erotic, beautiful, heart-breaking and powerful. Orsino was a fat, corrupt brute, living surrounded by his hos, but desperate that Olivia wouldn't put out. At the end, he flew over to her place in a helicopter and arrived surrounded by bodyguards. Olivia lived in a strange and beautiful world – Hockney's California would be the best approximation – all sky blue, with the only shadow a chorus of ladies wrapped head to foot in black. Sir Toby sat in a sitting room watching the television, drinking beer and picking fights. Viola and Sebastian wandered around in strictly conventional Elizabethan guise, and the moments when they just missed each other, but felt each other's presence wafting by, simply broke your heart. To cap all the fun, in the tavern scene with Sebastian and Antonio, staged in a sunken section of the orchestra pit, they put a perfectly re-created Shakespeare in the corner, reading a book and smoking a pipe.

They didn't miss a beat, primarily because they let every beat be. The sickness in English Shakespeare production, and in English theatre, is where a director chooses a style for a play and then relentlessly forces everything to fit. Find a world for the play and make it consistent, these halfwits spout. It is the revenge of the stupid on the beautiful. If you look at the world around you, you see no consistent style, no uniformity. People can be a bit two-dimensional; some can be complex; some are cut in an antique mould; some are loose and modern. If I look at a theatre audience, I see a teeming confusion of styles and types all co-existing together. So why present them with a life less interesting than their own? The world is not consistent. Why should the theatre be?

Shakespeare understood this more than any other. He mixed high and low, lyrical and prosaic, romantic and cynical, heroic and clumsy. He invited everyone to the party: he didn't try to create a salon for like-minded types. *Twelfth Night* is a masterpiece of variety. Beside the high lyrical strain of Olivia and Viola, he puts the sitcom antics of Toby and Andrew; beside the music-hall wit of Feste, he puts the psychological realism of Malvolio's disintegration. He mixes and he matches. A good production will play each strain as it is. A bad one will try to make it all one. Serban in Romania fully explored each possibility. And at the end, as a gift, Feste wrapped his arms around the world and sang the last song in a broken child's voice.

> When that I was and a little tiny boy
> With hey, ho, the wind and the rain
> A foolish thing was but a toy
> For the rain it raineth every day.

Performing Shakespeare in a foreign language is liberating. There is none of the hegemony of the iambic foot. No schoolteacher or drama critic or voice coach or Peter Hall figure standing over the production saying, 'No! No! No! That is not the way you say it!' They can just act out the emotional and political heart of each scene, play it clean and hard, without sounding like they've got a cucumber up their arses, or a naysayer over their shoulders.

It is equally releasing to watch in a foreign language. You watch the dreamscape more closely, without worrying about each verbal chime. The story, the myth elements, the dynamics of the relationships, the iconic nature of the plastic elements all come to the fore. In Georgia, we very happily watched the young Rustaveli company rehearse *Hamlet* for two weeks in Georgian. To see the performances evolving, to watch the directors and actors relating to each other, to witness moments coming to life and not to understand a blind word anyone was saying was hypnotic. The detachment of incomprehension left space for the mind to wander. The strength of the underpinning beneath all Shakespeare's work is enhanced when you see its magic stealing over people in a different language. What we love most – the texture, the cadence and the wit – is only half the story.

pub problems, plonky politicians and the arrival of James I

CLAUDIUS Now, Hamlet, where is Polonius?

HAMLET At supper

CLAUDIUS At supper! Where?

HAMLET Not where he eats, but where he is eaten: a certain convocation of politic worms are e'en at him. Your worm is your only emperor for diet: we fat all creatures else to fat us, and we fat ourselves for maggots: your fat beggar and your lean beggar is but variable service; two dishes, but to one table: that's the end.

CLAUDIUS Alas, alas!

HAMLET A man may fish with the worm that hath eat of a king, and eat of the fish that hath fed of that worm.

CLAUDIUS What dost thou mean by this?

HAMLET Nothing, but to show how a king may go a progress through the guts of a beggar.

As children, the distinctions we draw between people are crude. Some are large, some small. Some have scary voices, some whisper in the corner. As we grow and learn, we are taught further distinctions, finer and more subtle. Slowly we are indoctrinated into this bizarre and ineluctable nonsense known as status. Whatever the costume, whether the crown of a king or the shades of a footballer; whatever the attitude, whether the power of a president or the cool of a rock star, we are taught to see the signs, decode and respect them. Then, later in life, having spent decades having these signs and signifiers pushed into us, we suddenly realize they are all cock. And we labour for further decades unlearning them.

Our immediate landlord at the Bush was an enormous Flintstonelike New Zealander with a huge purported capacity for violence and a diminutive wife with a proportionate capacity for malice. They hated the theatre, they hated the punters, and they hated us. They felt much more at home with the usual clientele, an odd mix of antique drunks, feral junkies and sweaty policemen. Though the landlord was always recounting his dark deeds of brutishness, and threatening what he might do, the only violence we ever saw him enacting was towards an elderly drunk woman called Bridie. She would occasionally stumble in from the bedlam that was Shepherds Bush Green and with a regal pride unveil her very own bush. The landlord would bundle her out with an unseemly relish.

Our problems with the pub were perennial. They ranged from filth to violence against our punters to threatened violence against me to non-stop, ear-shattering tannoying of dreadful early-nineties pop music. The disjunction between theatreati drifting into the theatre upstairs to see the latest new writing and the madness down below was part of the headache of the place, and also part of the glory. One of the choicest moments was after the first preview of a striking piece set in post-Cromwell Ireland. As the audience of writers and agents and film producers reeled out, they enthused about the muscularity and Arthur Miller-like force of the work. One of the regular junkies started wandering around in their midst, listening in and offering nonsensical phrases of agreement. This would have been more annoying than funny had it not been for what he was wearing. He had blown up a condom and pulled it down on to his head to the level of his eyes. As the theatrefolk spoke earnestly of advances in dramaturgy, the rubber-bedecked junky nodded vigorously, the tip of his condom wobbling in agreement.

This is, of course, how theatre was meant to be. Art and life are supposed to bash rudely into each other. It is the model created and perfected by the theatre of Shakespeare's day. As Hamlet would be yadda-yaddaing away, prostitutes milled around amongst the groundlings, slipping their hands down the chap's jerkins. Thieves circled in the opposite direction, slipping their hands in elsewhere. Fights broke out and escalated into brawls. The horny of all sexes retired into nearby rooms for hasty relief. Salesmen, shops and stalls crowded into the nooks and crannies within and without the theatre. Beyond the walls of the theatre riots erupted. Only a hundred yards away, alternative entertainments, including bear baiting, prospered. The noise and the distraction were constant disruptions to the continuing thread of performance. Forget about suspension of disbelief, it was sufficient of a challenge to get to the end of the show. The acting had to be mighty, the voice clear, the force of will heroic, just to keep the thing afloat.

Contrast this with many of today's freeze-dried spaces. There is a vogue for insulating theatre further and further away from the reality it is supposed to represent. It began with Stanislavsky, who evolved a singularly bonkers theory of how theatre foyers should work. He proposed there should be three foyers between the outside world and the theatre, each painted in a shade more anaesthetizing than the one before. In this way, the average punter would slowly disengage from his own realities, become calmer and more meditative and more receptive to the world soon to be exposed to him.

You see the logical extension of this in today's smaller chic theatres. Exclusively the preserve of the modern millionaire class, they are designed specifically to give their audience the same security from reality as a jewellery store. The same calm colours, the same minimal decoration, the same sense of organic simplicity. Someone should sneak into these theatres in the middle of the night with a dustbin full of donkey do and a set of tins filled with vibrant-coloured paint and splash a bit of life and mess around. Shakespeare's theatre shoved your head into the toilet of life and showed how the most enduring beauty and exquisite fineness could emerge magically from rough mess. Today's theatres often seem more like a trip to the manicurist and do little but conceal the rot beneath the fingernail.

The Bush was never in danger of being mistaken for a boutique. Frequently the problems veered out of control, and at that point, we had to start complaining. This process became a lesson in power structures. The immediate level of authority above the pub was the brewery's area manager. The person filling this post changed on a six-monthly basis, but the type remained constant – a man in his mid-forties, with a fleshy, drink-soaked face, glasses tinted a variety of colours and fading hair sharked back across the scalp. We would present our problems to them, and they would tell us to bog off. The next level would be the managing director of the brewery itself. Again, this character filled out an archetype – a Dickensian gent, with a thick neck and bald round head. He told us to bog off as well.

So we had to go to the top. Our ultimate landlords at the Bush were an international corporation dealing largely in chains of pubs and off-licences and the industrial distribution of alcohol. Sitting at the top of this corporation was an enlightened figure who had the rubicund English features of one of those eighteenth-century scientists who pottered around with fuzzy wigs on, discovering the atomic weight of iron. We discovered a route through to him, so whenever we had one of our perennial problems with the pub, we went straight to him. He knew that, though we were a small concern, we had a hefty profile and were good publicity for his corporation. He told the brewery and the area manager to bog off. On one occasion, we, a scruffy crew of wrecks, were asked in for lunch with all the senior executives at the corporation. It was an odd encounter of paint-spattered jeans with crisp new suits. Theatre has always been an easy passport into all the inner sanctums, both of low-life and high, from shebeen to high table. The oscillation of the young Prince Hal from the drinking dens of Eastcheap to the court at Westminster is his own story, but it's also a testament to the dizzying freedom of the actor.

On another occasion, the same corporation was the reason for another trip to Stratford. They were generous sponsors of the Royal Shakespeare Company and were giving a marquee dinner, followed by a performance of a comedy. The show was execrable – bright, brash and stupid – another example of what an exotic gum tree the RSC were stuck up. What was more intriguing was the company at our table. There was a junior minister sitting with us, who was one of the most dazzlingly uninteresting people I have ever encountered. Every one of his actions seemed a fastidious attempt to be less exciting than he had been a minute before. These were the Major years, which were anecdotally grey, but this man was out in a grey zone all of his own. I remember two of his most promising conversational starters, which still chill the soul: 'I know an interesting story about a sommelier . . .' and 'Yes, but there is more than one way to make a bouillabaisse . . .'; and the looks of deadness that crossed everyone's face as he set off on another anecdote. All faces but one, since this monument to charmlessness had brought his secretary with him for the weekend. I hope, for her sake, he was more exciting in the sack than he was over the coronation chicken.

This wasn't my first encounter with politicians, but it was the bleakest. The Bush had a peculiar leverage way beyond its size. We managed to get two government ministers down to the Bush to have dinner and see shows. The first was fleet, fly and sharp; the second bluff, wise and charming. Neither was any disgrace to the human race, but nor was either a dazzling example of human brilliance. They were simply people who had been trained up for public office since they were in rugby shorts. They had chosen that path and walked steadily down it. Having only recently been an unemployed layabout, I was thrilled by the initial contact with the world of power. There was a sense of walking behind closed doors, of hearing whispered secrets, with its accompanying sense of entitlement. Yet it didn't take long for that thrill to give way to disillusionment in the face of the people who filled that world. The sheer weight of their ordinariness was flattening. They were so comprehensively less interesting than the world they purportedly represented. They were simply men who had bullied, charmed, cajoled, begged, lied and betrayed their way into power. And once they had attained that power, they stood lost in a wind of loneliness and purposelessness, having no idea what to do with it.

Everyone comes to the same insight in their own time. We spend so long being bamboozled by the paraphernalia around politicians – their accessories of power, their magnification through television, the careful stage management of their every appearance – that we lose sight of what a bunch of plonkers they largely are. It was a journey, from illusion to disillusion, which Shakespeare travelled at an extreme pitch. Arriving in the metropolis of London from the small market town of Stratford, he could not help but be struck by the glamour of the world he found, and the contacts he made. The theatre, with its magical and sordid web of connections, brought him into an impossibly self-celebrating world. Rich characters – Essex, Southampton, Ralegh, Cecil – jostled for the spotlight. Each vied to pull focus away from each of the others, charging off on batty adventures to big up their own myth. The New World, the Spanish fleet, Ireland, the country house and the dockland tavern were all playgrounds within which they could compete to create the best story of a life. And at the centre of this vivid ensemble was the great glittering lie herself, Elizabeth, a brilliant and cultured woman, creating a persona as distant from human reality as the crudest witch doctor in an African village. An elderly and ailing lady by the time Shakespeare came into contact with her, she still wigged and made herself up as a young debutante. Naturally repressive, she still had the wisdom to counter her own instincts and allow her world to be peopled by the most vivid, wild and tawdry collection of characters.

Shakespeare was acute enough to see the calculation behind the charisma of these figures, but it's hard to imagine he was not over-whelmed by the charisma itself. The public characters he wrote into his plays of the 1590s had a heroic scale and energy – Richard III, Mark Antony, Brutus, Titus, Bolingbroke and, most gloriously, the wild young Hal, who becomes Shakespeare's most unabashed celebra-tion of pure charisma, Henry V. The sheer headlong force of these people reflects the charge of electricity the author took off the public figures of his own time. He never lost his own critical intelligence, but there is a strong sense when these characters stride on stage that they merit their position. Their private magnitude deserves the public platforms they carved out for themselves. You can feel the fizz of the Stratford boy's infatuation with the cut and dash of the self-styled heroes of his age.

Then something turned. In his own life, domestic tragedies crowded in, as first a son, then a father, then a brother died. And a great light went out with Elizabeth's death. There is a strong sense that when James I rode down from Edinburgh to take over the English crown, he brought more than just his own courtiers. He also brought a slate-grey sky and a persistent drizzle. Shakespeare was assiduously careful to cultivate his new lord and master. He balances out even his bleakest critique of the brutality of power, *Macbeth*, with a bit of astonishingly blatant bum-sucking to the new king, as he outlines how James will one day accede to the English throne. But there is an overpowering sense of a scaling down of festivity. The politicians have lost their charisma and gained nothing but greed. Shakespeare, as he passed the forty-year-old mark, felt this disenchantment keenly.

It is the diminishing of credulity that goes with maturity in all of us. Heroes are harder to come by, politicians simply fall through the floor. Public figures who had shared some of the stardust of Elizabeth herself now, in the cold grey light of James' rule, just looked like indecent frauds.

In his later plays, Shakespeare puts the boot in, and he puts it in hard. In *King Lear*, once Lear has been stripped of authority, the world becomes painfully clear to him:

LEAR What, art mad? A man may see how this world goes with no eyes.
　Look with thine ears: see how yond justice rails upon yond simple thief.
　Hark, in thine ear: change places; and, handy-dandy, which is the justice,
　which is the thief? – Thou hast seen a farmer's dog bark at a beggar?
GLOUCESTER Ay, sir.
LEAR And the creature run from the cur? There thou mightst behold the
　great image of authority: a dog's obeyed in office. –
　　Thou rascal beadle, hold thy bloody hand!
　　Why dost thou lash that whore? Strip thine own back;
　　Thou hotly lust'st to use her in that kind
　　For which thou whipp'st her. The usurer hangs the cozener.
　　Through tatter'd clothes small vices do appear;
　　Robes and furr'd gowns hide all. Plate sin with gold,
　　And the strong lance of justice hurtless breaks;
　　Arm it in rags, a pygmy's straw does pierce it.
　　None does offend, none. – I say none; I'll able 'em:
　　Take that of me, my friend, who have the power
　　To seal the accuser's lips. Get thee glass eyes;
　　And, like a scurvy politician, seem
　　To see the things thou dost not.

There is a wilful aggression in the writing of *Lear*, from the author towards his characters, and towards himself. There is some deep-seated sickness with surfeit and luxury and fraudulence and fake love. The old anarch Shakespeare, sick of the bourgeois Shakespeare who co-habits with him, wants to take his characters, rid them of their comforts and hurl them out into the lashing rain and the stripping wind. As one ego, William the bank manager, went on piling up the money, and buying up ever greater tracts of land in and around

Stratford, his alter ego, Will the banshee, wanted to scream the house down. A desire burned to reject his own success and make the whole world follow Lear's progress from a tyrant in a palace to a beggar in a storm.

His profoundly subversive streak was bred in the English countryside, where a cider-fuelled strain of violence has always accompanied milder colours. It only grew as he grew richer and better connected. For every venal bishop whom he met and flattered and treated with an exaggerated seriousness, there would be a muttered 'cunt' as the man in purple walked away. The closer you get to power as you grow older, the more you realize how desperately it improvises its own definition. The more you see of the accoutrements of power and wealth, the more you realize the crimes necessary to put them on the table.

And yet, the terrible paradox of age is that the older palate learns the difference between the best wine and the cheap plonk. It understands better what it takes to get great wine into the glass and knows finally that once the good has been tasted it's harder and harder to accept the bad. This is the tension, between the appreciation of refinement and the knowledge of its cost, that tears Lear apart, and which he articulates so beautifully in 'O reason not the need . . .' It is the sickness of aspiration, the disease of wanting more than you had, or your father had. The loss of place that goes with that. It was ripping through Shakespeare when he wrote *Lear*. It is a crisis that speaks to us all, especially as we grow older. We love our comforts, but bewail the loss of purity that goes with them. We hang about with politicians and powerful men and feel a thrill of entitlement. But that is inevitably followed by a deep shame that we have been so blinded by lies so tawdrily constructed. It is a tension that Shakespeare refuses to resolve in *Lear*.

Even more fiercely in *Timon of Athens*, his road test for *Lear*, he gobs square in the eye of both the political world and its beating heart, the love of money. *Timon* is one of the greatest explosions of punk rage conceived prior to Johnny Rotten. Timon has been rejected by the world which he previously bestowed his largesse on and sits before a cave letting them all have it:

Raise me this beggar, and deny 't that lord;
The senator shall bear contempt hereditary,
The beggar native honour.
It is the pasture lards the rother's sides,
The want that makes him lean. Who dares, who dares,
In purity of manhood stand upright,
And say 'This man's a flatterer?' if one be,
So are they all; for every grise of fortune
Is smooth'd by that below: the learned pate
Ducks to the golden fool: all is oblique;
There's nothing level in our cursed natures,
But direct villany. Therefore, be abhorr'd
All feasts, societies, and throngs of men!
His semblable, yea, himself, Timon disdains:
Destruction fang mankind! Earth, yield me roots!
(*Digging*)
Who seeks for better of thee, sauce his palate
With thy most operant poison! What is here?
Gold? yellow, glittering, precious gold? No, gods,
I am no idle votarist: roots, you clear heavens!
Thus much of this will make black white, foul fair,
Wrong right, base noble, old young, coward valiant.
Ha, you gods! why this? what this, you gods? Why, this
Will lug your priests and servants from your sides,
Pluck stout men's pillows from below their heads:
This yellow slave
Will knit and break religions, bless the accursed,
Make the hoar leprosy adored, place thieves
And give them title, knee and approbation
With senators on the bench: this is it
That makes the wappen'd widow wed again;
She, whom the spital-house and ulcerous sores
Would cast the gorge at, this embalms and spices
To the April day again

There is an accumulated, accreted image of Shakespeare, as the
kindly soul, the champion of stability, the steady alderman, holding

England in the sure grip of normality. He had those qualities, and he had a self as greedy and acquisitive and power-hungry as the most craven politician. But it was constantly at war with another angrier spirit, which wanted to strip every veil of illusion and pretence from his own and others' eyes, and which would have been perfectly happy to see the whole fake fandango go up in flames.

Peter Hall and the first ten lines of the day

As I was drawing to the end of my time at the Bush, Sir Peter Hall requested a meeting. I suggested we met in the pub under the theatre. About five minutes late, I walked in quickly, glanced at the chorus of elderly toothless drunks who always occupied the tables by the door, and walked on. I looked round and couldn't see Peter. Then I looked back at the chorus of drunks, and there he was, sitting uncomfortably on the edge of the group. A small, wizened figure. I suggested we sat somewhere else – which he jumped at – and led him off to another cubicle. As we drank, he outlined his plans for a year of work at the Old Vic. As he continued, and as he grew in imagination and ambition and excitement, he literally grew bigger, puffing out his chest, throwing out his arms, until it seemed that the six-person cubicle we were in could hardly contain him. I started to wonder if he was real.

Like a cartoon superhero, Peter has a special, self-telescoping gift. He can be any size he wishes to be. It is often allied to his moral strength. If he has been naughty and been caught out, he will shrink, and his face will summon up the wet-eyed little boy lost, who is never too far from the surface of any theatre director. There are many stories of betrayed actors, directors and writers who have tracked Peter down for days with double-headed axes, then, once they have found him, have spent twenty minutes in his company and come out having signed up for fresh seasons of work. When the little boy lost appears, you just want to take care of him. Conversely, when he is angry, and he feels he has moral strength on his side, he inflates exponentially. At the end of our year together, we were at a huge arts do at the Savoy, and he decided to take on the government. Presented with a lifetime achievement thingy, he didn't get up and fondly reminisce about salad days with Ralph and Johnny. He increased himself up to an almost elephantine size and bellowed about the New Labour government's broken promise to the arts. 'This won't do,' he roared, 'this just won't do.' A crowd ranging from young trip-hop artists to elderly novelists rose to their feet.

Peter is the most complete Shakespearean figure I have ever met, in detail and in spirit. He even physically resembles him in some ways. The funny little moustache and beard arrangement that Peter favours, and that Trevor Nunn copied, together with several other directors, reflects many directors' desire to be caught somewhere between Jesus and William Shakespeare. And as Peter's hair recedes and his face fills out, the resemblance grows. Starting as a student, then as a freelance at Stratford, then running the newly founded Royal Shakespeare Company, then opening the National Theatre, and finally as a freelance international director, Peter has been drenched in Shakespeare all his life, and saturated in theatre. Towards the end of our year together at the Old Vic, I wearily told him that I needed a rest from the constant trundle of new shows, press nights and fights. He asked me how many shows I'd produced or directed. Oh, about ninety-five in the last seven years, I said in what I thought was a casually impressive manner. What about you, I asked. At the last count, 876, he replied with the glee of a small child with the biggest toy collection. He has directed almost all of Shakespeare's plays, many of them over and over, and the stories, myths and language are infused through his marrow.

Peter has taken to writing and teaching about Shakespeare. He has evolved a doctrinaire theory about the verse speaking, about hitting the rhythm regularly and hard, and about driving through to the end of each line. It's good as a corrective to much televisual mumbling, but it can lead to a stiffness of delivery which doesn't sit easy in the modern world. Its formality can be a straitjacket for the verse's tumble and switch. Peter does not just teach Shakespeare, in many ways he is an exemplar of him. He has the greed of the true Shakespearean; for food, for love, for children, for money, for marriages, for art, for thought. He is a glutton for anything that is passing and can be grabbed, a monster for life. Yet softer qualities temper the greed: a warmth for all people; a capacity to surprise himself, and enjoy being wrong; a mischievous and naughty humour; a passion for the aesthetically beautiful; and a discreet but probing moral sense.

What Peter could get away with, which hardly anyone else can, was to talk to Shakespeare almost on the level. There was no questioning his adoration, but through many years of dogged acquaintance, he had come to know him and come to enjoy his laziness and his faults. He had a theory about what he called the first ten lines of the day – sudden patches that appear throughout Shakespeare's plays of surprisingly turgid writing. Peter's take was that Shakespeare would wake up, bleary-eyed and hungover, think, 'Oh fuck, do I have to?', then settle down with quill and paper. 'Where was I?' he'd groan, then start scratching uncomfortably away, trying to revive the magic of the day before. The first ten lines are clumsy and deliberate and plonky. Then plot, character and image would start to dominate the front of the brain and steer the hand, and the writing would start to float. Twenty lines later the story and the ongoing dramatic momentum would release Shakespeare's great heap of images and sources and emotions. And he was elsewhere. Flying. Until the next morning, when he would have to scratch his way into life again.

Peter's favourite passage of this was one that unfortunately appears at the beginning of a play, so it's hard to disguise its clumsiness. It's the beginning of *Cymbeline*, and it's an exquisitely bad bit of writing. Check out the subtlety with which he tells you first the situation, then the back story, then a further back story. This is a piece from the car-crash school of exposition. Some suggested thoughts of Shakespeare as he was composing are appended.

(*Oh Christ, do I have to? What's this one then?* Cymbeline. *Oh well, here goes.*)
1ST GENT You do not meet a man but frowns:
(*Ouch*)

our bloods

No more obey the heavens than our courtiers
Still seem as does the king.
(*Not great. How shall we move this along?*)
2ND GENT But what's the matter?
(*Subtle as the plague. Oh well, who cares? First few lines. They'll still be pushing latecomers in.*)

1ST GENT His daughter, and the heir of's kingdom, whom
   He purposed to his wife's sole son – a widow
   That late he married – hath referr'd herself
   Unto a poor but worthy gentleman: she's wedded;
   Her husband banish'd; she imprison'd: all
   Is outward sorrow; though I think the king
   Be touch'd at very heart.

(*Well, that's the story dealt with. In record time. Complicated history, seven lines. Get me. Who the hell's going to understand all that? Oh well . . . Onwards and upwards.*)

2ND GENT None but the king?

(*Double ouch.*)

1ST GENT He that hath lost her too; so is the queen,
   That most desired the match; but not a courtier,
   Although they wear their faces to the bent
   Of the king's looks, hath a heart that is not
   Glad at the thing they scowl at.

(*Better.*)

2ND GENT And why so?

(*Mmm, intriguing.*)

1ST GENT He that hath miss'd the princess is a thing
   Too bad for bad report: and he that hath her –
   I mean, that married her – alack, good man!
   And therefore banish'd –

(*Blown it. Arse.*)

                     – is a creature such
   As, to seek through the regions of the earth
   For one his like, there would be something failing
   In him that should compare. I do not think
   So fair an outward and such stuff within
   Endows a man but he.

(*What's that last bit about? Search me. Shall I give this second guy a character? The first one's turning out to be a right fuckwit.*)

2ND GENT You speak him far.

(*Nah, fuck him.*)

1ST GENT I do extend him, sir, within himself,

187

Crush him together rather than unfold

His measure duly.

(*What? Help. He's talking Swahili again. Someone get me out of this scene.*
This really isn't going well. Oh well, plot, plot, plot.)

2ND GENT What's his name and birth?

(*Triple ouch.*)

1ST GENT I cannot delve him to the root: his father

Was call'd Sicilius, who did join his honour

Against the Romans with Cassibelan,

But had his titles by Tenantius whom

He served with glory and admired success,

So gain'd the sur-addition Leonatus . . .

(*Do you think my research is showing? A few Roman names usually shuts*
them up. That should impress Boring Ben.)

                . . . to his mistress,

For whom he now is banish'd, her own price

Proclaims how she esteem'd him and his virtue;

By her election may be truly read

What kind of man he is.

(*What's this play about again? I'd better give this second guy something,*
or the actor will be whingeing.)

2ND GENT   I honour him

Even out of your report.

(*Nah, can't be bothered. Back to the questions.*)

                  But, pray you, tell me,

Is she sole child to the king?

1ST GENT   His only child.

He had two sons: if this be worth your hearing,

(*Don't think so, matey.*)

Mark it: the eldest of them at three years old,

I' the swathing-clothes the other, from their nursery

Were stol'n, and to this hour no guess in knowledge

Which way they went.

(*Who's going to buy that?*)

2ND GENT   How long is this ago?

(*Ouch with cherries on.*)

1ST GENT Some twenty years.

(Oh, please let this scene be over. Do you think they'll believe all this rubbish? I'd better let them know I'm in on the joke.)

2ND GENT That a king's children should be so convey'd,

So slackly guarded, and the search so slow,

That could not trace them!

(That should do it.)

1ST GENT   Howsoe'er 'tis strange,

Or that the negligence may well be laugh'd at,

Yet is it true, sir.

(Yeah, so yah boo sucks to all you disbelievers.)

2ND GENT   I do well believe you.

(Not much choice, matey. That's enough. I'm off down the pub. Better luck tomorrow.)

1ST GENT We must forbear: here comes the gentleman,

The queen, and princess.

(And you lot can all . . .)

Exeunt.

It couldn't be said that the Second Gentleman is his most finely realized creation. This is basically an example, and there are many, of a form of writing that could be called 'shutting your eyes and getting on with it'. It's a glorious example of how there are no rules to great writing. And how close bad art walks to great art.

It was something of a revelation when Peter lightly told me this theory. I had heard pompous directors, and arsey kids, dissing Shakespeare before and just thought they were fools. I had done it myself, and blushed later at the thought. The director of our student *Romeo and Juliet* had said that he thought his production suffered from being occasionally superior to the play. But for Peter to say it after such lengthy acquaintance released a flood of new thoughts. That Shakespeare was not a god, or a divinely ordained authority. That he was a man, and a writer, like any of the writers I had worked with at the Bush. That he made mistakes and wrote badly. That he wrote at speed and never bothered to revise it. And that that was a glory rather than a fault. His imperfections were all wrapped up in his humanity, and were what made him unique. And the mountains of exegesis finding rational explanations for his bad writing were simply mountains of nonsense. He was sometimes a lazy arse, and that was part and parcel of his greatness. It was liberating.

a *Dream* in the garden and the joys of amateurism

Rain was on its way, a long black cloud bearing down from the Bristol Channel. No one even glanced in its direction. Everyone was skittering around the garden I grew up in, from bush to apple tree, from the house to the dairy, from barn to barn. They were adjusting costumes, trying to remember lines, stopping for urgent conferences, swapping flirty glances. Not one of them was an actor – farmers, postwomen, teachers, doctors, farm labourers and their children – but all swept up in the same excitement. They secreted themselves as the audience started to arrive and take their seats in the garden.

Since my parents' separation my mother had brought herself and our old home into the centre of the village life. The old uneasy relationship between a small-holding farming community and 'thicky there buggers from television' had dissolved, and thanks largely to her effervescent gathering of people, everybody was in and out of each other's homes like a soap opera on speed. The main agency of this was the creation of the local drama club. Each January, a lavish and fairly bonkers show would be presented. These were principally either pantos or musicals, but idiosyncratically structured. Each show would be halted at regular intervals for compulsory turns. Hayward Rossiter would give a recital of a poem. His wife Molly would tell a joke, if she could conquer her giggling problem, which meant she rarely reached the punchline. The young farmers would inevitably stop the proceedings twice for two displays of cross dressing.

And it would always stop, no matter what the show, for a five-minute display of old-time dancing from the unsubtly named Theale Old Time Dancing Troupe. Five or six couples, all over seventy, would walk on, the ladies in long skirts, the chaps in white shirt and black trousers, with a garish cummerbund as the only flash of colour. They would grip each other tightly, the men's rigid stare fixed above the ladies' right shoulders, the ladies the same. The music would start and they would slowly walk each other round the floor for five minutes. No surprises, no bursts of paso doble, no sudden tangos, just a slow, rigidly undemonstrative walk around the floor, a small bow and then off. It was easy not to be sentimental about these couples, easy to project that if the woman stepped out of line at home she'd get a clout, easy to imagine that some of the men would be on a slow diet of mouse poison in their minestrone. But as they stiffly, and rigidly, turned each other round the floor, it was always hard not to cry.

But this night was going to be special: tonight they were trying on Shakespeare. Tonight they were doing *A Midsummer Night's Dream*. The set was all in place, supplied by nature and husbandry. Straight ahead, an old pear tree with a wooden swing hanging from a lichen-covered branch. The backdrop, the gently rising hill and a wood which swallowed the dusk into darkness. To stage left, an old stone wall. To stage right, more trees and an old dairy. The floorcloth of grass was sprinkled with buttercups and daisies, ignoring the action and quietly folding themselves up for the evening.

Much of the garden and barns had been taken over by factions from all over the village, not least the caterers, who, for £1, would give you a cup of wine, and for £2.50 a cardboard baker's box of snacks in a mid-Somerset equivalent of Glyndebourne: chocolate crispy cakes, egg sandwiches and sausage rolls. A black market in chocolate crispy cakes quickly sprung up, while sausage rolls were deemed disgaaaasting, and discovered by the roots of bushes for weeks afterwards. The audience was a motley crew, from two months old to nearing a ton. They sat on the grass, on chairs and benches, old blankets wrapped round them. Our babies slept in our laps. In such a ludicrously idyllic English setting, only one thing could happen. Rain. And it came. A fair torrent. But it deterred neither actors nor audience, freshening their spirits, and increasing their determination to be happy. And after the rain came the compensation of a clear sky, and early stars pinpricking their way into the black carpet.

In the absence of enough young bloods to animate the whole of the play, my mother had cut the young lovers and twisted the play towards Bottom and his mechanicals, Titania, Oberon and the fairies. She had renamed it *Bottom's Dream*. There had been problems with the cast. The girl playing Puck had had a big row with Titania and Bottom, her mother and father, and had stropped out of the production. A last-minute replacement was drafted in. The replacement could certainly act Puckish, but suffered from being a little on the tall side. When not generously crouching in a squat, she did tend to tower over everyone else. She certainly seemed most likely of anyone to manage a girdle around the earth in forty minutes. Oberon was great, although a little on the female side, being a woman. Titania was adored stiffly by Oberon, hardly at all by Puck, subduedly by the fairies, extravagantly and demonstrably by Bottom (her husband) and chiefly by Titania. The Indian prince was my niece, exotically got up in Chinese silk pyjamas and an enormous purple turban, secured with a jewel. My niece was my mother's first granddaughter, and the apple of her and much of the village's eye. As was customary in early Theale Players programming, rehearsals would take place without her and she would, like Pavarotti, fly in from London, stand where she liked, while the actors flexed around her, then accept the most extravagant bouquets and biggest cheers at the end.

All were full of good spirits, but many were intimidated by the language. Some came out and bellowed it, without a care, which worked beautifully. Others felt the terrible pressure of its importance and were either inaudibly precious with it or frightened into not being able to make any sense of it at all. The fairies were wonderful, a troop of children who scattered around the garden then drew back together and sang out their lines with bright clear Somerset voices:

> Over hill, over dale,
> Thorough bush, thorough brier,
> Over park, over pale,
> Thorough flood, thorough fire,
> I do wander everywhere,
> Swifter than the moon's sphere

At the end of the play they walked down from the hill, slowly emerging out of the darkness, led by Molly Rossiter, the giggling fairy godmother of all the pantos. An ample woman, her face, after a couple of drinks or when on stage, is a beacon of mischievous delight. She led the chorus of fairies in the song:

> Where the bee sucks, there suck I:
> In a cowslip's bell I lie;
> There I couch when owls do cry.
> On the bat's back I do fly
> After summer merrily.
> Merrily, merrily shall I live now
> Under the blossom that hangs on the bough

This was exquisite, if a little textually corrupt, the song not being part of *A Midsummer Night's Dream* at all, but an import from *The Tempest*. But, as they say in Somerset, a fairy is a fairy is a fairy. At the instruction of Oberon,

> Through the house give glimmering light,
> By the dead and drowsy fire:
> Every elf and fairy sprite
> Hop as light as bird from brier . . .
> Now, until the break of day,
> Through this house each fairy stray.

The fairies processed past the audience and into the house I grew up in.

One of the glories of Shakespeare and one of the proofs of his richness is that during this final track of *A Midsummer Night's Dream*, one of the most sincerely sweet and kind passages of literature ever written, he drops in a few lines of miserably toxic inhumanity. Just as you are holding your breath in the hope that this sustained sublimity can remain aloft, you suddenly find yourself listening to a small-minded middle-Englander hoping that his pregnant wife doesn't need an amniocentesis.

> To the best bride-bed will we,
> Which by us shall blessed be;
> And the issue there create
> Ever shall be fortunate.

So shall all the couples three
Ever true in loving be;
And the blots of Nature's hand
Shall not in their issue stand;
Never mole, hare lip, nor scar,
Nor mark prodigious, such as are
Despised in nativity,
Shall upon their children be.

You would have thought the man who came up with 'what a piece of work is a man' and 'Hath not a Jew eyes . . .', could have been a bit kinder to anyone unfortunate enough to be born with a hair lip. But Shakespeare was the child of the moment he was in. If a small-minded thought passed through his head, he put it into verse; if a humane one, the same.

If the fairies were a delight, the mechanicals were spectacular. *A Midsummer Night's Dream* is Shakespeare's great hymn to amateurism. A country boy himself, who had fallen into the big time, he never lost his sense of the spirit that got him there, nor his pride in its inherent generosity. When he was eleven, it's probable he went to see the Earl of Leicester's extravagant shows at Kenilworth to entertain the visiting Queen Elizabeth. At one point a dolphin emerged from the lake, ridden by a sea fairy. The spectacular illusion was slightly broken by the actor playing the fairy stopping the show and shouting to the audience that they weren't to be afraid, he wasn't really a fairy. A moment whose echo in the mechanicals play in *A Midsummer Night's Dream* speaks of the child's joy in the raggedy dignity of such unabashed amateurism. There's a certain sort of colleague in the theatre community who uses the word 'professional' with a special venomous sting. 'It's just not professional', 'we in the profession', 'well, that's how the professionals do it'. Speaking on behalf of a tradition leading from well before Shakespeare and well beyond me, I wish all those people could be herded into a boat, sailed out into the mid-Atlantic and sunk. Theatre is an offering of the heart and the spirit; it has nothing to do with qualifications, or careers.

Some people are more able at it than others; some people make a living out of it. That doesn't make them uniquely qualified. Anyone who wants to dress up and tell a story is entitled. In the scene at the end of the play when the mechanicals present Pyramus and Thisbe, Shakespeare manipulates our sympathies gently. We start out laughing at them with the young lovers at the Athenian court. Then, as the scene progresses, the jibes of the courtiers become excessive and annoying and unkind. At that moment our sympathies move to the players, and the presentation of their play becomes an act of heroism. Amateur as they are, clumsy and lost, their goodwill redeems their offering.

When Shakespeare arrived in London it was dominated by the university wits, a tearaway gang of scholarly writers who combined furious creation with fast living. They were carving out the new drama with a rock rebel arrogance, a 'look what we can do' ostentation. Their plays opened the door for Shakespeare but lacked a crucial quality. They were certainly full of erudite wit and mythological reference, but also cripplingly pleased with themselves. Shakespeare saw that theatre should be a resource open for all, not the educated few; and that its crucial ingredient was generosity of spirit. When characters approach the audience at the end of a comedy asking for applause, they are not being winsome or political, they are expressing the spirit at the heart of their theatre. My nephew, unable yet to enunciate his *l*s, had some of this spirit when, at the end of a family nativity, he shouted at us to 'crap harder'. 'We are doing this for you, and we hope you like it' is the idea. Shakespeare was also capable of saying, 'I hope you rot in hell, scratching yourselves,' as he does at the end of *Troilus and Cressida*; or of saying a gentle farewell as he does at the end of *The Tempest*. But crucially, he talked to everyone, not to himself. The mechanicals are the rebuff to the university wits.

I've never seen that final scene better played than it was in my mother's garden by a farmer, a postwoman, a doctor, an unemployed man and a kid who was trying to start a rock band. Bottom was full of mild pomposity and good humour; Quince had the perfect mix of someone who wants to appear very knowledgeable but is in fact very stupid; Starveling was stupendous, a farmer's daughter who had no problem with Shakespeare at all. Flute was played by a schoolboy probably more interested in his rock music than Shakespeare. He had suffered 'the Blot of Nature's Hand' and been born with a slightly maimed hand with missing fingers. But he acted with such ease and honesty and natural comedy, he spoiled the part for anyone who will come after. Thisbe was played by a man as timid as he was meant to be. The village had come out to laugh at their neighbours and friends. No extra effort was needed to bring the old jokes to life.

So the spite, humour and magic of the play were all there in equal part. The sun subsiding and the lamps coming on, the natural magic of an English dusk meant the midsummer evening was there for real and with all reality's occasional effortlessness. The setting of the play seemed to be this night and this house. The countryside around seemed to transport itself to the imaginary realm of the play. The violets were still nodding and there was the oxslip, and the smell of musk rose, and Oberon did indeed lie down on a bank where the wild thyme grew. The smells and noises described were those that filled our senses, no sleight of hand, but a true spell, cast over us all by this flirtation between Art and Life.

When the fairies blessed the house at the end we all turned to look at Barrows Farm. There was a fairy at every window and each window lit by a candle against the now black night. It was a kind moment, a benediction over the house and a statement of pride by the household gods.

> With this field-dew consecrate,
> Every fairy take his gait;
> And each several chamber bless,
> Through this palace, with sweet peace;
> And the owner of it blest
> Ever shall in safety rest.
> Trip away; make no stay;
> Meet me all by break of day

And it seemed that Shakespeare's fairies had actually conjured themselves into the 500-year-old flagstoned kitchen of the farm that night.

> And we fairies, that do run
> By the triple Hecate's team,
> From the presence of the sun,
> Following darkness like a dream,

> Now are frolic: not a mouse
> Shall disturb this hallow'd house:
> I am sent with broom before,
> To sweep the dust behind the door.

came Puck's lines, and I realized the fairies were the guardians of homespun magic, the play an ode to the ancient lore, and the crude realism, of English country life.

For my mother, who had rebuilt a new life after the departure of first us and then my father, it was a gentle vindication of her achievement. It was opening a door on something new and all her own. Robin had restored amends.

an election rally and a naming ceremony

Scraps of poetry stick in you at different moments. Some loosen their hold as time and circumstance shifts. Some retain their grip through crisis and all the different identities of maturity. One sonnet has never shifted.

> When in disgrace with fortune and men's eyes,
> I all alone beweep my outcast state,
> And trouble deaf Heaven with my bootless cries,
> And look upon myself, and curse my fate,
> Wishing me like to one more rich in hope,
> Featur'd like him, like him with friends possess'd,
> Desiring this man's art, and that man's scope,
> With what I most enjoy contented least;
> Yet in these thoughts myself almost despising,
> Haply I think on thee, – and then my state
> (Like to the lark at break of day arising
> From sullen earth) sings hymns at heaven's gate;
> For thy sweet love remember'd such wealth brings
> That then I scorn to change my state with kings.

It's a great mantra to mutter to oneself at bleak moments. Its Hopkins-esque leap into the abyss of self-pity is the perfect match for any unloved moment. Its delicate, frail rise back to hope is the perfect whisper of sunshine. It's a poem for real men with a small murmur of girlie in them. It's also a great pulling poem. It sufficiently displays one's understanding, sensitive nature, even indulges it, before flipping itself over with the bold stare, 'Haply I think on THEE', and then finishing with the clinching couplet.

It didn't first sink in as a means of seduction. It was sponged in at school or university as an aspirin to break the grip of some black dog or other. But it stayed. The 'thees', the subjects of inspiration, changed, from friend to lover, from work of art to religious icon, but the poem was always there to pivot me out of the depressed downward gaze and towards the horizon line.

It also stuck around because it's so often used. It's a favourite at large public events. It's as seductive for a crowd as it is for an individual. There was a 'luvvies for Labour' do at Millbank in 1992. It was a week before the general election and the *Observer* had just printed a poll with Labour a clean four per cent ahead of the Tories. The mood was high and fresh. After thirteen years of Tory mismanagement, there was a genuine feeling that it might just be over. Within ten minutes of the entertainment starting, it had plunged. It was a ramshackle mess. Witless songs about Maggie and Major, daft poems about 'factories opening like flowers' and clonky comedy routines bore witness to the fact that a political revolution was a long way away. If this was the show, then it was hard to imagine what the electoral machine was like. By the time Lord Attenborough introduced Neil Kinnock as 'the next Prime Minister of Britain' the mood in the audience was very ho-hum indeed. He stood there at a podium half-way up a sweeping staircase. Beneath him, backs against the wall, not looking at Kinnock but staring out at the crowd, stood Harold Pinter and Edna O'Brien. They added considerably to the weirdness of the event – Pinter with his heavy shades looking like a Stasi agent about to arrest everyone, and O'Brien looking flushed and delicate as if she'd just had a multiple orgasm.

Kinnock stood up and said some warm and witty guff – a cunning mix of politics and showbiz. Then, as a climax, he launched into 'When in disgrace . . .' It could have been ghastly, the politician playing actor in front of the actors. But he spoke it magnificently – all of the Welsh Methodist fire and intelligence in the phrasing and his own particular public honesty. His 'thee' was broad and open, all of the friends who had supported him on the way. It was simple and moving. By the end, anyone in the room who had the faintest delusion that Labour might win should have been in no doubt at all. They hadn't a chance. It's a great poem, but it's a loser's poem. It's a realist's poem, a human's poem. There's little point in advertising your humanity if you want to win the *Daily Mail* middle ground. You wouldn't catch Tony Blair spouting anything like a sonnet. He might give you a belt of *Henry V*'s jingoism, or some of the paranoid messianic sulking of *Coriolanus*. That's what makes him a winner. Kinnock was too decent a human being for the political process.

A week after the election Kinnock turned up at the Bush for a gala night charity doodah. It was a public display of great courage. The election had been humiliating for every idiot, including me, who had convinced themselves that Labour might win. For Kinnock it had been excruciating. Yet, in a room full of the celebrities who had backed him, he bore it as lightly as if it had been a trifle. The occasional crease of worry betrayed the fact that it wasn't, but he wasn't going to give in to bitterness. Too good for politics.

It was at the Bush in a very different context that I next heard a public rendition of 'When in disgrace . . .' My first child had been born, a gale of an event which blew many of the remaining scraps of nonsense out of my brain. All the lack of connect was hurricanoed away when the purple angry head screamed its way out into the air, and the precious, lifelong panic of being a parent began.

We decided to name the child in a humanist ceremony at the theatre. We took over the two pubs downstairs for a day, decking out the grimy fixtures and fittings with autumn branches. A giddy over-excitement filled the air as a couple of hundred guests poured in to be regaled by a string quartet in a corner of a smelly old pub. We had to do two separate renditions of the ceremony, since we couldn't squeeze everyone in. I had chosen to contribute nothing to the proceedings, just to sit, with my baby in my lap, and for both of us to gurgle happily. There was a catechism spoken by the godparents, a specially composed poem, a couple of songs. Then, before the final set piece, my Sasha singing my baby to sleep with some sweet soaring Schubert, my father stepped up to the plate.

Beforehand he approached me and told me he had written a poem. He proudly told me its first line: 'It's a shame you were not born a boy . . .' I told him to bin it, and if he tried that on, the lights would go out on him and stage management would bundle him off the stage. He accepted my authority in the matter and promised he'd come up with something else. When the time came, he was nervous. It was partly because he was up there in front of the broad church of all my family's friends, many of whom were still angry at him for leaving my mother. Partly because there was a weight of emotion in the air, and he had to match it. And mainly because the grandparent moment is a peculiar one. The child appears as a strange, distorting mirror of its grandparent, simultaneously ensuring a continuity down through time and reminding the elder that time is moving on.

Something odd happened to Shakespeare after the birth of his first grandchild in 1608. A sense of peace settled on his spirit. It was also the moment of the move from the large public space of the Globe to the more intimate confines of the Blackfriars Theatre. This accounts for some of the formal difference in the last stretch of his work, and its more discursive intellectual voice. But there is a sense of hope and redemption that floods through the last stretch of his work – *Pericles*, *Cymbeline*, *The Winter's Tale* and *The Tempest* – which is a substantial volte-face after the plays that preceded it – *Timon*, *Coriolanus* and *Macbeth*. Something significant happened within the base of his spirit. His beloved elder daughter Susanna had married in 1607, an event that must have drawn him back to Stratford. A big public wedding must have been a forcible reminder of the warmth and cohesion of the world he had neglected. His wife would have stood beside him as well, sharing in his pride.

Two of his late plays deal powerfully with the reconnection with a daughter and a wife. Pericles searches the Mediterranean shores for his lost daughter Marina and finds her. He also soon after rediscovers a wife he had presumed dead. On confirmation of who she is, he exclaims:

> This, this! No more, you gods! Your present kindness
> Makes my past miseries sports. You shall do well
> That on the touching of her lips I may
> Melt and no more be seen. O, come, be buried
> A second time within these arms.

It's hard to imagine the matrimonial bed is not being rewarmed after a long absence from Stratford. At the conclusion of *The Winter's Tale*, Leontes, who believes his wife Hermione dead, and his daughter lost, is reunited with the daughter, and sees the wife transform from a statue to a living being. It is clear that Shakespeare's wife Anne and his two daughters had come alive to him again. Through all his last plays, there is the powerful sense of a long and lost and displacing journey, and an overpowering need to belong again. The inspiration for this could well have been the moment when he held the youngest female in his family, the baby Elizabeth, up above him and saw the peculiar recognition in her eyes that told him that he was old, that he was loved, and that it was time to come home.

My father stood in front of the crowd and launched gently into 'When in disgrace . . .' He was hesitant. There was a penitent air to it, as he explained to friends he had lost that he maybe wasn't as bumptious and greedy for pleasure as they liked to think. He lost his way in the middle – which made me wince – but no one else noticed. His training in the Parks kicked in and he improvised his way out of trouble in fluent Shakespearean. Then, on the 'thee', he turned to his new granddaughter, and his strength and confidence kicked in. It wasn't a barnstorming, sobby-sobby turn. There was still many a dry eye in the house. But it was a gentle reminder, through Shakespeare, that there is something sacred in the bond between human and human that no church can match. And that the sustenance of family love is one of the most sacred of all.

hubris, hangovers and a car crash of a *Troilus and Cressida*

One of the most laughable of the conventional wisdoms about Shakespeare, and indeed all tragedy, is that suffering and experience make you wise. The imagined trajectory is a rosy one, where life is a steady walk up a slope towards a mountain plateau from where you look out at the world with a saintly sagacity. And that all our errors, our crimes and our grief help us towards inner peace and an absence of folly. Ha! In fact, double Ha! Why do they teach this garbage at school? Every day is a succession of pratfalls; every month a revisiting of old sins and old stupidities; every year a deletion of memory as large as its store of new experience. The old man doesn't end up wise, he ends up 'sans teeth, sans everything . . .' From childhood I had the word hubris drummed into me. For the same length of years, the motto 'pride comes before a fall' had been chanted around me. None of that accumulated wisdom stopped me from wanting to produce *Troilus and Cressida* in enormous theatres with actors who had no experience in Shakespeare.

With two beautiful children, another on the way, a nest and a love whose depth of joy I could never have dreamed of deserving, I should have been protected, ring-fenced, contained from mishaps and disasters. But the Shakespearean way is the greedy way, the 'and' way, the wanting more of everything way. If things were going well, go for more; if there was a big Sunday roast on the table, ask for a Chinese to go with it. Keep going for more, until you bust it all wide open and go back to nothing again. There was a desire to wreck as well: to wreck a happiness and wreck a career. It walks hand in hand in the theatre with all the endless building. It's an exhausted response to the years of cheerfully standing things up. Producing plays is an endless process of goodwilled construction, of night after night garnering the forces on stage and in the audience to produce something collective in the air in between. No one understood this better than Shakespeare, no one slaved at it harder than him. Occasionally, after all that building, you just want to pick up a sledgehammer and knock it all down. If you're going to take a weapon to happiness, there's no better play to do it with than *Troilus*. It is a wrecker's delight, a stock-car rally smash-up of a play, where all positive or delightful human emotions are gleefully Semtexed to oblivion. Love, loyalty and life are blown apart.

The first mistake was beginning rehearsals two days after our new millennium had dawned. New Year by itself would have been bad enough, the millennium proved a disaster. On the very first morning it was clear a majority of the actors assembled had been drinking for the whole of the last week. Few had slept for the last forty-eight hours. Menelaus asked Helen for a fuck two hours after the read-through, which is something of a record. No waiting for a cold night in Manchester on tour for him, he just steamed right in. The whole of the first week, as we sat studying Shakespeare's labyrinthine text, was lost, as the cast negotiated their historic hangovers. They smiled at me politely, as I continued my enthusiastic exegesis, not wanting to disturb the troubled waters of their cerebellum. A four-week rehearsal period rapidly became three weeks, as week one was lost in the fog of crapulence.

Actually, the first mistake was earlier with the casting. I had recently started at the Oxford Stage Company, a touring company subsidized by the Arts Council. I had opened with a bang, negotiating a contract with a West End theatre for a year, mounting several successful productions and directing a lovely and very happy production of *Three Sisters*. For our next challenge, I thought nothing of directing Shakespeare's most intractable work, touring 2,000-seat theatres, usually reserved for musicals or opera, then bringing it into the Old Vic. Just to make it a proper challenge, I wasn't going to work with any overly trained, Shakespearean actors with trilling voices. No, that would have been far too easy. I was going to corral together the roughest Irish and English actors. A brutal *Nil by Mouth* of a production. Violent, wild and tender. Auditions were surprising, to put it mildly. Nutcase after geezer after psycho trooped in, with a few RADA graduates and film starlets interspersed nervously in the middle. While waiting for one actor, we were rung by his agent and told that his client couldn't attend because he was in court. He'd been so excited by the prospect of the audition that he'd gone out, got pissed and pulled a knife on someone. Eventually, I ended up with a fine collection of actors, from the distinctly softer end of the spectrum. The mistake was in ignoring their lack of Shakespeare experience. I could teach them all that, I thought. Twitbrain.

Week two, after the hangovers had cleared, and the cast had stopped shaking, we ran into the Shakespeare problem. Several actors, brilliant on stage in modern plays, or on film, had a defensive reaction to a lump of blank verse. Instead of bringing it into themselves, and letting it come through with a muscular simplicity, they kicked off with a strange parody of Victorian acting. They raised their arms stiffly, rolled their eyes and spoke with a constipated reverence. It was the sad switchback of centuries of posh Shakespeare, of Shakespeare the other, the strange, the only admitted to an elite few. It's a poisonous prejudice, and a persuasive one. These actors – quick, intelligent and alive though they were – felt they could not be themselves. They felt compelled to assume a weird artificiality to be worthy of the work. This took a lot of unlearning. With some of them it was quick and easy, and they took to it fast, with electrifying results. With some it was torture.

The problem could have been superable if I'd had enough time, but I'd built my own prison. The play was too big, and too rangy, for the time allotted to it. If you nailed one bit, another would squeeze through your fingers. When it was just about to open, it was at a delicate stage. With a positive and rhythmic technical period, and a warm opening house, it could have flown. Well, it had a stumbling, error-strewn technical time, and it opened in Oxford. There are wonderful, generous, easy people in Oxford, and there are tight, neurotic and intellectually superior folk who are so full of opinions they've lost sight of where life is. If you get a preponderance of the former you can have a good night; if you get a preponderance of the latter, you might as well be telling your best joke to a gerbil. We had all of the latter. If they'd booed, it would have been a blessed relief. Instead we had the chilled contempt of 600 eggheads beamed in our general direction. It was an experience the show would never recover from. Though, to be honest, it probably didn't deserve to.

There were rallies. The show improved radically in Oxford, until Hector broke his ankle entering a night club. We had him on stage in plaster the next day, but he ceased to be history's most terrifying warrior. His final climatic duel with Achilles swiftly metamorphosed from being a bloodthirsty battle to a strange bit of stylized Noh theatre with crutches. It rallied again on tour, where some of the cast did some beautiful work. When it hit the huge barns I had insisted it played to, it suffered from the fact that an audience of 400 would be lost in an auditorium that held 3,000. It also suffered from the nocturnal habits of the cast, which were, basically, nocturnal. Hardly one of them had a daytime habit. When I tried to act the scoutmaster with them, it didn't help that they could point out that I was habitually the last to bed.

A keener political animal would have buried the show outside London, found some artful way to pretend it had never happened. I was the opposite. I cajoled, blackmailed, begged and whined to get this sickly animal into town, where it was inevitably going to be massacred, together with what little respect I had engendered. I secured the Old Vic, and the money to present. The board of my company told me not to do it; my friends begged me not to; something in me knew it was mad, but there was a greater determination to see it through. I wanted the wreckage to be complete. This shouldn't be a discreet disaster: it should be a big, squalid, tawdry one. I got what I wanted. Sitting at the back on press night, a thousand people watching, thirty-odd critics licking their lips, I watched the show falter, stumble and fall. It had no confidence, no strength and no muscle. It was a timid thing at the end of the room inviting a kicking. Something inside me was grateful. I'd reached the end of a certain sort of road, a certain hubristic sense of myself. The car crash in front of me was ample proof. It was a charmless, unwieldy play in a charmless, unwieldy production.

Something inside me had to be cauterized and ripped out, like the buds of horns which I helped to burn out of the heads of calves as a boy. It was a self-administered professional ticking-off. The proud antlers of the esteemed Shakespeare director, garlanded with arty respect, and admired by leagues of eager students, were something I'd always wanted to wear. But they weren't right for me, and I wasn't right for them. The truth won out. It was a violent way to learn it, but a relief. If I was going to approach Shakespeare again, I was going to have to work harder and be honest to the person I was, rather than a person I might want to be.

It was also a reminder to live and enjoy where there was already comfort and blessings, and not to chase more. It was probably also time, as I nudged forty, to stop being an adolescent. *Troilus and Cressida* had a link for me with my teen years from having performed Pandarus, but it's also the great sulking play. It's all negativity, all posturing, all disillusion, all slipped reality. All the big questions, and no comfortable answers. Now, though still poor, I had happiness and connections and all the linkage that made me a bit of a bourgeois burgher. My inner berserk was fighting for air and starting to look a bit silly surrounded by peers who were all choosing to wear woolly jumpers. Doing *Troilus*, doing it violently, wrecking my own success was a last hurrah for that inner punk. He won't have disappeared completely, none of our noisy inhabitants ever do, but he won't be allowed to dominate proceedings again.

Another Shakespearean turnaround. The day after the reviews popped out – merrily hanging, drawing and quartering me – and feeling as blue as can be, I went morosely for lunch at my regular Thai bolt-hole. I sat down hidden within papers full of gleeful reports of what an idiot I was and waited for my crispy fried pomfret. I was dragged out of my introversion by the bold attention of the proprietor. We'd exchanged pleasantries, but never really sat down before. That day, she was more wired than usual and needed to talk. She sat opposite and talked for a couple of hours. She unwrapped a story of such ill-starred fortunes and crossed love, with such a comic plethora of tragic outcomes, that it made what the *Evening Standard* said about *Troilus and Cressida* seem as harmful as a gnat's nibble. It was a Shakespeare story, full of misunderstandings, a love lost and then found and then lost to the drowning of the waters, and children maimed but still growing. It was told with a sharp English humour that took self-pity away but lost none of its emotional soar. It was strong medicine, as all great tragic-comic stories are.

open-air joy and children's faces

My chance encounter after the *Troilus* debacle lifted my spirit temporarily and threw a more mature light on events. But it was still a debacle and hurt my company badly. We were plunged into debt. Various other outstanding problems had been hidden rather than dealt with. It was too soon to process why I'd screwed up so spectacularly over *Troilus and Cressida*. I was still in a great wrap-around mess. I felt the impetus to run, but I had to stand and help the company through its troubles. The only break in the year was three days in midsummer. We thought we'd drive up through England to Scotland. The first stop would be Oxford, where I was mired dealing with auditors, bank managers, arts administrators and board members. A hotel room was booked for the family and, for want of anything else to do, tickets to an open-air *Midsummer Night's Dream* in Magdalen School gardens.

Expectations of the show were low. My experiences of open-air theatre were generally disappointing. I had once directed an al fresco production of a Jacobean comedy by Middleton at university. It was after our final exams, and rehearsal attendance was minimal. We never managed a dress rehearsal. On the first night two principal actors went on for the last act not only ignorant of their lines but also largely innocent of the plot. They required a lot of steering. Subsequent to the first night, we worked out the narrative, but still were very reluctant performers. At the first whisper of rain, we would all rush out and shout, 'Cancelled!' and 'Refunds over there!' before disappearing into the night.

So hopes weren't high. It was a lovely summer's evening, with that wisp of mischievous humour in the particles of the warmly failing light which is unique to middle England. A soft spryness of fizzy drinks and hay bales and green trees hung in the air and enlivened some naughtiness in the spirit. We walked through beautiful gardens, crossing miniature bridges over tiny streams, and passing peeling cricket pavilions. In a corner, a makeshift grandstand had been built, directed at a corner of a meadow, surrounded on two sides by tree-covered streams. It was an Edwardian idyll of a setting. Still managing to damp down our expectations, we purchased our vintage burger and our fresh red wine and sat down to watch.

It wasn't great. It was a production from the wham-bam school. Lots of charging about at the beginning (some battle scene I didn't even know was in the play); bright, almost Bollywood, costumes; lots of front foot shouting; and some stunts. Oberon and Titania came in on huge stilts. They weren't great with the language, but who cared, they were impressively tall. And there was a moment when Titania slept, when she seemed to levitate, having no means of visible support. It was cheap and tacky and gimmicky, but it was honest, and it knocked my socks off. I was sick of sophisticated and polished and academic and smart Shakespeare. I wanted Billy Smart's. I wanted a pensionable ringmaster and mangy lions and bad trapeze artists who really scare you and clowns who have got nothing but their own despair. I wanted the real thing, and I wanted my children to enjoy the real thing. And we got it. Shakespeare with brio and spirit and good intentions. Poetry shouted at us by good-souled people, bright with amateur hope, not highly trained nitwits, marinaded in professional sourness. Stories told as if they mattered, not as if their interpretation mattered. Magic occurring as if it was magic, not in some meta-theatrical discussion between actors and audience. That night, in a cheesy setting, the thing itself was on display.

My children were electrified. They were agog, their mouths permanently open, their eyes bursting out of their sockets. Their faces were lit up, taken elsewhere. Their ears were pricked alert, like quivering antennae, urgently awaiting the next pulse of poetry. Magic was stirred into their brains. Fairies and love and potions and rage – all the staples of their own games – all in an adult world. They could see the adults sitting all around them just as stupidly happy. They knew this was some sort of guarantee that the stories which were sustaining them now as children would be allowed to last a lifetime. The next day they remembered it moment for moment. The next year they remembered large chunks of it. They still clutch on to fragments. The sight of their faces, held taut by their drawn breath of excitement, will never leave me. Filled as I was with toxins at the time, it was a draught of pure antidote.

The next day we drove up to Derby, where I secured a company-saving deal with the theatre there. That night we stayed in a farmhouse in the Peak District, a lovely Georgian house beside an old medieval ruin. We climbed the huge hill beside it and had a good look out. The huge expanse of rolling Peak District stretched away, all scrubby green and browned in the sun. It helped mightily with perspective. Things had got bad, and then better. Things had hurt, and then they healed. All through my life, when wounds had opened, Shakespeare had appeared with comic balm or tragic suture, to patch things up. There was going to be no great final completing disaster, until the last one. No final triumphs or redemptions or catastrophes. Just the life oscillating giddily between each in a minor key. Just as in Shakespeare, always the same chaotic mess, and always the same imperceptible movement within that chaos, inching forwards, towards being able to walk calmly into the last goodnight.

So I stood there, my family dotted around on a great bluff of land above and below, and breathed in the landscape, settled in the knowledge that I was still capable of piling things up, and still capable of pulling them down. And that the only viable resolution was to go forward, open to anything, wiping each slate clean at the end of each day, eagerly awaiting the nonsense of the next. I had been an idiot, but you have to be an idiot to be wise again. You have to be empty to refresh the tanks. For the first time in my life I could admit I was a happy man, and that maybe admitting that didn't harm the future. I owed it to the shine in my daughter's faces as they stared at *A Midsummer Night's Dream*.

Shakespeare supposedly died after catching a cold, having been out to get horrendously rat-arsed with his friends Ben Jonson and Michael Drayton. He was pissed off because his new son-in-law was a nitwit who had just got the town whore pregnant, and she had died in childbirth. Even his professional career ended sourly. Having mapped out and delivered the perfect farewell of *The Tempest*, with its casting-aside of the book of magic, he then snuck back in and wrote a couple more not very good plays, just to show those young bucks, Beaumont and Fletcher, a thing or two. It's not exactly a martyr's farewell. It's messy and it's human and it's unapologetic. It's as inclusive as every other moment in his story, inclusive of failure. Everything was allowed.

The Walk

Monday

Good friend, for Jesu's sake forbear
To dig the dust enclos'd here.
Blest be the man who spares these stones,
And curst be he that moves my bones.

'Who wrote that doggerel?' my friend Quentin asks. 'Shakespeare,' I reply. 'Ooops.' On a cool summer's morning, we mill around the enclave at the end of Holy Trinity church, Stratford. We stop before the tomb with its inscription. These four lines are the last forceful plea of a steadfastly private man, demanding to have his identity and his secrets left undisturbed long after death. The man who spent his life disappearing into the worlds he created wants that vanishing act to prolong into eternity. It would be impossible to ignore the instruction. Shakespeare knew how to curse. The man who wrote *Macbeth* and knew as much as him about witchcraft (those spells weren't copied off the back of a cereal packet) is not a man to cross in the afterlife. Beside him lies his much-maligned wife Anne. All the world contends she held little attraction for him, yet they share a deeper secret, and a closer companionship, for as long as stones cover them.

Four of us are standing there, one who will peel off soon, another, Mark, after a couple of days, and two others, myself and Quentin, who are determined to see our task through to the end – a long march from Holy Trinity church, Stratford-upon-Avon, to the Globe Theatre in Southwark, London. Walking through Oxford as we intend, and ignoring all roads, it's a distance of around 140 miles, intended to take seven days. Myself, a mildly podgy and squat forty-year-old; my companion superior to me by about a foot in height and twenty years in age. With his long stride, tall carriage and horizon-splitting stare, for the next seven days he will maintain a steady pace ahead of me, sometimes by a few feet, sometimes a few hundred feet, sometimes a mile. With my spasmodic gait, porky physique and eyes fixed on the ground, I will stumble along behind. He is to play the Don Quixote of the shires. I am to be his Sancho Panza.

It was an idea born of drunken enthusiasm two months before. Quentin is an ardent walker, eager Shakespearean and great company; I am feeling the pressure of age and wondering, if I don't do ludicrous things like this now, when will I ever? There is a muted element of pilgrimage to it. An attempt to more sharply understand something that has been fundamental but blurred for too long. The two months since have been spent on spasmodic research into Shakespeare's route. We have decided, with some historical justification, that this boiled down to straight south to Oxford, climbing up into the Chiltern hills, a descent to the Thames around Maidenhead and the final stretch along the river into London. I have equipped myself with a rucksack, boots, walking sandals, a fold-up hat, a compact version of the *Complete Works* and more maps than I have previously owned in my entire life. Having never been one of nature's ramblers, I'm uneasily comfortable with this new uniform. As we prepare to set out, though it's far from a short walk across the Hindu Kush, and may lack some of the macho glamour of Ewan McGregor with 1000cc between his legs (OK, all of it), it still feels like an adventurous jaunt.

Before we leave the church, an elderly volunteer guide approaches us and offers to show us around. Bumptious with independence, we decline, but he's as deaf as a post, so starts helping anyway. He immediately points us towards a killer fact. In the desert of facts relating to Shakespeare, the two principal oases are the birth register and the death register in this church. Both scrawled messages, declaring first his screaming into the world and later his whispering out, they are holy objects in Bardology. Our guide points out how the formula for the first shows how Shakespeare was born into a recently Catholic country, and the second shows he passed away in a Protestant land. The central division that snaked through his life expressed at arrival and departure. Quentin says an ominous 'Aha!' and looks mysterious.

It's a holy and pure, damp-in-the-air, clean, green morning outside the church. We bumble around for a second, fussing with maps, waiting for one of us to say something propitious. None of us do, so we simply set off, away down a lane and towards the Avon. Quentin immediately marks my card, in a tone more Holmes to Watson than Quixote to Panza: 'I've been doing some research, Dominic, and think I have cracked the heart of the issue. However, this is going to be a long week, and I don't want to shoot my wad too early. So I'm going to hold on to my theory until Thursday afternoon.'

We cross the bridge over the Avon and plunge down into the riverside walk, a high canopy of green patchworking the sunlight over our heads, the wild garlic and cow parsley smells of England filling our nostrils. The distance from the town to Arcadia is a very short one. Only twenty minutes after his last statement, Quentin returns to the fray: 'It's an important theory, and it may well influence our thinking for the whole week. I think it might be necessary to bring it out into the open earlier than originally planned. I shall tell you after lunch today.' We pass a weir a half a mile outside Stratford and strike out away from the river, finding an old green lane running alongside a thick hedge. One of our group of four, an actor working in Stratford, leaves us to return to rehearsals. Quentin gives in: 'Do you want to hear my theory, then?' We assent and Quentin begins monologuing. Having been variously in his life a historian, a publisher, a farmer, a journalist, a broadcaster and a whimsical philosopher, Quentin has an enormous and eccentric field of reference, together with a huge wit. Listening to him monologuing is one of the great pleasures of my life, so he is given free rein.

His theory on Shakespeare is influenced by the Ted Hughes book *Shakespeare and the Goddess of Complete Being*. It centres round the bi-polar contrast between two Eurasian myths, fully expressed in 'Venus and Adonis' and 'The Rape of Lucrece'. Hughes' theory expanded by Quentin is that, at a certain point in Shakespeare's playwriting life, he became consumed by these myths and spent the rest of his life trying to resolve the polarity between the two. The first myth, expressed in 'Venus and Adonis', is of the female dominant, the mother goddess swamping the man and letting him pass through her, the man himself dying in the winter, a new son being born in the spring. The goddess is the eternal and the constant, the man is passing through. The second myth, expressed in 'The Rape of Lucrece', is of the male dominant, the aggressor, forcefully scattering his sexuality wherever and however he may, and in the process killing the goddess. Historically, this is allied to the spirit of patriarchy destroying the dangerous powers and sexuality of the female. Quite a lot to chew on for so early in the journey.

Resistant to theory as I am, and being an argumentative bugger, I store up reasons to disagree as the monologue continues and elaborates. But it is striking as a model for Shakespeare's life. 'Venus and Adonis' serves as an abstract for the young man and Anne Hathaway. She is a powerful mother earth icon. An older, no doubt stronger, woman, teaching her junior first to begin and later to relish sexual acts; nurturing children, feeding them from her own breasts since they had no money for a wetnurse, two at a time with the twins; remaining forever in rural Stratford, surrounded by fruit and fertility; her constancy to her husband both repulsive, because it enclosed and entrapped, and beautiful, because it supported and liberated. 'The Rape of Lucrece' also serves as an abstract for the adventures of the liberated Shakespeare, charging away from his home and his base, getting into scraps, glamorized by the world, falling into love and lust with men and women, scattering himself hither and thither. This was another great tension from his life, the home and the away, the domestic and the wild, the bourgeois gent and the libertine, Stratford and London. Maintaining a balance between the two was his lifelong work. The connecting tissue is what we have chosen to walk along.

Though not that successfully at the moment. As chief navigator I have planned a cunning cross-country route, along what I think will be natural walks, bouncing in a carefree A. E. Housman manner from country village to country village. In fact we seem to be spending an unnatural amount of time trudging through ploughed fields and forcing our way through hedges. Three disasters happen in close succession. First we are confronted by a seemingly unfordable stream. Quentin strides through it carelessly. I pick my way across gingerly. Mark elaborately removes socks and shoes, before tip-toeing across barefoot. He then changes to a new pair of shoes. Soon after we are confronted by a thick bush, which requires a good deal of hacking through and unpicking from briar and thorn. Mark goes through another shoe ritual. He is declared the Imelda Marcos of country ramblers. It is only when we are stopped by the third obstacle that the true culprit is discovered, me. Standing in a farm yard and looking along a brambled-over sewage canal, I insist that that is our route. A farmer emerges and, having looked at our map, informs us that we are trying to walk along a parish boundary. We have in fact been walking along parish boundaries all morning. My pathfinding skills have been humbled. It takes a great effort of will to retain control of the maps. I plan a new route through more hedges.

Quentin moves on from Eurasian myths, ground on which he is surprisingly secure, to ground on which he is more naturally secure – history. 'Venus and Adonis' describes the destruction of the god, and 'The Rape of Lucrece' that of the goddess. Hughes and Quentin claim the first is the founding myth of Catholicism, the second of Puritanism. And this elides invisibly into the Protestant and Catholic divide which kept Europe jangly for several centuries. From the moment Luther sat constipated on his toilet and dreamed up a more direct relationship with God through to the moment when Europe chose to chuck in the towel on all gods – plain, frilly or otherwise – the diaphragm of the whole continent was stretched tight in the war for hearts and souls between the grumpy northern Prods and the louche southern Papists. And at the nexus of this crisis was Shakespeare himself, a covert Catholic in a repressively Protestant world. Quentin's thesis is that this and other discordant notes fouled the music in Shakespeare's head, and his life's work was to resolve them into some form of harmony. His plays are rites within which he rehearses these conflicts and finds partial solutions. Although Quentin has hurried his way into presenting his theory – we still haven't had lunch on the first day – it's an impressive beginning. His first-round flurry of punches has landed several telling blows.

We arrive at an absurdly pretty village, a Hollywood version of the ideal England. It has even gone so far as to put a maypole in the middle. It has no pub, but does have a post office, which looks like a set from a 1950s children's film – shelves full of antique sweets in tall glass jars. We settle down to ginger beer and sandwiches like a group of dubious elders still living out their Enid Blyton fantasies. We brag a little to the post mistress about how far we're going and what a tough morning we've had of it. 'How far is Stratford actually?' we ask with a butch nonchalance, as if making light of a jog up and down Kilimanjaro. 'Oh, about two miles,' she tells us with a giggle, and we splutter out our Eccles cakes. She laughs even louder at us. She is far from impressed.

The afternoon is a modest triumph on the directional front, as I manage to secure a continuity of decent paths. We open out into big and broad country, walking over the fertile earth of South Warwickshire, much of it now turned over to industrial farming. There are great expanses of field, untouched by hedge or fence, with great hectares of ripening wheat and barley lazing their way upwards in the sun. At one point we find ourselves in a field as wide as the eye can scan filled with elaborate bamboo wigwam constructions. The tendrils of young beans curl around their bases. Each construction is too delicate to be placed by machine, yet there are thousands stretching out to the horizon. Quentin's old farming instincts are brought alive, and his nostrils twitch with curiosity. 'Extraordinary. It would take an army to do this.' Sure enough, in the middle of a field we find three minibuses beside two Portaloos. A young man emerges from one, whom we try to engage in conversation, but to no avail. He speaks no English, but is able to get out the word Poland, and point to the brow of a distant hill where we can pick out about sixty of his co-workers. Our path away from the roads has detached us from modern England, and this sudden injection of modernity – migrant labour having the arse exploited off it by industry – seems a brutal anachronism.

This momentary mood of defeat, of prose in poetry, prompts a pessimistic conversation about the point of the walk. This seems a little early in the week for such existential purposelessness. Mark and Quentin keenly question whether Shakespeare would have walked to London anyway.

'Wouldn't he have ridden a horse?'

'No, he couldn't have afforded a horse. At the end of his life, when he was well off, he would have ridden a horse from staging post to post. But at the beginning he didn't have a bean.'

'Mmm, sounds suspiciously Dick Whittington for historical analysis. Wouldn't he have travelled with his theatre company in a coach of some sort?'

'Well, yes, there is a myth that he left Stratford with some players. Ran away with the circus, as it were. The Earl of Leicester's men lost an actor in a pub fight just before they reached Stratford. The idea is that Shakespeare filled in and travelled away with the troupe. But that's all a bit sweet and convenient for the truth. Anyway, wherever he went in his unknown years between 1584 and the early 1590s, whether it was teaching in a recusant house in Lancashire or fighting in the Netherlands or on a tour of Northern Italy or dressed up as Mickey Mouse at EuroDisney, wherever it was that he went, in order to change from being a glover's son with an overenthusiastic prick to being the greatest dramatist who ever lived, he must have come back to see his wife and young kids. Every now and then. He wasn't a monster.'

'But he wasn't mad. He wouldn't have walked.'

'Well, there wasn't a fucking train to travel on. Most probably he walked the drove roads, the old roads which brought cattle down from the West Country and Wales to London. There may have been some cart and coach traffic, and he may have been an early hitch-hiker, but the roads were notoriously rubbish, and in his youth he would have had to walk a fair amount of the way.'

'So, there is a point to this walk.'

'Yes, this is the land he would have crossed, this is the arch of the hills, these clustered buildings are the same villages, these church spires are the same church spires. There is a point.'

The argument is won, not by me, but by the landscape, which has taken a turn for the seriously picturesque. As we cross little hills, spurt through small woods, traverse gentle slopes, hidden valleys are suddenly revealed to us. All is human in scale, all intimate, all domestic. Each tree is the home of its own warm and gathered ecosystem; each stream has its own circle of friends along its banks; each sward seems alive with its own efficiently ordered insect society. The *Wind in the Willows* ethos of the English countryside risks being a twee archetype, but we are walking through that green warmth and magic. We crest a low hill and find ourselves in a discreet vale, where a cluster of wild willows surrounds a stagnant pond. We stop for a second and lie back. Mark reads from *Hamlet*, as Gertrude tells of the spot where Ophelia has drowned herself:

> There is a willow grows aslant a brook,
> That shows his hoar leaves in the glassy stream;
> There with fantastic garlands did she come
> Of crow-flowers, nettles, daisies, and long purples
> That liberal shepherds give a grosser name,
> But our cold maids do dead men's fingers call them:
> There, on the pendent boughs her coronet weeds
> Clambering to hang, an envious sliver broke;
> When down her weedy trophies and herself
> Fell in the weeping brook.

And I read Desdemona's song to Emilia before she is going to her certain death with Othello:

> The poor soul sat sighing by a sycamore tree,
> Sing all a green willow:
> Her hand on her bosom, her head on her knee,
> Sing willow, willow, willow:
> The fresh streams ran by her, and murmur'd her moans;
> Sing willow, willow, willow;
> Her salt tears fell from her, and soften'd the stones.

If a gang of Hell's Angels had stumbled across us at this moment with vacancies, we may well have failed the interview. But, lying on logs, under the shade of that wild willow, and feeling a current of memory running in the air between those words and that place, it wasn't hard to find a point for the walk.

We press on, passing a picture-perfect little town called Ilmington, nestled into a cleft of hills. There's a steep climb as we emerge from the town. Quentin announces that the only way to approach a steep hill is at your own pace, and there is no purpose in walking together. He and Mark swiftly disappear into the distance, leaving me lagging and puffing behind. This is patently unfair. Quentin is twenty years older than me, and Mark half a foot shorter. It must be the maps. They compound the insult by turning and shouting, 'Come on, Piggy' at me. We are now playing at *Lord of the Flies*, which is a worrying development. Piggy was thrown off a steep rock. It would be better to get back to Shakespeare. From the top of the hill, we descend towards an extremely grand house.

There is a sudden burst of wild flowers – sharp blues and delicate purples. This fills me with a spread of delight, but is the occasion for a brief treatise from Quentin on the decline in flora since Shakespeare's day. He sums up how rich and varied the colours and textures would have been, and how they have been dulled and made uniform by centuries of brutalizing agriculture. Our imaginations, spurred on by the few colours present, fill up with the wilder kaleidoscope of four centuries before. I remember the best sequence from the Eminem film, *Eight Mile*. Away from the aggressive braggadocio of the singing competitions, there is a passage where we watch him travelling around in the back of the bus. The collapsed businesses, burned-out shops, seedy clip joints – all the desperate detritus of late capitalism in downtown Detroit – parade past the window. He stares out on it, his face blank, and the view sinks into his eyes. In a neutral vein he writes images and instances down in his notebook. He is building up inside himself 'the great heap of images' that Ted Hughes identified within Shakespeare. It's the heap they draw on throughout their life to colour in the gaps in their imagination, and to manifest their understanding of the world. For Eminem, Detroit, for Shakespeare, Warwickshire and Oxfordshire, with all its teeming, elegant and delicate life. Flowers and sheep and willows and brooks are Shakespeare's sustenance.

We walk past the grand house, recently acquired by an American who made his fortune from selling knickers, and pass on through a cool and colonnaded wood towards our destination. We descend a hill towards a modestly beautiful Elizabethan farmhouse. This will be our first port of call. It belongs to an ex-press grandee, who has now taken up farming. He is an old friend of Quentin and has offered to put us up. It is walkers' heaven. After some fragrant tea, we are told of the facilities on hand. A steam bath. A sauna. A heated swimming pool. We practically faint with relief. We avail ourselves of all three. The swimming pool is a quick step to nirvana. It has long, low windows on each side looking out over the landscape, and a peaceful ganesh squatting at one end. It may be a long way from the rough-housing of Shakespeare's day, it may not be the ditch the boy poet collapsed into under the canopy of stars, but you have to take what's offered.

It's followed by some slugs of home-brewed mulberry gin, which slip down with an ease which begins to alarm our hosts. A gentle dinner full of chat of Shakespeare follows. At one point, we start to steer towards unnecessary controversy in a discussion of how anti-Semitic is *The Merchant of Venice*. I am in no mood for controversy, so I hijack the conversation with a long, confused and addling monologue about how Venice was the New York or the Los Angeles of Shakespeare's day, how it was a cultural and commercial epicentre, and how he clearly had a very ambivalent attitude towards it, portraying the Venetians as by and large ghastly and venal. I lose my thread somewhere in the middle of the argument but plough on regardless. I am determined not to return to anything sour after such an exquisite day. By the time I've finished, everyone is doing the washing-up.

Tuesday

A quietly formal garden falls away plateau by plateau from the manor house where we slept. We leave the next morning by the gate at the end, waved off by our hosts. There is a pleasantly Shakespearean feel to it, a night stopping off with a rich patron on the endless to and fro between Stratford and London, delighting the hosts with some theatre discussion and gossip, then steaming on. Each of us, despite the mulberry gin and the much wine, is big of lung and ready for the stride-out. Quentin, drawing on his walking experience, has insisted that we each have a boiled egg. 'A little packet of energy', he describes them as, sternly. Before us is a huge expanse of open and slowly rising hill. Our home for the night slowly dwindles as we keep pushing away from it; and we diminish for them from vivid humans saying loud farewells to ants scurrying around on distant horizons. I think of Donne's 'Valediction Forbidding Mourning' and its idea of lovers stretched apart by separation but held together by the thread between them, with its prolonged conceit of a compass. A mathematical instrument should be poetically unpromising, but Donne extracts beauty from it:

> Our two souls therefore, which are one,
>   Though I must go, endure not yet
> A breach, but an expansion,
>   Like gold to aery thinness beat.
>
> If they be two, they are two so
>   As stiff twin compasses are two;
> Thy soul, the fix'd foot, makes no show
>   To move, but doth, if th' other do.

And though it in the centre sit,
   Yet, when the other far doth roam,
It leans, and hearkens after it,
   And grows erect, as that comes home.

Such wilt thou be to me, who must,
   Like th' other foot, obliquely run;
Thy firmness makes my circle just,
   And makes me end where I begun.

Walking away from the house up a long hill, you feel the sense of God's compass slowly widening as you inch away. And I think of all the farewells in Shakespeare's plays: Romeo and Juliet's sweet sorrow; Antony and Cleopatra's delight in the theatricality of their arrivals and their departures; Othello and Desdemona's fear at parting, and delight at rediscovering, before it all goes tits-up. A farewell was something then, it was a slow human dwindling as eyes watched and hands waved. It had an emotional juice. An arrival was even better. A steady march towards each other from a distance, absence and silence and loneliness all falling away, as separation shrank between people. What do we do now? Jump in a car and vroom away. Nor in the age of the mobile and the great virtual conversation in the ether are we ever properly absent any more.

We hit the horizon, and after an animated discussion of what constitutes a reservoir and where we should cross a road, we top the rise and look out over a huge basin of earth, full of modest bumps and gentle rises. We plunge down. Mark, who has not satisfactorily resolved his shoe issues – we suggest high heels at one point – is beginning to grimace and limp. He decides the best way to settle his problems is to charge in short bursts then wait for us, rather than match our steady but grinding rhythm. We have a brief stretch of road. It feels alienating after all the switch and scratch of the country up to this point. Sports cars peopled by flash chaps, looking like bit-parts in detective series, whizz past, leaving us feeling subtly foolish and subtly proud.

The alienation between road and path, between walker and car, brings Quentin back to his Ted Hughes theories and beyond them to his own gentle obsession, separation and attachment. These were the central words for an early twentieth-century psychoanalyst, John Bowlby, and for Quentin they constitute the central tension within humanity. From the moment we pop our heads out into the world we all need our attachments, the first most powerful one being our mother's breast. Much of the rest of our lives is a search to find other attachments to replace that. Yet we need to separate from our mother, as from many other ties that bind, if we are not to become dependent or weak or imprisoned. For Quentin, as for Bowlby, life is a constant search for the right balance of separation and attachment, a prolonged attempt to keep the two in proper harmony. As he puts it, 'Shakespeare knew it all 400 years before Bowlby told us: once the umbilicus is cut we need new cords of secure attachment to anchor us, new ties to make us confident and secure – Mum cuddles me, I cuddle her, we cuddle; cuddlo, cuddlet, cuddlemus – until the time comes to fly off on our own into a new life of renewed cuddles with another.' This is his summary of the pleasures of attachment. In counterpoint he presents the anxieties of separation: 'Parturition is a dangerous game to play – a parent living in a hall of cracked mirrors – disfiguring her, disfiguring me, disfiguring us. It splits us from our growing points, distorts our senses. It leaves us unfeeling, unknowing and uncaring.' It is Quentin's contention, and, he claims, Ted Hughes', that these are the orienting poles of all the plays from *As You Like It* on, and that Shakespeare's mission in life was to bring separation and attachment into sweet harmony with each other.

We are off the separating road by the time this theory comes to an end, and enjoying earth under foot again. Back in the scenic graces of South Warwickshire. Our journey is defined on a map, but is dictated in our green three-dimensional reality by country spires. Over low hills, or through breaks in the earth or gaps in the woods, church spires appear. These thin stone elegant fingers, pointing up to god, orient us on our way. They also lock us back into history. We are in concert with every trudger who has ever used them to make sense of the landscape. Though Mark's foot is now worse, the landscape is a buoyant electrifier of mood.

Parting and homecoming, separation and attachment, walking the line between the two. Walking is a supportive platform for slow conversations. The hypnotic rhythm of the walk dictates the pace of the conversation, the breath on the foot becoming the breath on the word. When you're walking in file, discussions tend towards alternate monologues. The person in front or middle or at the back throws a stream of connected thoughts – an argument, some illustrations, some random observations – out into the air, and the other two listen as the country rolls past. Listening is liberated by the lack of necessity to respond. We cannot see each other's faces, so there is no requirement for the nod of understanding or the knitted brow of pretend concentration or the crinkled forehead of surprise. The words drift in and are filtered for truth or use. Responses can be held for moments, hours or days. We find ourselves saying, 'As you were saying four fields ago . . .' or 'I want to pick up a point from Monday afternoon . . .' It's a mobile Socratic dialogue, dredging up a little insight, securing some, losing it again.

We set to in a gentle way on Quentin's and Bowlby's attachment and separation theorem. It's a metaphor for any number of scenarios. In a psycho-geographical sense, its truth is explicit in the topographical journey we are making. It's trite to point out how the countryside is a warmer and more nurturing environment than the city, but it's also true. The land we have been moving through attaches you to nature, links you into an original form of the self; the great urban metropolis we are moving towards separates you, detaching the spirit from its antique state. If this is true now, how much more would it have been true in Shakespeare's day. The Stratford he came from was a minor country town, where everyone would have known each other. They practically shared a bed. Beyond the town's edge was fertile ground feeding human and animal. Further than that, within the town's cosmology, the great beyond was filled with spritely goblins, air fleets of fairies and woods concealing witches summoning darkness out of light. This was the reality Shakespeare came from, a physical world of dirt in the fingernails, milk on the lips and stillborn sheep left in the fields for pigs to munch on; and an imaginary world, rich with primitive superstitions, as real as the carrots they dug up.

He walked, hitched and later rode away from that place of clammy actuality towards a great metropolis. London was still in its infancy but it was already a couple of centuries distant from Stratford. Whitehall palace loomed large on the eyeline before the traveller descended into the great mess of the city. Grand mansion houses lined the banks of the Thames; the Tower sent out its grim messages of repression; churches and cathedrals stabbed at the air; within the narrow streets houses climbed over each other as if they were playing Twister, and down at the docks ships jostled for space, their masts and rigging filling the sky like a great spider's web. And the cargo those ships brought in delivered a world of terror and surprise to London – silks, spices and exotic wonders like the potato.

Yet greater and stranger were the human cargoes. For the Stratford boy, a town teeming with Italian peacocks, Dutch gloomyboots and French sophisticates (to indulge in a little gentle Shakespearean stereotyping) would have seemed like the Tower of Babel. To hear the explosions of other languages pouring out of inns and courts and bedrooms would have scattered the linguistic bearings of a boy who grew up listening to Warwickshire uncles moaning about the barley crop. Beyond the Europeans were people from far further shores to extend the imaginative possibilities of creation. Ralegh had brought back a Native American from one of his speculative outings, who became the wonder of London and Elizabeth's court. African slaves and the very occasional freed man were a significant part of the town's population. For Will, on entering London, a world rich in his imagination suddenly became richer in fact. It's no surprise his early plays are so powerfully driven by a continuous sense of wonder, and so frequently illuminated by a joy at what the world has to offer. In a late play, the child Miranda explodes with:

> O, wonder!
> How many goodly creatures are there here!
> How beauteous mankind is! O brave new world,
> That has such people in't!

and her father Prospero replies ruefully with ' 'Tis new to thee'. He remembers the enchantment of youth and understands the price of it.

The price of wonder was detachment. An Irish writer, Billy Roche, whom I worked with at the Bush, said of his own many trips to London, 'You come to London the first time and you want to go back. You're sick for home. The next time you feel uneasy. The next time you feel better. Then one time you find yourself walking down a London street and you feel relaxed, you feel that you belong. And the moment that happens, something inside you flies away.' All his life Shakespeare journeyed between attachment and separation on his lonely treks and trudges between Stratford and London.

By the time we have meandered our way through this topic, we have risen to a point above a small and ancient village called Long Compton, a stopping-off point for Shakespeare on his route. The view is handsome. Walking into it is like stepping into a Constable painting. Before we get to Long Compton there are a couple of hundred acres of jungly patch to get through. It's hard to read this from a distance. Once we get close, it becomes clear it is the world's biggest clump of broad bean plants. Rising to about eight or nine feet in height, they cover the whole of a plain. We skirt round the edges for a while, then find a path through the middle. We feel like Dr Who penetrating some infinite mass of vegetation. There's the slightest fear that if you cast aspersions on the pulse genus, there might be a stirring in the branches, a crunching underfoot, and the mother bean herself would loom up and suck us into her greenness. After a mile of consistent broad beanery, we are feeling all too attached, and urgently in need of separation.

We escape and find ourselves in a walled meadow approaching the church of Long Compton. It's a hot day. In front of the church, a classic oak spreads itself generously. Beneath its shade, fifteen or twenty sheep sit in placid calm. It's a little vision of eternity – sun, church, oak, shade, sheep – to stumble across. It prints itself on my inner eye. We say nothing, we don't stop, it's just one of those mild and mellow epiphanies which the English country throws up as you pass through. Modest, simple, perfect.

We stop at a farm shop which had been recommended. There are other people here. Their presence reminds us of their absence over the last few hours. We become giggly and over-excited. We start relating what we're doing to anyone and everyone. We start flirting unaccountably with the rather portly middle-aged woman behind the counter. We look slightly crazed. After five hours' walking we seem to have all the manic desire for company and repressed sexual desire of a group of escaped convicts. Once we have bought our authentic lemonade and our game pies, the shop is pleased to see the back of us.

If we made such a fuss over a farm shop, how would Shakespeare have behaved when he arrived in Oxford or London? The contrast after sustained periods of loneliness must have been overwhelming. Yet the loneliness served its purpose. It was there for stockpiling his great heap of images as he moved along in the iambic rhythm, the rhythm of a foot's tread or a horse's slow clomp. Then the cities were there for unloading them. Mark had recently directed *The Taming of the Shrew* and remembered the figure of the father returning to the city or arriving from another town. It's a trope which appears in many plays. The passage from country to town is one we hardly observe these days. But the Elizabethans would have enjoyed a massively expanded sense of personal space as they wandered through open land. And an equal sense of claustrophobia when they squeezed themselves into the contracted bustles of life that were the towns of the day.

We decide to break apart for a forced march up a heavy hill. Quentin and Mark disappear into the distance, throwing back the occasional cry of 'Hurry up, Piggy', as I break into a sweat. The pack on my back is laden with the extra weight of a pair of smart walking boots which I bought the week before. So far, I have stuck it out in sandals, through small bursts of rain, and ploughed fields. The footwear has grown with mud and ears of corn and barley, as have the bottoms of my trousers. I'm starting to look like an eccentric entry in a 'spirit of the country' fancy dress competition. The walking is hard, heavy step after heavy step up a steep incline. Thighs are starting to stiffen, and stabbing pains punch into the feet.

We reconvene at the top of the hill and look for the Rollright Stones, our lunchtime destination. We find them behind a hedge. We are a little underwhelmed. They are a sort of low-key Stonehenge, an almost perfect circle of three-foot-high, weather-bashed and -beaten, prehistoric stones. The diameter of the circle is about a hundred feet – exactly the same as the Globe, by a strange coincidence. A desultory girl in a shed sells us tickets. We walk in and settle on the far side of the stones for a quick picnic, followed by a quicker collapse. For Quentin into sleep, and some of his deep, resonant snoring; for myself into a blissfully calm contemplation of the tree over my head, and the light scattering through it; and for Mark observation of the world around him. A deep calm descends, a profoundly pleasant nothingness. Some buried stillness which permeates the place settles into us.

We resurface from our various reveries to see that a small crowd of sightseers have gathered. They are wandering around with makeshift divining rods, wooden cylinders with lengths of thick wire suspended from them. Everyone is heading off in the wrong direction, walking round the circle, around the stones, or at funny angles. Quentin points out that the only successful way to use them is to walk right across the diameter, passing over the various concentric circles which work their magic beneath the ground. Something of a sceptic, I purloin some rods and set out across the middle. At regular intervals, every three paces, the wire rod twangs violently in one direction then another. Gratified, I cross back, and they twang with perfect symmetry in the opposite direction. Brought up near Glastonbury, and over-burdened with ley-line, hippy-dippy mythology as I had been, I had always successfully rejected the idea of earth forces. The crude instruments in my hand contradict me. Quentin gives me a long 'There are more things in heaven and earth than are dreamt of in your philosophy' look, and we move on.

The physical difficulties have travelled up the body and are now establishing themselves largely in the genital area. Mark announces that his thighs seem to think that his scrotum is a cactus. There seems to be an unsavoury war waging between stiff thighs and scraped gonads. On top of fucked feet. Various discussions ensue about the right sort of underwear to use on a long walk such as this. This subject is attacked with the same rigour we have brought to anything else. The conclusion is uncertain, but definite in that Mark got it wrong. We struggle on, but as we continue, our legs slowly get further and further apart. We are turning from humans into ducks.

Quentin starts in again. He states that three layers of meaning can be applied to interpreting Shakespeare's work. One is mythical, the Eurasian earth goddess stuff, as laid out in 'Venus and Adonis' and 'The Rape of Lucrece'. The second is national/cultural, which revolves around the Catholic/Protestant divide. And the third is psycho-biographical, his work reflecting his life and the growth of his soul within him.

We spin a few examples of psycho-biographical readings of the works into the air. From *A Midsummer Night's Dream*, there is Egeus' violent, possessive love for his daughter and the ongoing battle over correct parenting between Oberon and Titania. If Shakespeare wrote this in the late 1590s, as is supposed, his elder daughter, Judith, would have been just developing a sexual appetite. Little wonder that he expresses with such ferocity the feelings of a father terrified by the onset of freedom. He doesn't condone such patriarchal jealousy, but he understands it and lets it come out into the open. Similarly, if he was an infrequent but steady returner to Stratford, it's not hard to imagine what skirmishes there would have been between him and his wife over their children's proper education. Just as between Oberon and Titania, so Will the London celebrity would return to find proud Anne the matriarch running the ever-growing country home. Uncertain of his status, would he stride in with decisions about which tapestries to hang, what time the children should go to bed and who were suitable friends? Would Anne grit her teeth and wait for him to go or boil up and tell him to bog off, and what right did he have when he was away all the time being a smartypants in London? Hot or cold, before long there would be war in the home.

I push the psycho-biographical theme as hard as I can. My legs are turning into a vicious blend of cement and raw nerve endings. A good ranty monologue is one of the few ways to distract myself. In the absence of beer. The central misunderstanding with Shakespeare has been in the relationship between Stratford and London. Historically, academics have come down on one side or the other. The Victorians wanted him to be the good, upright family man. For them he was all Stratford, a sound and sober country gent, amassing a fortune, tending to his wife and children, visiting the Anglican church and writing moral fables. His stays in London were a necessary distraction from his solid bourgeois life. Even when he was there he managed to keep his rectitude while surrounded by sin and temptation.

The twentieth century read him in a counter direction. They flung every scrap of tortured artist iconography at him they could pluck out of the ether. He was a feverishly paranoid Catholic in a repressive Protestant world; a wild sexual libertine, rampaging through the orifices of men and women with an uncontrollable sexual energy; an early Marxist, pitilessly observing the class movements around him and savagely indicting the world he lived in; and a heartless anarch, dispassionately watching friends and family die, break hearts and grieve, and recording their emotions with a scientific detachment. For them, he loathed Stratford and all its values, as he loathed his family life and the incarceration it represented. This is the polarity between the different readings. Academics, critics and all other decisive whatnots tend to position themselves at one end or the other.

A third reading is the most difficult to encompass, but the easiest to prove. This is that he was all of those things. He was as everything as he possibly could be. He was Stratford and London. He was bank manager and robber. People believe that because he spent a lot of time away from Stratford that means that he did not care for his family. Those who pursue that theory do not understand how artists work. An artist needs an emotional life, needs a source of genuine emotional resource. They need a well from which to get their water. However, more often than not, they need it over there. They find it impossible to live within it.

It is impossible to read Shakespeare and not believe that he loved, protected and cared for his family with a concrete passion. The large events in his family's life – the death of his son, the loss of his father, the loss of his brothers, the appearance of his grandchildren – all occasioned profound red shifts within his work. They spun him off into emotional areas whose surprising new landscapes he translated into his plays. It is equally impossible to trace the pattern within the scattered fragments of fact we know about him and not credit his attachment to Stratford. He continued to buy new homes there, acquire large tracts of land around the town and do business with other Stratfordians right through his life. Biographers have tradition-ally got over-excited about whether he loved the Earl of Southampton or not; how great was his connection to the Earl of Essex; his fallings in and out with Christopher Marlowe, Will Kemp and Richard Burbage. They practise a sort of celebrity 'Who Had Who' out of the pages of *Heat* magazine. But they miss the real story. The emotional story of his life was based in his home and his family. It was always his security, the strong part of himself. He gave most of his time away – his art required it – but not most of his heart.

However, this is not to say that any of the contraries aren't true. He did go to London; he did enjoy the freedom; he did fuck about; he could be dispassionate; he did like hanging out with the wealthy and the powerful. Vicious, ugly, treacherous thoughts flitted through his head with the same frequency as kinder ones. He spent large tracts of time away from home. He gave most of his life to the theatre in London – acting, producing, managing, writing; he toured the country with shows; he languished in large country piles.

The soaring passions that drive the sonnets are not Stratford passions. The burgeoning love for the beautiful youth traces the pattern of his separation from Stratford. He is intoxicated by the company of elegant young earls, giddy with walking through magnificent country seats. He looks upwards in these residences and sees Italianate orgies of vibrant colour in ceiling frescos and looks down to see gracefully confected young men and women gliding through their hallowed habitat. He falls in love with both, and the sonnets are a record of that infatuation. Written early in his career, the flight and swoop of the sonnets bears witness to the joy of floating on the love of the soul for the first time. He is away from home and in the full onrush of first eye-widening love. His passion for the dark lady is a record of first lust, of an ungovernable desire to fuck over and over and over again. And then again. The sonnets are a testament to the joys of love and lust and the price to be paid for it. London passions fund them. They also embellish the plays.

We all, in our own lives, know the possession and the ferocity of those feelings. We also know that they are wild forest fires, sitting on the great hills thrown up by our more profound emotional landscape, the tectonic one produced by fathers, mothers, brothers, sisters, wives, sons, daughters and grandchildren. The vivacity and rococo decoration of Shakespeare's plays comes from his London passions. The under-structure comes from the seismic movements of heart that only family, and only Stratford, could bring.

Mark challenges these thoughts energetically and with a simple but pertinent observation. He says what I am describing is as much my father's life as it is Shakespeare's. There is little argument with this. My father did put us on a farm in Somerset in my infancy. He spent much of his own time away putting on plays in London and working in television in Bristol. We did see him infrequently and yet we never doubted how profoundly we mattered to him. It is also to a certain extent my own life. Within a family, yet keeping something private and elsewhere. Within my work, yet drawing on my understanding of family as an emotional resource. As with everyone else, I have made a Shakespeare in my own image. I think of the ending of Anthony Burgess' book about Shakespeare with its poetic coda:

We need not repine at the lack of a satisfactory Shakespeare portrait. To see his face we need only look in a mirror. He is ourselves, ordinary suffering humanity, fired by moderate ambitions, concerned with money, the victim of desire, all too mortal. To his back, like a hump, was strapped a miraculous but somehow irrelevant talent. It is a talent which, more than any that the world has seen, reconciles us to being human beings, unsatisfactory hybrids, not good enough for gods and not good enough for animals. We are all Will. Shakespeare is the name of one of our redeemers.

One of the capacities that distinguished him most from all of us was that, when he imagined others, he gave them their own imaginations. When we imagine others, even when we try to imagine Shakespeare himself, we give them our own.

These thoughts have washed to and fro for a couple of hours as we have walked along a continuous green lane. A rutted path with walls and a ceiling of interlocked trees and shrubs. It is a path as old as the argument. By the time we come to the end of the line and the talk, Mark is in severe trouble and I am little better. He is walking like a cowboy who's been in the saddle for a decade. He considers giving up and calling a taxi. We come out of the green lane and head along a large road. Our mood dips the moment we hit tarmac. The easy connectedness of earth, thought, talk, air and history crumbles the moment we start dodging juggernauts. A long, low, black cloud is lowering in towards us at the same time. The dipped mood creates a little temper, as we try and settle on the right route. There is much staring at the map, walking in one direction, then walking back. Every time we do this Mark tinges the air purple with muted expletives.

Eventually we find the forest we are looking for, full of high some-thing or others, and good clear air within it. A small brook runs through the middle. Another absurdly perfect rendition of an English fantasy. Quentin and I revive, but Mark is still troubled. We were talking earlier about *A Midsummer Night's Dream* and fairies, and Mark had told us of the life in shtetls near forests in Eastern Europe, where his ancestors lived. He had offered it up as an equivalent lifestyle to the hobgoblin-fearing village dwellers of Shakespeare's time. For both societies, the supernatural became a way of giving names to fears and a means of articulating the darkness. Now we are in the depths of a light-denying wood, he returns to atavistic fears of fantasy dybbuks, and of all-too-real raiding Cossacks. Quentin and I are insufficiently sympathetic and start pretending to see Cossacks behind every tree trunk.

To reroute us back to Shakespeare, Mark gets out the *Complete Works* and starts belting out some sonnets. This is hard enough at the best of times, but yet harder when nettles and brambles pull you back. But, however much we are hobbled and cobbled, and whatever ancestral fears assault us as we walk through a wood beside dancing water, the sonnets pull our spirits up and out again. Three raggedy nitwits stumbling through a forest, shouting with a lung of joy,

> As an unperfect actor on the stage,
> Who with his fear is put besides his part . . .

and

> When in disgrace with fortune and men's eyes
> I all alone beweep my outcast state . . .

and

> Tir'd with all these, for restful death I cry
> As to behold desert a beggar born . . .

and

> Shall I compare thee to a summer's day?
> Thou art more lovely and more temperate

and

> When to the sessions of sweet silent thought
> I summon up remembrance of things past . . .

Somehow every single sonnet misread as we stumble through the fresh-scented gloom gives us a bounce. Shakespeare's great love affair with language is our companion on the march.

Its medicinal effect does wonders for all but Mark's feet. Once out of the forest, he storms ahead, believing that running will get him there faster and lessen the pain. With his bow-legged, fast-footed gait he looks an increasingly odd figure as he disappears into the distance. We catch up with him at a village close to our eventual destination. Sadly, we get rather confused here and seem to walk around a church and large graveyard about five times. Quentin is quite blithe, remarking with interest on a rare breed of cattle each time we pass them. I am fairly bonny since the sonnets are still buoying me up. Mark is neither blithe nor bonny. He keeps thinking the town we are approaching, Charlbury, is round the next corner. When he finally crests yet another hill, and sees before him yet another huge field with no sign of town in it, he finally flips. We are a field behind him, but can hear his cries: 'Where the fuck are we? What the fuck are we doing? When are we going to get out of this fucking place?' We read between the lines of his companionable banter that Mark is not very attached to the countryside and is feeling somewhat separated from his North London habitat.

We are saved by a sweet young American girl who rides up on a pony, blonde hair flying behind her. She points us to Charlbury, and soon we are sprinting down a slope and across a stream towards it. Quentin has put one thought in our heads – pint – for the last couple of hours, and the possibility of that spurs us on. Mark gets further directions from a bevy of young girls standing provocatively outside their amateur dramatic shed, looking out for whatever trouble life may be so kind as to bring them. Soon he is sitting in a pub, nursing a pint, insane from the consistency of pain, most of his habitual gaiety snuffed out of him. Quentin and I nurse two pints each. We are following Quentin's maxim of one for thirst, which disappears in a matter of seconds, and one for taste, over which we take time.

Wednesday

We wake slowly, stiff limbs stirring unhappily into life. Quentin, believing we are alone, goes downstairs stark bollock naked to make himself some tea. He is confronted in a large stone-floored kitchen by a Rabelaisian figure of a woman. They gasp at each other, and Quentin scuttles back upstairs. Our absent hosts have sent along their daily woman to make sure we have everything we need. When he returns, she doesn't bat an eye. She kindly shows us how to get a breakfast, then fills us with gloom with some classic English countryside fatalism. Everything in her universe is tending to the bad: the weather won't hold, there'll be storms all day, we'll never make it to Oxford that night, there'll be flash floods, none of our suggested routes are the right ones, the police will arrest us for trespassing, our limbs will fall off. She says all this with a glad heart, and with a sure conviction that small clouds full of failure follow everyone around and rain disappointment on their heads.

This is the psychological soil which Shakespeare emerged from, a vigorous cast-iron pessimism. Quentin knows it well, having farmed much of his life, and I grew up with it, a daily oral gazette of mishap, disease and accident. For Mark it's a surprise. It's the natural mindset of those who work the earth. Each morning they rise and look at the sky, and deduce whether it means a lot of work, a ridiculous amount of work or so much work they die. It's not a melancholy, since that smacks of sophistication and the town. It's more a hard, practical, definite sense that all will go wrong. It's the counterpoint to Will's capacity for joy and makes that joy all the more remarkable. It is often drawn from the weather. Academics write of the poet's pathetic fallacy, the objective correlative, which exemplifies his character's moods in the elements and the changing sky. I see a farmer's eye.

We are to walk Mark to the station, or rather hobble him there. His legs are now as far apart as a pregnant dairy cow's. His feet are similarly wrecked and look weirdly misshapen. He winces on every step. We have time for one last squabble before he goes. Partly to forestall the return of the Ted Hughes theorem, which I have enjoyed but feel has had its time, and partly to have a day free from the intellectual, I decide to put the boot into scholarly assessments early. The world is too full, I assert, of over-analytical nincompoops hell-bent on stuffing weird intentions into the plays. Intentions which would never have occurred to the author in a million years. The bird is now so stuffed with this nonsense it is almost impossible to taste the meat any more, so overpowering is the sage and onion and forcemeat within. Shakespeare was not a self-conscious or a deliberate artist. He was like any of the playwrights I have known over the years – an instinctive, impulsive, creative animal.

He took situations from other plays, from books, from life, from his imagination and worked them into a new and wilder life. He never sat down and said, '*Today I shall be discussing contemporary politics and interweaving that with themes of loss and redemption. And all the while, in a formal sense, I shall be extending the possibilities of the neo-classical model by breaking it up with a little English realism.*' He not only did not have that language, he did not have the capacity for thinking in that way. He wrote blind, stealing merrily from what-ever his magpie mind picked up in books, and drawing from within himself. Particularly in England, we have a terrible problem with instinctual genius. Our country and our culture is and always has been run by a highly educated elite (not necessarily a bad thing), and we have always found it hard to credit the fact that education and genius are separate things. So we try to ascribe to a natural gift the same deliberate plodding the rest of us are saddled with.

Noel Coward wrote *Hayfever*, one of the great comic masterpieces of the early twentieth century, in a weekend. There was no time for thought or deliberation. It just bubbled up. David Storey wrote *Home* and *The Contractor*, two of the greatest Chekhovian masterpieces of the late twentieth century, in two days each. Chekhov himself wrote his plays in little more than a fortnight. In ten years of working with over fifty playwrights, I have never met a single good one who knew what they were setting out to achieve when they began to write a play. They take a story or an image or an emotional sense and let it rip. Shakespeare was of that ilk. But he has been lost as a writer of plays to the academics, who have transformed him into someone strangely like themselves. We steal Shakespeare from Shakespeare by disabling him with our own lack of freedom and self-consciousness. When he wrote the plays, he wrote blind.

Mark counters hard with the Harold Bloom argument about Shakespeare's greatest achievement being one of creative 'reading', how he took work from the canon of literature and reinterpreted it for a new world, and in the process created a whole new consciousness. This idea is picked up by Jonathan Bate in recent years, who brilliantly writes of how much of Shakespeare's work is a response to the work of Christopher Marlowe. Yet, however persuasive this theory may be, and it's impossible to deny the degree to which Shakespeare begged, stole and borrowed from other sources, it still seems an extremely depressing example of people trying to cut down a giant to their own size. The very word 'reading' seems unfortunately reductive for a man who imagined, understood and expressed with such free range. Mark's clinching example for the proof of self-consciousness is a moment in *Titus Andronicus* which draws on Ovid extensively and at one point most graphically refers to its own source. Lavinia, who has been raped and had her hands and tongue cut off, is keen to communicate her sufferings to Titus:

(*Lavinia turns over with her stumps the books which Lucius has let fall.*)
TITUS How now, Lavinia! Marcus, what means this?
  Some book there is that she desires to see.
  Which is it, girl, of these? – Open them, boy . . .
  . . . Lucius, what book is that she tosseth so?
BOY Grandsire, 'tis Ovid's Metamophoses;
  My mother gave it me.
MARCUS   For love of her that's gone,
  Perhaps she culled it from among the rest.
TITUS Soft! So busily she turns the leaves! Help her.

What would she find? Lavinia, shall I read?
This is the tragic tale of Philomel
And treats of Tereus' treason and his rape;
And rape I fear was the root of her annoy.
MARCUS See, brother, see! Note how she quotes the leaves.

This is excellent proof of Mark's argument, since there is little doubt it is a deliberate piece of referencing to a canonical work. But it's not an arch bit of post-modern intellectual self-satisfaction. It has all the earnest clumsiness of a grammar-school boy, in the early stages of his career, before he had learned to bury his education within him. 'Look at what I've read! Aren't I clever?' It also serves a purpose as a bit of detective work, using the book not in an ornate literary way, but as a means of solving a mystery. It is also the most penetratingly anti-intellectual image. A beautiful gilded book which a damaged girl with stumps for arms tries painfully to turn the pages of; sweetly confected Latin phrases which a girl with no tongue tries frantically to speak. It is the most perverse piece of quotation.

Towards the end of this argument, which descends into a 'That's not what I mean', 'You're contradicting yourself', 'Of course I'm contradicting myself, Shakespeare contradicted himself all the time, why can't I?' sort of argument, Quentin suddenly thunders out in a huge deep voice:

> Do I contradict myself?
> Very well then I contradict myself
> (I am large, I contain multitudes)

We are taken aback by this and ask him to repeat it. He does, with an even greater thunderous authority, booming it out to Charlbury:

> Do I contradict myself?
> Very well then I contradict myself
> (I am large, I contain multitudes)

We think for a brief second this is a sudden attack of lunatic megalomania. Quentin was once heard to shout 'I am big, I am strong / I have got a penis six foot long' at an excessively gobby American artist, who was boring the arse off a group of people, before he dived on the said artist and wrestled with him as a means of shutting him up. Perhaps he is having an attack of the same impatience and imagining himself as a god. He bursts this bubble of thought by announcing, 'Walt Whitman. "Song of Myself",' and marching on ahead of us. A big light goes on within my head. It is the perfect quotation for all my understanding of Shakespeare. It is Shakespeare. We are at the railway station.

At the station we swap Mark for Will, an actor of irrepressible good spirits. He is to accompany us for the day's trek into Oxford. Mark tries his best to look sad about leaving us, but he is in such acute pain that the joyous prospect of public transport, home and a long bath is not far from his face. We will miss his exuberance and his intellectual contrariness. Quentin immediately presses Will to teach him the lyrics of Cole Porter's 'Brush Up Your Shakespeare' from *Kiss Me Kate*, but Will is as ignorant of this as anyone else under the age of fifty. The day takes on a less discursive aspect, as we settle into a brisk pace. Quentin and Will start playing fart tennis, a game where each fart is counted as a tennis point. So the first loud bottom-burp will be counted as 'fifteen-love', and on until the cry of 'Game.' I am not equipped for such competition.

After passing through another picturesque village, we start on another long, covered green lane, riding the ridge of a hill. Shortly after, we pass a young couple who are tongue-locked and grinding in a way you don't associate with ten-thirty in the morning. A few minutes after, a dog blithely trots past. Five minutes later the couple jog up to us nervously and ask if we have seen the dog. We say he went thataway, and watch them jog off. Shortly after, an elderly couple, sweating and nervous, tear past screaming the name of the dog and blowing on silent whistles. When we finally come to a clearing there are two cars which have disgorged seven or more dog-searchers. They are all frantically charging about as if they were SAS men and had just been told that Osama was in the vicinity. It seems we have stumbled across a dog-worshipping fraternity, and that the happy little pointer who bounced past us is the prince of dogs. There is a raw pain in the faces of the searchers, which is hard for a dog hater to sympathize with. It is the first example of loss that day.

We are soon in industrial farmland again. In a vicious and relentless cross-wind we walk along the ridge of a hill without any cover. On either side is a great expanse of ripe barley. In great tidal waves of motion it sways and swirls. Ahead of us it is gold as the heads bow to us, and behind all silver as the awns flow off downwind. All the curving and turning of a Van Gogh. Nature outworking fancy. I ask Quentin what the countryside which Shakespeare traversed would have looked like. 'Scrub woodland, probably, flowery meadows with tall waving grasses, and around the villages the old strip cultivation of oats, barley and wheat. Tall wheat to counter the vigorous competition of

> . . . rank fumitor and furrow weeds
> With burdock, hemlock, nettles, cuckoo flowers,
> Darnel, and all the idle weeds that grow
> In our sustaining corn.

In those days they would perhaps yield only ten bushels an acre – a tenth of what their short-strawed, modern, weed-free counterparts are capable of.' And shortly after, when we see a flowery meadow which has the breadth and technicolor variety of hundreds of years before, a burst of colour, after a monochrome continuum, Quentin explains how this has been achieved: 'You see, here, the soil fertility has deliberately been exhausted. That is the only way to achieve variety. To starve the earth. The only way to restore some of the old botanical exuberance. If you make life too easy by artificially upping the fertility with chemicals and what have you, you give variety no chance. The greedier, more aggressive plants strangle and swamp all the others. The meeker, milder species can only appear where there isn't too much competition. The competition will see them off.' We have found a new metaphor for the modern age. Where markets are supported and deregulated and made easy and accessible for everyone, does variety flourish? Does it hell. The few most aggressive, most competitive, most vicious behemoths see off all the smaller concerns. The struggles and privations and non-stop danger of Elizabethan England gave us Shakespeare, Marlowe, Jonson, Beaumont, Fletcher, Webster, Decker, Drayton, Chapman, Marston: the riches of modernity are monopolized by Disneyland.

A long stone wall appears before us as wide as the horizon. Our path leads us to a rickety ladder by which we can climb the wall and pass into the vast estate of Blenheim, the first great swathe of privately owned country we have come across. Immediately across the wall, we are lost in the cool shelter of a tall and spare wood. The escape from the buffeting wind is a relief. The contrast from the openness of the ridge to the enclosure of the woodland brings relief, and a flush of that subdued, fresh magic that lives within the enclosed light of trees. Will caps the feeling with some of the most delicate descriptive writing Shakespeare achieved. It comes from *The Merchant of Venice*. In one of those peculiar tonal excursions which Shakespeare delights in, after four acts of tight and riven social melodrama, he spins the fifth act off the previous axis and casts his net for the sublime:

> The moon shines bright: in such a night as this,
> When the sweet wind did gently kiss the trees
> And they did make no noise, in such a night
> Troilus methinks mounted the Trojan walls,
> And sighed his soul towards the Grecian tents,
> Where Cressid lay that night.

And then swiftly followed by:

> How sweet the moonlight sleeps upon this bank!
> Here will we sit, and let the sounds of music
> Creep in our ears: soft stillness and the night
> Become the touches of sweet harmony.

The lines that woke my mother up to all the potential in Shakespeare. The artificiality of the verse, summoning beauty through confidence and charm, rather than through truth, is the perfect complement to Blenheim.

For now we are out of real country and into the grandest confection of the eighteenth century's greatest dreamer, Capability Brown. The jagged clumps and bumps and zigzagging ridges of the past two days give way to euphonious sculpted parkland. This is not the country that Shakespeare would have passed through: this is the creation of the Cecil B. de Mille of Georgian England, a landscape built by thousands of labourers attempting to emulate the French landscape masterpieces painted by Poussin and Claude. Those paintings, exhibited so sensationally in London in the early eighteenth century, were themselves artificial, an attempt to re-create the landscape described in classical verse. Verse which was itself describing a mythical and imaginary world. So the woodland, the parks and the long swooping hills we are walking through are the imitation of an imitation of an imitation, and all in the higher cause of being natural. What would Shakespeare have made of that?

The sense of alienation induced by Brown's grandiose fakery is enhanced by the number of signs planted everywhere telling us to not to go here and not there, stop this and stop that. The Marlborough family are clearly reluctant to have ramblers marauding across their land. We are truly in the land of the *Merchant of Venice*'s Belmont, full of snotty Venetians, beautiful but too manicured, too constructed. Relief is provided by another unbroken stretch through a long wood. There is no chance for Mr Brown's rearrangement here. Many of the trees have stood longer than him or Shakespeare or any number of meddlers who have passed them by. There are enormous, thick-necked, ancient, stag-headed oaks. Quentin labels these anything up to five or six hundred years old, already mature when Shakespeare struggled, sore-footed, by. They have spectacularly knotted and gnarled faces like the twisted and angry gargoyles of country churches. Quentin supplies us with another telling metaphor, when he describes how the insides of these trees die, yet the husks survive, continuing to draw the goodness of the earth up, out and towards the sun. Like the life of a Shakespearean play, as it cleaves tenaciously on to relevance and life as the centuries pass by.

We collapse under a tree looking out over the lake and try to read 'A Lover's Complaint'. It has us all asleep within seconds. When we wake, Quentin is determined we find a pub and make the afternoon's long stretch more plausible by anaesthetizing ourselves with some pints. But beyond Blenheim, we fall into a bleak heartless no man's land full of roundabouts and strips of motorway, flat plains and airfields. The good-heartedness that has been inculcated by earth and air is snuffed out in an instant by the first full gusts of carbon monoxide and the roar of exhausts. Each gate seems to be garnished by a sign with a skull on it, warning of dropping aircraft or chemical filth or huge electrical currents. Hungry and publess, we have to resort to a garage for lunch – fizzy drinks and processed pork pies munched on the garage wall. I have a desperate need for a toilet and have to rush into the freeze-dried blankness of a car show-room. I see myself in the mirror, unshaven, sweating, filthy, shoes and legs covered in leaves and ears of corn, and realize how quickly I have fallen out of step with my own world. When I rejoin Quentin and Will outside there is a general feeling that we are in hell, and the sooner we escape the better.

Relief comes as ever from a church spire which points the way to the canal, and the towpath that will take us into Oxford. Only another eight miles and we'll be there. Pain is setting in again and steadily accumulating. It works by a peculiar ratio where the physical discomfort relates directly to the depletion of spirit that accompanies it. As the pain goes up the will power to combat it passes on the way down. When we reach the canal, a barge sits there, holding a theatre company. A diminutive impresario hails us from his longboat, which holds the entire company, wardrobe and scenery of the Mikron Theatre, the smallest travelling theatre in the world. We ask them if they play Shakespeare. No, he says, they play *A History of the Railways over the Last 200 Years*, written and directed by our jovial friend. As he speaks, the rain begins. That's several hundred quid gone begging, he complains. They are playing that night in the courtyard of the nearby pub. So the oldest form of theatre in England, pub theatre presented by travelling companies moving from courtyard to courtyard, still survives.

The towpath gives clarity of direction but no relief for legs. In fact, since the landscape is so uniform, trees crowding in either side of the canal, the pain only becomes sharper. And with it, all thoughts of Shakespeare and time and history dissolve, and the mind turns on nothing but the hammer thump in my legs every time I land my feet. The *Complete Works* are handed back to Will. I instruct him what to read and tell him to belt it. He screams out in the gloom and the downpour, with what Quentin describes as a sergeant-major parade-ground fortissimo, my father's old speech for the Israeli troops:

Once more unto the breach, dear friends, once more;
Or close the wall up with our English dead!
In peace there's nothing so becomes a man
As modest stillness and humility;
But when the blast of war blows in our ears,
Then imitate the action of the tiger;
Stiffen the sinews, summon up the blood,
Disguise fair nature with hard-favoured rage . . .

Will, Quentin commends, that was as good for the legs as a jolt of electricity and a shot of Napoleon brandy. More please. So Will follows with:

If we are mark'd to die, we are enow
To do our country loss; and if to live,
The fewer men, the greater share of honour.
God's will! I pray thee, wish not one man more . . .

And yet more blood is sent tingling through tiring limbs.

Our second case of loss in the day is more disturbing than the first. We are passing through the North Oxford canal community, a collection of crusties and hairy, tattooed folk living out a squalid dream of non-engagement, growing tomatoes all over their cracked and leaking barges. A young man wearing an Arsenal shirt stands by a bridge as we pass, shaking. He tries to speak to us, but is inhibited both by mental difficulties and what is clearly great upset. 'Have you seen my brother? My little brother. Have you seen my little brother? He's wearing an Arsenal shirt like me, my little brother.' We speak to him briefly and try to calm him down. Soon his father arrives, with two policemen. They head off into a huge scrap yard. The sense of terror and grief runs ahead of us up the towpath, and each new cluster of people we meet is in a fresh state of fear and shock. Mothers are crying and grabbing their children to them, men are charging about. There is a hysteria of self-dramatization in their reactions which I remember from my childhood days near hippy communities. When reality hits flimsy utopias, there is often little equipment around to deal with it. A police helicopter starts hovering above our heads. We meet the lost boy's gran standing outside her house, full of over-excitement and good cheer, her toothless mouth cracked open in a broad grin. Behind her an enormous young woman stands staring blankly, her pupils dilated unnaturally, her head lolling slightly. We have moved from Cotswold pastoral to hillbilly Gothic. We move on and through.

Warm rain starts to pour. Bodies and spirits are dampened, and the long industrial and distribution area of Kidlington, just north of Oxford, is not going to raise any hearts. We struggle into Oxford, cross the river and trudge around looking for a pub. It takes us for ever to find one, Oxford having conspired to create zones without them to frustrate us. When we do, we sit in silence, swallowing pints in great long gulps. Will leaves us, having charmed and fortified, and we are almost incapable of saying a decent farewell, so leg-focused are we. I give in to frailty, and we order a cab across the 200 yards we have to cover to get to the pub we are staying in for the night.

On arrival there, we go to check in and hear a warm and husky northern voice behind us exclaiming, 'Bloody hell, you look like two refugees from *Waiting for Godot*.' We turn and see the hotel manager, a young woman, who sprays sexuality around her. We hadn't considered what we looked like, but the pain and the earth and the rain and the endless rhythm must have lent us a little of the rogue and vagabond aspect. We are now partly qualified tramps. Though checking into a hotel disqualifies us a bit. I clamber into a bath, pass out and wake with not nearly enough of the pain having left me. I meet Quentin downstairs, scrubbed and brushed, and we tear into more beer and monster steaks. We talk of our brothers and ourselves and the conversation becomes thrilling in its insight and depth, a brilliant examination of the social forces that create the outer human, and the spiritual moulds that shape the inner human. It is one of the most sustained and revealing conversations I have ever had, and I cannot to this day remember a blind word of what was said. Such is the folly of alcohol.

Our charming manager comes and joins us and invites us to come and drink with her, her husband and a friend at her table. We tell them of our journey, and it delights them, so they tell us of epic journeys of their own through Africa. I become monopolized by their friend, a hale and hearty chap in a too-tight jacket and tie. It turns out he has been filming all day for a programme about a criminal case. He has a dark charisma, which he frequently tries to bellow off with coarseness and jokes. He is a forensic geologist, he claims the best in the country. He tells me he could take a piece of dirt off my shoe and trace that piece of dirt to the back garden of any house in England. We are soon heavily into our cups, and he brags, but brags with a subdued intensity suitable to his boasts. He has helped convict many of England's worst murderers, by tracing earth on their clothes or shoes or under the wheels of their cars. He has visited murder sites and dug around for imported soil or vegetation. He speaks bluffly of it all, but it clearly troubles him. The earth gives up its secrets, he tells me. Earth and blood and the solving of mysteries. After the day I've had, it's all a little too much for my feverish brain. I reel away from this chat and sink into a drunken and aimless flirt with the hotel manager. She tells me of her brief days as an actress – oh why did she have to say that? – and of her eventual desire to be a novelist – oh why does she want to be that? Dark thoughts crowd into my head, unimpeded by the presence of her husband sitting next to her, who is now fielding the unburdening of the Poirot of the topsoil. The early hours have now been entered, and a sense of futility overcomes a desire to flirt. I crawl upstairs.

Thursday

I wake to a darkened hotel. There's no light from the lamps, no comforting banalities from morning television, no heat in the water. The breakfast is apologetic and peremptory. There's been a power cut, and it seems irreparable. Everyone's wattage seems to have decreased in sympathy. After the over-excitement of the night before, there's that awkward English embarrassment. People stand around not quite knowing what to say. Once the bill has been settled, another friend arrives, a theatre designer, Michael, with whom I am working on the design for a play. Quentin tacitly disapproves. His view is that the invasion of work compromises the purity of the walk. He has been strict about mobile usage throughout, though this has ceased to be a problem, since I lost mine in the drunken energy of the night before.

We set off down the Thames footpath. Where the canal path north of Oxford had been all dereliction and decay – industrial warehouses and motorways overhead, peopled by the marginalized and the lost – south of Oxford is more of a home counties comfort zone. Boat-houses line the river, and teams of eight power up and down, full of the focused and futile energy of youth. Large houses, with gardens running down to the river bank, appear behind high fuck-off walls. Complicated systems of weir and footbridge and inlet crossings appear with all the self-conscious charm of *The Wind in the Willows*. It's the charm that permeates all the country we walk through south of Oxford, apart from the Chilterns. A strained presentation of nature, cutely unkempt.

Michael tells of how whenever he goes on a long walk in the country, there's always a moment when someone spots a kingfisher and points it out, but by the time he looks it will have flashed its technicolor dreamcoat and moved on. True to form, ten minutes later, Quentin blurts out, 'Kingfisher!' but by the time we look it has gone. We talk of the colours in nature, and how the most vivid and lustrous tones are often hidden. The light-catching halcyon blues of the king-fisher in flight; the ferocious reds and purples on the underside of a reef; the incredible tree of deep scarlets and blues that branches its way through a placenta. As if some experiences of colour are too rich and too startling and need to be rationed.

Within an hour, Michael and I have settled the essentials for our design. We cross the river and leave Michael to walk back to Oxford. We leave the river path and head in-country, up into the Chilterns. We strike out through fields into wide-open and farmed country. Quentin and I are alone now for the first time on our walk. This is how it will remain for the rest of the week. Various others who have been invited to join us have failed or will fail to show, put off by the weather or the exertion, who knows.

We are not in the mood for Shakespeare. We have had a glut and need a rest. I don't know if Quentin is taking the opportunity afforded by us being alone, or whether he simply has nothing else to say, but he slips into Ancient Mariner mode. He begins a monologue which continues for much of the day, with the occasional break and the occasional detour. It is the story of his life in vivid and illuminating detail. The Proustian madeleine, which kick-starts it, turns out to be the post office we encountered three days before. His grandparents had run a similar all-purpose post office, and it is a resort of numinous magic in the treasure box of his memory. It sets in motion a long and fascinating story.

It is a walk through family and travel and adventure, loves that fail and loves that succeed, terrible loss and not quite compensating gain, failures that have to be swallowed and successes that come out of nowhere. It has resonances with the pattern of my own life; it has resonances with Shakespeare's; it has resonances with the lives of those Shakespeare created. A human life. His monologue underpins our understanding of Shakespeare. Finally, to understand his work, you have to understand yourself. To look properly at his complete and ever-expanding universe, you have to look hard at the infinite possibilities within yourself, the big bang of your own creation. Quentin's decision to tell his story, conscious or not, opens the door to greater insight. Every academic should do the same: it may spell the eradication of a certain wearying scientific tone.

As he talks on, my mind goes happily to the places the story takes me. We go to Africa in the sixties, full of idealistic youth following in the colonial service of their parents under a different guise; to Australia in the seventies, where expat English let their hair and all else down as the world turns itself upside down; we even travel on a paradisal trip to Tahiti. Vivid details are hologrammed into existence: two gin and tonics with a twinkly uncle on a Sunday morning when everyone else was in church, a kiss full of parting and promise outside a hotel on a London street, and an early-morning walk up some stairs full of a desperate foreboding. We travel far and wide and into the most hidden nooks and crannies. Some of it is banal, some mysterious. There is no creation of hierarchies, no 'this-is-a-good-bit', nor any self-dramatization. It is told without tears, or too much laughter, or any 'hear my confession' pride. The hypnotic regularity of the tread, the story unfolding on an iambic beat, and the levelling presence of whatever gods or greater spirits live in the line of the horizon, flatten out any vanity in the storytelling. There is no agenda behind it, no conscious intellectual patterning, just the story.

This is the Shakespearean way, the telling of a story of truth, and if true any story is as wide as the universe. Truth doesn't mean plain or real. *Pericles*, as mad a story as was ever told, is true to its own intentions, and to its own world, and by extension to our world. The moment you start lying, the moment you start creating patterns from thought rather than from life, is the moment that universe starts contracting. It is the lack of seeming arrangement, the honesty of the recounting, which constantly widens the scope and opens out the possibilities. With Ben Jonson, with Kit Marlowe, with John Webster, we are made to feel the presence of the author. There is a controlling intelligence, telling us discreetly or explicitly how they arrange the world. With Shakespeare the intention is to liberate, not to enclose. As Quentin tells his story, I am reminded of my father's response to my questioning of Shakespeare's realism: 'Of course, it's realism. You don't need big detailed sets for realism. You just need one man standing there saying, "I am real, and so is my story." That's realism.'

We walk continuously, listening to this story, through field and cross hill, for three or four hours. I stop briefly in an über-posh gastro-pub to buy some water. It is slowly starting to fill with Oxfordshire Ladies Who Lunch. They find my grisliness as alienating as I found their couthness. I am ushered out quickly. We skirt around a manor house with its own cricket pitch. Soon after, exactly at the halfway point of our walk, we reach a point where we should be crossing a large stream across a bridleway. Unfortunately, I have forgotten that we don't have a horse. The water is considerably too high and fast for us alone. There is the promise of another crossing called 'Stepping Stones' not far beyond. We dive into a jungle of brambles and bush to try and find this. Each site we find fails to qualify. Finally we find a few scattered rocks, rearranged by the winter storms into a flotsam of branches and plastic, stretched out over a wide and deep and fast stream. Quentin says it's impossible, I say it's not. Quentin says we shouldn't do it, I say we should. I prevail, but on the insistence that Quentin does it first. I feel slight shame as he sets out, twenty years my senior, to take the chance. My conscience is eased with the thought that he's had a long life. He makes it to the other side. His journey across is a model of English courage and decorum compared to mine. I squawk and wail and beg for advice all the way across. Quentin kindly talks me through it. We beam with self-satisfaction once we are over. It is a symbolic crossing, halfway through and obstacles overcome.

The process from hubris to nemesis is swift. Full of myself after the stream escapade, I immediately revert to the half-witted map reading of the first morning and plunge us into long fields of wheat with no means of escape. We have to skirt the edges of a mile of fields. Each is sodden from recent rain, each is recently ploughed. Every hundred yards we have to stop to scrape off the mud, which clings to our shoes like a red octopus trying to pull us back down under the earth. My sandals metamorphose into diver's boots pulling me to the bottom. My map reading, my propensity to attract mud and my general all-round slowness are starting to break down Quentin's even temper. To put some distance between himself and the object of that temper, he strides out towards the village on the hill ahead of us. I follow lamely.

Quentin is discovered in a low-ceilinged nook of a pub, sitting before four pints, and with several steak sandwiches on order. His spirits revive swiftly. There are only the two of us, the barman, and two pickled and pink country gents. Quentin launches into a wide repertoire of music-hall and Victorian songs in response to the beer's balm. The two drunks join in the good cheer and engage with our mission, pontificating grandly on the distance we have to go and the difficulty of our route. We need to reach a village up in the Chilterns called Turville. One of them obsessively repeats with the urgent self-importance of the sozzled, 'I'll tell you the thing about Turville . . .' and then later, 'Now Turville, the thing about Turville . . . I'll tell you the thing about Turville.' I go to the loo and come out and he is standing there, jabbing his finger at me. 'I want to tell you something about Turville . . . I'm going to tell you . . .' We sit down and change our socks and clean our shoes, and he carries on with the same refrain. Eventually our good humour snaps, and we shout, 'What? What about Turville?' 'Well, Turville, I'll tell you, they've got some nice houses there.' His face crumples into disappointment at the banality of his own secret.

Before we escape this village, we are struck by a monsoon of oriental proportions. We take refuge in the snug of an old-fashioned red phone-box. A thick sheet of rain conceals the rest of the world from us. We stand, cut off from the universe, steaming up a three foot by three foot red box.

The route planned for the afternoon is straight and good. It is another ancient road, now turned into a well-carved-out country path, and it goes on for ever. It is fucking endless. There are no pubs, no stopping points. The next village is always several fields away and is passed by without stopping. The plain we are on seems to be eternal, and the Chiltern hills we are heading towards seem to stretch ever further and further away. It's four hours of continuous walking along the flat. The conversation dries a little once Quentin's life story has taken a rest. There is an attempt to prompt me to reciprocate, but I haven't got the puff or the clarity of thought, and Quentin, after his steady unemptying, hasn't got the ear to listen. It is now just our bodies, and the landscape, and our failing will.

We hit the base of the Chilterns at about seven. A county-long wall of raised earth confronts us. The early part of the incline is going to be lengthy and slow, with a sudden and silly rise to follow. To counter the yowl of pain now screaming up from solid legs and nerve-end feet, I return to my childhood and read Mark Antony's oration to the crowd in a loud and belting voice. When we reach the base of the steep bit, Quentin follows his rule of separation and tears off alone. The only way I can conquer this excruciatingly steep passage is by taking tiny steps of a foot or so. Somehow, this is the way my muscles have arranged themselves. I lean into the slope and force myself upwards. Halfway up, I stop and turn to see the plain beneath and the last two days' walking stretching behind. There's too much pain for pride, but the humanity of the landscape strikes me again.

A red kite suddenly appears overhead. Its wide wings are spread taut, and it banks warily on the air currents. It looks watchful and cautious. With a flick of energy, it twists itself up and down. Quentin later tells me that kites have only recently begun to reappear in these parts, as more farming country returns to wilderness. This broad and balanced bird looks like it still feels unfamiliar here, but has a wary hope that it will soon feel at home. Perhaps I'm projecting insanely. I continue my ludicrous shuffle up the hill. At the top I find Quentin seated on a bench.

We have hit the plateau at the top and walk out of a small wood into a field. It is covered in a fine evening mist that floats seven or eight feet above the ground. The grass is a rich and deep green the like of which we haven't seen yet, walking through sunburned yellows and browns as we have. The vaporous shroud and the lustre of the green plunge us back in time. We half expect a horse to break through the horizontal curtain of mist with an armed knight upright on it. Falstaff's exquisite death scene breaks into my mind, a scene played out without its main character. Crony after crony of Falstaff's shuffle out of the room that contains him and describe his losing battle with life:

Nay, sure, he's not in hell; he's in Arthur's bosom, if ever man went to Arthur's bosom. 'A made a finer end, and went away an it had been any christom child; 'a parted ev'n just between twelve and one, ev'n at the turning o' th' tide; for after I saw him fumble with the sheets, and play with flowers, and smile upon his fingers' end, I knew there was but one way; for his nose was as sharp as a pen, and 'a babbled of green fields.

That detail of babbling of green fields always finishes me off. It is the perfect match to the addled mysticism of an old English drunk.

In my clearest dream of death, I was searching for a lost child while being driven round a mountainous landscape in a beaten-up old Morris Minor. The driver was an old stage manager of mine (always take a stage manager into death). We found the child in a sort of Buddhist monastery on the top of the hill and returned her to her parents. Afterwards I walked over the top of a small mountain and found myself walking down into an endless valley, rich with the lushest and most dazzling green. I knew I was dead and felt, in the presence of this great pour of green life, as well as I have ever felt. I'd thought the vision was unique until stumbling over that line of Falstaff's. And I thought I'd never see a green to match it, until I walked into that misted field.

My legs are now locked into the pattern of walking they concocted to make it up the hill. The tight shuffle that suited then is now hardwired into them. They refuse to do anything else now they're on the flat. I look like a sweaty overweight geisha girl, mincing forward small step by small step. Quentin is buggered if he'll wait for me and speeds ahead towards the pub in a hamlet called Christmas Common. I inch my way along the road, as cars fly by, laughter booming out of them. I fall into another snug pub and pull a chair up in front of the fire. Quentin is equally silent and plops the obligatory two pints – one for thirst, one for taste – in front of me. I peel off my mud-, bush- and grass-encrusted sandals, and splay my wet and rotting toes out in front of the fire. Quentin does the same with socks and shoes. A lounge bar full of people is silenced by the weight of our silence. We have acquired the presence of the wholly exhausted and the completely fucked. We have the charisma of the blinkered tramp who stumbles into the drinks party and makes a beeline for the trifle.

Several pints and another lump of burned meat in, and we are ready to engage with our fellow drinkers. An elderly couple who clearly nurse the same drinks in silence over several hours every night; a pint man with his lemonade son; some bluff and burned-cheek farmers, and a tattooed malcontent farm labourer. The classic blend for any small country pub. We buy drinks for people; they buy drinks for us; we talk of our silly mission; they tell us about Christmas Common. Cromwell signed a major treaty here in the seventeenth century. The Civil War has shadowed us everywhere over the last four days. Sites of battles and conferences and refuges have been dotted around us. Quentin's theories about the tensions that pulled England tight in Shakespeare's time, political and religious, is borne out by all around us.

Quentin tells everyone what a terrible walker I am and threatens to walk off without me, then rescinds. Everyone finds this very amusing but me. They think he's joking, I think he may be serious. An inane elation fills the room similar to that we experienced with our guests on the first night, in the farm shop in Long Compton, in the pub in Oxford, in the pub at lunchtime and now here. There is a benevolent effect that goes with acts of gentle pottiness. Especially ones that pass through. Ones that hang around probably get a little wearisome.

I ring ahead to the bed and breakfast we've arranged to stay in. The woman I speak to has an excessively refined and delicate English accent. We've spoken before, and she always addresses me as though she were a lady arranging a reception for a visiting lord. This is pleasing but a little worrying. We think the village we're heading on to is only a mile away, but of course, as with everything on a long walk, it turns out further than expected. We clatter on through high woodland in the dark, and the many pints elevate and excite the chat. The Civil War trigger has Quentin off and away again on his theories about polarities. He has stiffened in his resolve that Shakespeare was a diviner of tangled knots that messed with the hair of Western civilization, and that his great mission in life was to comb these knots smooth. A cultural chiropractor straightening the twisted spine of humanity. I am still not sure about all this. It sounds too deliberate for my instinctual artist. But I hold my fire.

He continues to outline how Jung said our task in life was to express the self – the totality of our historical inheritance and our personal lifetime experience. Occasionally people are born – Buddha, Christ, Shakespeare, Mohammed – with a near-cosmic range of inheritance and near-uninhibited range of experiences, who are thus able to express something close to human totality. These few prophets, or shamen, or genii, or what you will, were in some way, by virtue of their gift, outside of humanity, above the immersion in conflict between yin and yang that afflicts the rest of us.

The musical accompaniment to these discourses is the unearthly screeching of a vixen which seems to walk beside us at a distance of a hundred yards or so. Whether in a state of rage or lust or pain, it screams a husky but savage and high-pitched whine for a good five minutes or so. The hairs on the back of our necks stand up. The vixen's screams, the inky black, the wind rustling the tree tops. All the dark imaginings of the night come rushing on fast. Peace returns when we turn into Turville Heath. 'Billionaire's row', the tattooed malcontent had dubbed it in the pub, and all the signs of ludicrous wealth are everywhere. Silence, and the invisibility of any houses. The central street of Turville Heath is a masterpiece of modern art. Not a single house is visible, not a man-made thing. The whole road is lined by the most magnificent avenue of giant limes, stretching up in random harmony to about sixty feet, and spreading out their broad arms at the base. In the night they give off a soft, lambent green light, and they occlude all behind them. In the middle of this avenue, as a jokey concession to modernity, a solitary pint-sized letterbox.

We find our destination after nosing around a while. When we knock on the door of what is a moderately grand-looking house, I hear the voice I know from the phone calls behind it. As the door opens Quentin and I are both mildly taken aback by the sight of a black woman. This would not be remotely surprising in the context of our lives or our work, but in the context of this walk it is. Airlifted out of multicultural London, we have seen hardly any non-white faces for the last four days. It also explains some of the extreme refinement from the telephone. This is not a place to be street. It turns out we are not in a bed and breakfast but in this woman's home, and that I have only got her number by a circuitous route. But she is determined to make us happy and welcomes us as if we were old friends.

I try to watch some television, but *Newsnight* with its self-importance and its opinions looks a thousand miles away. Eventually choosing to turn in, I fall into a small camp bed beside Quentin's larger bed. This is the first time we have shared a room. Quentin's snore is legendary, but I've never been so close to it before. We slept in the same house in France once which had thin walls, and much of the fabric of the house seemed to tremble at the force of his snore. But nothing quite prepares you for a shared room. I had foolishly drunk a jug of coffee which our hostess had prepared. This compounds the problem. Sleep is just not an option. Overtired as I am and full of beer and coffee and too many novel thoughts, I become over-involved imaginatively in the snore. I seem to be shrinking into a small particle which is sucked into Quentin's nose on a long inhale of breath and blown out again into the world on a long exhale. I am living out Bowlby's scheme of attachment and separation drawn into a nostril and then sent away again. Hours pass as I ride the aural ebb and flow of this monster noise, boogie-boarding on a wave that flows continually in and out. At about three in the morning, I resolve for my own sanity that I have to leave the room and collapse on the floor on the landing.

Friday

The sensation of a dressing gown passing over my head brushes me awake. Our hostess is gingerly attempting not to step on me. I pretend to remain asleep. Soon after, Quentin appears. 'Dominic, what are you doing on the floor?' 'Ermmm . . . aaaahhh . . . ermmm . . .' 'Was it anything to do with my snoring?' 'It might have had something to do with that. Can I hop into your bed for an hour's kip?' 'Go ahead.' I scurry into his bed. Morning light has filled the room. It is a child's room, festooned with pictures of a young woman – sailing, partying, graduating, fooling about, receiving presents. There is an irrepressible gaiety that fills everything she does. It infuses a little joy before I sink back into sleep.

The smell of bacon perks me up again, the twitch of the nose pulling the body into the world. I walk down to find Quentin extolling the virtues of his breakfast. It is special. Fresh leaves of mint garland the grapefruit. The eggs are recently laid and full of yellow richness. Even the bacon is home grown. It's all a little too much. Our hostess' nerves seem attenuated. She herself is from Trinidad. Her husband is away sailing, she knows not where. I haven't the wit to understand this means something is wrong, so, buoyed up by my breakfast, I plough cheerfully into, 'How is your daughter?' referring to the girl in the photos. 'Well, that is why my husband is away. He is grieving, and does not know how to . . .' and the story of the daughter trickles out. She was young and vibrant and alive, then was diagnosed with cancer and went into an inexorable decline. We sit over our eggs and bacon, frozen with respect for her grief, as tears leak out and then are pulled back. The bed and breakfast operation is a way of escaping her grief and bringing new life into the house. We murmur phrases of inadequacy. When her story is done, we rise to pack our things.

When we return downstairs, she wants to show us something. Hanging in her lounge, and expensively framed, is a poem her daughter composed just before she died and wrote out by hand for her mother and father. Our hostess reads it out to us aloud. It is technically clumsy but charged moment to moment with a freight of emotion that is hard to witness, and throughout has an easy natural grace. In some strange and democratic way we are all poets now. It is hugely generous, giving thanks for a greatly enjoyed life, no matter it is finishing early, and sternly warning the parents to be happy, and live, and feel no regrets. It is a modest and small act of saintliness tucked away in a country village. There are tears at the end, and that terrible awkwardness of not knowing what to do. I give our hostess an inadequate peck on the cheek, we mutter some phrases, then set off down the road with a backward wave.

We are silenced for a while. My mind passes over the lost children that have permeated the texture of the walk. The frantic search for the lost boy on the towpath north of Oxford; Quentin's tale was underpinned in sorrow by the loss of a child; the soil detective had helped solve a celebrated case where two children had been abducted and murdered; and now we have inadvertently slept the night (or failed to sleep) in a shrine to a lost daughter. I shiver in terror for my own children and clasp both hands round the trunk of a tree in hope for some arcane life-spirit blessing.

Shakespeare comes to mind vividly, and my imagination fills with a picture of him, standing over the grave of his adored son Hamnet on a wet Stratford day, watching the dank clods of earth piling up on top of one of his greatest hopes. The backstop of his happiness had always been his son. When audiences yawned at his plays, or actors whinged at him, or lovers tired of him, or his muse failed him, his last resort of joy had been the thought of his son. The bright boy, now a pallid corpse in the wooden box, had been his mainstay, even in absence. And here he was pitched into despair, after an inadequate Protestant burial service, which not only lacked the ritual beauty of the old church but also might, for want of the proper rites, leave his child's soul lost in purgatory for ever. Here he was, his wife lost in her own grief, his daughters clinging to their mother and ignoring the man they loved but were not accustomed to. Standing alone in the rain, his old Stratford friends estranged from him by his success, his London glister and gold as empty as a blown eggshell and falling into the blackest hole he ever imagined possible. The same year he wrote in *King John* the words for a mother, Constance, grieving the loss of her young son, Arthur:

> Grief fills the room up of my absent child,
> Lies in his bed, walks up and down with me,
> Puts on his pretty looks, repeats his words,
> Remembers me of all his gracious parts,
> Stuffs out his vacant garments with his form . . .
> . . . O Lord!, my boy, my Arthur, my fair son!
> My life, my joy, my food, my all the world!
> My widow-comfort and my sorrow's cure!

Lost children.

We get beyond the manicured and fragrantly perfumed hamlet we were in and move into Chiltern country, passing through a beech wood to reveal one large valley within the hills. Windmills appear to confirm the area's status as an English idyll. We skirt above a series of villages along a ridge and look down into their lives. The kite from the night before returns, this time with a friend. They fly above us, watchful and alert, protecting us. The horizon they cut in clean decisive lines is empty of the steeples we enjoyed in the Cotswolds. In the early stages of our walk fine churches and architecture were pushed in our face; here they are hidden behind trees. We descend into a village on the way to a large forest. We ask directions of a hawthorn cutter. He is paralysing in his confusing vagueness, but neither Quentin nor I want to admit we didn't understand a word he said, so we both form our own understanding of his gibberish. This is perilous. We have to cross a wide meadow to get to the forest, and it is here that our greatest argument begins.

It begins with a compliment of mine on Quentin's snore. Being a great believer in accentuating the positive, I choose not to bemoan my midnight tormentor but to praise it. It is, I tell Quentin, the snore of a deeply balanced and contented man, its deep basso profundo rumble showing no signs of neurosis. It comes from the depths of him and passes out through the top. It is a great sign of well-arranged yin and yang, where no preponderance of the one or the other blocks the passage of this Emperor of Snores. Quentin inflates gently on listening to this paean of commendation, but it also seems to sharpen his appetite for another intellectual scrap. The phrase I shouldn't have mentioned is yin and yang, since this starts Quentin off on his attachment and separation, reconciling of opposites rasp again.

'Dom, Elizabethan England was split down the middle – indeed all of Europe was. Shakespeare was at the heart of that schism. Contradictions abounded in him. He came from an area riven by factionalism. His father was a covert Catholic, carrying out a Prot-estant public office, while simultaneously receiving mass in secret. He passionately opposed the illegitimacy of the concentration of political power in a hereditary few, yet he spent most of his life sucking up to it. He was a member of the recently empowered mercantile class, who were gradually eroding the power base of the old aristocracy. He was in the centre of all those conflicts. He was driven to explore those divisions for himself, for the theatre-going public, and beyond for us.

'The same splits under different guises last through to today. If the factions change their names or costumes, the heart of them remains the same. The split cuts through the centre of us. You can call it being and knowing, spirit and matter, mind and body, reason and unreason, conscious and unconscious, yin and yang, male and female, separation and attachment, whatever you call it, and whatever new names they choose to invent in the future, that division will always be there. We are the cleft and cloven species, Dom. That will never change. All we can ever do is try to pull those separate poles together, try to help them to live with each other. Shakespeare knew that. He spent his life in the attempt to reunite us. But he could do nothing unless he knew those two poles, and observed the life within them.'

'Well, that's just it, "WITHIN", that's where you're wrong, Quent, "within!". It's all contained in that word "within". Shakespeare did not understand divisions and conflicts, and write about the life *within* those polarities. The opposite was the case. He wrote about those divisions *within* a greater life. He knew that life is larger than any of the passing squabbles or quarrels which flare up within it. Shakespeare was about everything, about allness, the great chaos and the great song of the universe. He was a sponge absorbing myth, literature, history, nature, natter, chatter and grace notes. He had a gargantuan appetite for whatever he could lay his hands on, a new edition of Ovid or a cheap joke down the pub, a history of Rome or a bit of court gossip. He re-created that everything in his work, building a confused, accidental and beautiful totality – Shakespeare's universe – which with its random beauty somehow matches the totality of life. His conflicts are *within* that totality; he does not create an argument then orchestrate a life within it.'

We are now within the forest and floundering. Our various interpretations of the hawthorn cutter's mutters have all proven roads to nowhere. The Ordnance Survey map in my hand is inadequate for the chaos of fallen trees, forks in pathways and branching lanes which confronts us. We keep stopping at long extensions of meshed wire, or come to sudden drops in the earth, or to small reservoirs. We retrace our steps and then have to work out where to try next. Quent picks up the theme.

'You've got a map in your hand. Ignoring the fact that you are singularly useless at reading it, how without a map would you be able to find your way? Through centuries we have been discovering ways to navigate via the stars or the sun, or writing directions or drawing maps. Shakespeare in the same way was an explorer into the world, and he created maps to help us find our way about.'

'No. No, he didn't create a map, he created the territory. He didn't aim to show us the way, he aimed to teach us to accept being lost. He absorbed whatever he could, wherever he could, and made a new heaven and earth for newly overflowing Renaissance humanity. He took the ambition of that time, and reflected it in the spills and surges of his work. The everything was what mattered, the allness. Many of his characters begin by trying to understand the world and finish by learning the only route to health is to give up and accept it, all of it. Hamlet has to learn that 'Readiness is all', Gloucester in *King Lear* that 'Ripeness is all'. There is no route map, no understanding, simply an acceptance of the everything on offer.

'If there is a conflict, it is between people who can live without pattern and those who have to discriminate, to live in small, enclosed

niches of understanding, walled zones of taste. He loved and enjoyed
the former; he felt contempt for the latter. All those filled with fierce
and meaningless positions. "A plague on both their houses", be they
Capulet or Montague, be they Bush or Osama. They are ludicrously
reducing the humanity within themselves. They steal it from the
dolts who choose to follow them. None of his characters has any
worthwhile plan, they all flounder in a floundering world. What is
shown is that life itself is way beyond any petty human idea of what
it is. It is a horrific and savage mess, where old men occasionally wake
to music and find their beloved daughter, whom they thought lost,
sitting by their bed. No, Quent, he made his own totality, the Shakespeare universe, to match the totality of nature.'

'Nonsense, what's that speech they're always quoting at Conservative conferences to scare people into submission?'

'Take but degree away . . .'

'That's the one. From *Troilus and Cressida*. Let's hear it.'

We pause for a second in a clearing in the forest, the *Complete
Works* are dug out, and Ulysses' great justification of political order
is read out:

> The heavens themselves, the planets, and this centre,
> Observe degree, priority and place,
> Insisture, course, proportion, season, form,
> Office, and custom, in all line of order;
> And therefore is the glorious planet, Sol
> In noble eminence enthron'd and sphered
> Amidst the other, whose med'cinable eye
> Corrects the ill aspects of planets evil,
> And posts, like the commandment of a king,
> Sans check, to good and bad. But when the planets
> In evil mixture to disorder wander,
> What plagues and what portents, what mutiny,
> What raging of the sea, shaking of earth,
> Commotion in the winds! Frights, changes, horrors,
> Divert and crack, rend and deracinate,
> The unity and married calm of states
> Quite from their fixture! O when degree is shaked,

Which is the ladder to all high designs,
The enterprise is sick! How could communities,
Degrees in schools and brotherhoods in cities,
Peaceful commerce from dividable shores,
The primogenitive and due of birth,
Prerogative of age, crowns, sceptres, laurels,
But by degree, stand in authentic place?
Take but degree away, untune that string,
And, hark, what discord follows! each thing meets
In mere oppugnancy: the bounded waters
Should lift their bosoms higher than the shores
And make a sop of all this solid globe:
Strength should be lord of imbecility,
And the rude son should strike his father dead . . .
Then every thing includes itself in power,
Power into will, will into appetite;
And appetite, an universal wolf,
So doubly seconded with will and power,
Must make perforce an universal prey,
And last eat up himself.

'Well, Dom, if Shakespeare was a sponge, he might have made a sop of all this solid globe, but I'm not sure he would have written *Troilus and Cressida*. That's not just a speech about political order . . .'

'Yes, a speech by a dishonest politician, who plots great schemes which eventually come to nothing . . .'

'Regardless of that . . .'

'You can't disregard that, Quent. That is one character's particular nonsense in a grander scheme . . .'

'Rather elegantly expressed nonsense, though, and fairly intellectually coherent. Regardless of who it is, that is not only about politics, it is also about physical matter. Nothing binds or holds or coheres unless it follows certain rules, rules of society, rules of nature, rules of physics. Those rules require articulation. Making a life within them requires resolution. His plays are about discovering and living within those rules. There is too much direction in his work for a wanderer. Too many layers for a sponge.

'He's more like a miner who knows where pay dirt lurks, what tools to use, how fire, explosion, acids, alkalis or plain water refine the mineral from the ore. He is mining not metals but the dark unconscious, bringing it up into the light of the theatre. His work is a means to create a new totality, his work cannot be a totality in itself.'

I haven't admitted up to this point that I'm not sure what the word totality actually means, but I enjoy the roll of it in my mouth, so keep pitching it in.

'No, his work was a totality. That is the purpose of creation. To make a new world. One that corresponds to the actual one, whatever actual means, and to everyone else's. There is no intention in the work . . .'

'Yes, there is Dom . . .'

'No, Quent. There is no moral purpose. No "Gosh, I must sort this out." No "Golly, I have to reconcile these opposites." There is just creation itself. As mysterious and wonderful as the creation of a child. And if good and true, a work of art will be as mysterious and as complex as nature itself.'

'Dominic, that is nonsense. Look around you. Look at the infinitely complex ecosystem here. Look at the trees and the soil and the roots. Imagine the myriad of small ecosystems within each one of those ecosystems. Try and imagine the variety and the strangeness and the difference in each strip of bark. Multiply that by itself and look around you within this forest at all the different living things, animal and vegetable, which are somehow making a life together. The world is infinite in all directions. Go as small as you will, the path is infinite; ditto when you go big. We're stuck in the middle (not a bad place to be, by the way) and can never grasp the extremes. So we're stuck with choosing from our own, uncomfortably narrow range. How can something so confused possibly be represented in art? It is impossible. Art is about shaping and refining. Art is about finding a way of giving meaning to mess.'

'No, I couldn't, couldn't, couldn't disagree more.'

'It doesn't matter if you disagree or not, you're still wrong.'

The argument is getting well beyond tetchy. It is not helped by the totality of our lostness. By this time in our argument we have travelled in two circles and down about ten blocked paths. On a long walk this becomes more than a distraction. You know that at the end of the day your legs will make you pay for all the extra yards. The sun is invisible because of the thick foliage, so we can't find our bearings. The confusion has become a source of fear. The creeping dread we may never get out has started to take hold. Fear and anger are funding the argument.

'I can't agree, Quent. Art is not about giving meaning to mess. It's about reflecting mess, it's about "holding, as it were, the mirror up to nature", mirroring the everything beyond. That is the base of Shakespeare's achievement . . .'

'Impossible. He constructed arguments between positions and resolved arguments. He reconciled opposites towards a totality.'

'That might be conceivable or true if his work had a unity or a design, but it doesn't. It is too attacked by life. Every weird cul-de-sac he travels down is proof of his genius, every stupid fart joke, every ludicrous nonsensical non-sequitur. They are the essence of Shakespeare because they deny shape or order. They are exactly what makes him different from the beautiful French stylists, Racine and Corneille, and from the rolling thunder of the Greeks, and what makes him finally more comprehensive. It is the invasion of stupid, silly life. He meanders, he loses his way, he refinds it. Just as we are now. Just as we always will be. His plays are a celebration of allness, a criticism of discriminations and a terrified examination of the nothingness from which any allness emanates. To celebrate that allness they have to create it.'

'But they create it by giving it form.'

'No, by losing form in content.'

'Come on, Dominic, form is the essence of all art.'

'No, it isn't.'

'Yes, it is.'

'No.'

'Yes.'

'NO.'

'YES.'

'NO.'

'YES.'

And there we are shouting yes and no at each other in the middle of a dark forest. Lost in a pantomime of intellectual vapidity. No, Yes, No, Yes, No, Yes. Lost in a wood, lost in our arguments, our silly shouts heard by nothing but the shifting trees. Eventually the silliness of our present positions strikes even us quite forcibly. We call a halt to our argument. There is no laughter, no shame either, however stupid we may look to the rooks or the squirrels or the beetles. There is a quiet relish of the lunacy of our position, an enjoyment of the fiery insignificance of our rhetoric. We enjoy the silence for a long moment.

Then we have to make a plan to get out. This is, of course, a metaphysical concession to Quentin. I could argue that we stay there and enjoy the chaos. But I want my pints. We find a path that is marked on the map, follow it until we find a decent clearing, look at the sun and work out which way is east and which west. As a punishment for all our intellectual footling, when we emerge from the forest we are faced with a long and steep slope. This squashes the argument out of us. At the top of our path we are faced with a second obstacle, a thick hedge. We are running low on time and patience, so instead of seeking a long way round, we both run at the hedge and force a way through, pushing through bramble and briar like second-row forwards blasting an opposing scrum out of the way. We emerge scratched and bloody, covered in thorns and sticks, and cleansed of our intellectual rage.

A long stretch of road curves past a garden centre. I nip into a café for a quick trip to the toilet and to buy a surreptitious fizzy drink or two, which I down quickly behind the succulents, since Quentin doesn't approve of these. I get momentarily completely confused by some automatic glass doors and stand staring at them like a Neanderthal. Soon after, we are on another long, green lane, trekking perilously close to the roar and whine of the M40 as it ferries its human cargo between Oxford and London. We are now as close as we've ever been to Shakespeare's actual route, but the motorway blasts any sense of history out of its environment.

We trudge across a field to a pub. We are now on the borders of the M25 and the weird world of the London orbital is starting to make itself manifest. Bowlby's separation is everywhere. The menu is of food that only needs to be microwaved. The chairs are in that strange light brown nowhere world between wood and plastic. The beer is standard syndicated piss. Two boys stand at a fruit machine playing with an absence of joy that would make an angel weep. Their eyes are long dead. This pub is trapped in the grey zone in between the country and London. Yet no matter, beer and fried fish does no shortage of good, and we gossip of friends we know. The intellectual gaminess has been extinguished for a day.

Four pints to the good, we career down a long hill towards our next obvious destination, the Thames. We left it a day and a half ago in Oxford and now are picking it up again. From the Chiltern hills we can see some of its long and lazy arc through the home counties. The Thames is the last way we can keep our minds out of the present day, its towpath winding its historical way right into the heart of London. The moment we hit the Thames we are back in the world of the well-to-do; well-heeled houses backing on to the river and week-end boats for bourgeois fantasists moored up.

The rhythm we set ourselves is brisk and monotonous. Pain begins to grip again. Each curve of the river looks near, but proves to be far. Each landmark on the map seems to be just round the corner, but the corner is a mile long. I am starting to suffer again. We pass through Cookham, the home of Stanley Spencer and Noel Coward's *Hayfever*, but my legs forbid me to even think about enjoying its quaint Edwardian flavour. We pass idyllic weirs shrouded in gentle greens, and quaint locks with hail-fellow-well-met boat owners operating them with their delirious amateurism. Why does everyone on a river always look so cheerful?

I tell Quentin one of my favourite actor jokes. A London actor was engaged to work in Birmingham early in the last century. He discovered that the cheapest way to get there was by canal, so he found passage on a barge. What he didn't know was that the other cargo was an enormous heap of manure. Whenever they came to a tollbooth, the local man would call out in time-honoured custom, 'What have you got on board?' and the bargee would reply, 'A heap of shit and an actor.' Ten miles down the same: 'What have you got on board?' 'A heap of shit and an actor.' And the same each ten miles for the next fifty. Shortly before they reached Birmingham, they were approaching their last tollbooth. The actor edged up towards the bargee and spoke confidentially to him, 'Dear sir. A word about the billing . . .'

I call a halt to our struggles since the legs are going wobbly, and I need a little rest. We have found a pleasant stretch of river, unencumbered by millionaires' homes or boathouses. It is just river, a long wood opposite, a long wood behind. A dazzling spray of light-green foliage all along the opposite bank catches the late-afternoon sun and turns a tender yellow. We are fucked and at peace. We dig out the *Complete Works* and enjoy a gentle rendition of Enobarbus' description of Antony and Cleopatra's meeting, the most excessively sublime bit of poetry he ever wrote:

> The barge she sat in, like a burnish'd throne,
> Burn'd on the water: the poop was beaten gold;
> Purple the sails, and so perfumed that
> The winds were love-sick with them; the oars were silver,
> Which to the tune of flutes kept stroke, and made
> The water which they beat to follow faster,
> As amorous of their strokes. For her own person,
> It beggar'd all description: she did lie
> In her pavilion – cloth-of-gold of tissue –
> O'er-picturing that Venus where we see
> The fancy outwork nature: on each side her
> Stood pretty dimpled boys, like smiling Cupids,
> With divers-colour'd fans, whose wind did seem
> To glow the delicate cheeks which they did cool,
> And what they undid did . . .
> Her gentlewomen, like the Nereides,
> So many mermaids, tended her i' the eyes,
> And made their bends adornings: at the helm
> A seeming mermaid steers: the silken tackle
> Swell with the touches of those flower-soft hands,
> That yarely frame the office. From the barge
> A strange invisible perfume hits the sense
> Of the adjacent wharfs. The city cast
> Her people out upon her; and Antony,
> Enthroned i' the market-place, did sit alone,

Whistling to the air; which, but for vacancy,
Had gone to gaze on Cleopatra too,
And made a gap in nature . . .
Upon her landing, Antony sent to her,
Invited her to supper: she replied,
It should be better he became her guest;
Which she entreated: our courteous Antony,
Whom ne'er the word of 'No' woman heard speak,
Being barber'd ten times o'er, goes to the feast,
And for his ordinary pays his heart
For what his eyes eat only . . .
                                                      I saw her once
Hop forty paces through the public street;
And, having lost her breath, she spoke, and panted,
That she did make defect perfection,
And, breathless, power breathe forth . . .
Age cannot wither her, nor custom stale
Her infinite variety: other women cloy
The appetites they feed; but she makes hungry
Where most she satisfies; for vilest things
Become themselves in her: that the holy priests
Bless her when she is riggish.

There are things to say about this: how he stole whole chunks of it
from a translation of Plutarch, and by the turning and twisting of
a few details transformed it from lumpen prose to gilded air; how
he plays with metaphysical conceits to show matter itself, the water,
the air, transformed by the charisma of the event; how through the
medium of Enobarbus' own adoration of the events, Shakespeare
reveals his own capacity for being, well, a fan. There is no aggrandize-
ment here, no look at me. This is all *look at this*, Shakespeare's most
particular quality. There are all these things to say, but none of them
are said. We spoke too much this morning. As the water of the dirty
old Thames flies by, between two green river banks in the late sun,
we just let the words settle on us, and let that great fake, Cleopatra,
float by.

Then back to the hobble and the stumble and the struggle. Quentin, as is his way whenever my late-afternoon impression of Richard III becomes too pronounced, walks away into the far distance. This never seems fair, since he never seems to be walking appreciably faster than I am, but somehow he just disappears. I limp in behind. We finally reach our stopping point, Bray. We descend into a brash chrome, leather and mirror bar. It is a prime further example of separation. Many people so far adrift from their moorings, you wonder if they still know where their journey began. There is a coked-up petty gangster sitting on the table next to us, firing his banal instructions at his consiglieri, a spotty boy, and scandalizing his hos, two fat women, with clumsy gropes. It feels all a long way from Long Compton and Shipton-on-Stour in the Cotswolds. We still haven't resolved where we are to stay the night. One look at our surroundings decides us quickly we are going to book a cab home and then drive back out the next morning.

An enormously fat and strangely asexual cabbie with a high-pitched voice drives us home to Shepherds Bush. He is amazed by the length of our journey. Hardly surprising given your girth, mutters Quentin to me. We push our way into the house and are dived on by children and my wife. It feels a small cop-out coming home before the end of the walk, but an enormous comfort. Sasha says how strange we look, haunted and pure. I suppose we are, five days with eyes trained on a distant horizon – maybe not the Kalahari, but it's not the Askew Road either. Walking like pack horses for twenty to twenty-five miles each day and talking nonsense certainly jolts you out of your domestic rhythm. We sit down to a bubbling stew, my blistered and swollen feet sunk in a large basin full of hot water and vinegar. We drink wine and tell stories and feel that slight sense of loss when something special is told, and its uniqueness diminishes.

Saturday

We wake at home the next morning to a feeling of security, but, for all the gain, an equal amount of the magic has gone. We had been on an adventure, and some of the strangeness has evaporated. There is a warm but subdued mood as Sasha drives us out to Bray. We are adjusting ourselves back into our walking headspace. As with every morning through the week, it is another lovely early summer's day, sunshine, a light cool and dampness in the air. All the elements gently arguing over which should predominate, with none winning, but each letting the others have their say.

We hit the towpath again, and head along the Thames. Much of the privacy we enjoyed earlier in the week has gone. Bicyclists now crowd the path, jostling for space with joggers, dog-walkers and the great tribe of ramblers we have now joined. Neither Quentin nor I have ever been great gang-joiners, but it is hard to resist the relentless bonhomie of the other ramblers we meet along the way. A hail of comments falls on us such as 'Nice day for it,' 'Not far to Windsor,' 'Don't mind the dog,' 'Going far?' We do our best to respond in kind. There's no hiding the fact we are in London's suburbs, the home of the British sitcom. We are engaged in an inescapably bourgeois activity, we are inescapably bourgeois, we'd better live with it.

We talk about the difficulty of communing with a dead writer, the distance of understanding and how hard it is to approach Shakespeare. I tell Quentin of how I met Chekhov in a dream once. I was in the middle of rehearsals for *Three Sisters*, a prolonged period of joy and life-enhancement. In my dream, I saw a low-slung and modest barn sitting on the prow of a hill, across a muddy field. I crossed the field and opened a door set in a corner of a wall. A small fat woman in a 1970s trouser suit greeted me modestly and told me to come with her. She led me down a series of corridors, and up several flights of stairs, all rather flat and neutral. Eventually she stopped by a door, knocked and showed me in.

The room was Spartan, a window, a table, two chairs and, beside the window, a man half in the light, half out. He looked almost precisely 140 years old, Chekhov's age at that moment, had he not died. He gestured for me to sit opposite. He was taciturn, reserved and sparing with his presence. He asked me how the production was going. I told him how much I was enjoying it. He asked me about each of the actresses playing the sisters, and there was a spectral flicker of something greater than curiosity. Then he asked if I was having any problems. I said just one. In the first act, Chebutykin with an ostentatious display gives Irina a new samovar for her birthday, and everyone present disapproves vehemently. I didn't understand this. Was it because it was too expensive? Too cheap? Too vulgar? He told me the region that manufactured samovars had recently been highly troublesome, and to buy samovars was seen as unpatriotic. After that I could see he was tired and made my excuses and left, trudging back across the ploughed field. It was a suitably Chekhovian encounter, delicate and discreet.

Quentin is taken with this, and delighted by it, being as big a Chekhov nut as me. He asks if there had been any similar encounter with Shakespeare. At some point during the week, I had been in a half sleep and had seen a figure in shadows, behind an old wall hanging, an arras I suppose. He had pulled the curtain slightly to one side and brought his face closer to the light, but only closer. It was still in shadow. The presence felt shy, yet overwhelmingly curious. Not much to base an understanding on. The scraps we use to build lives are particularly scarce with Shakespeare. This is not an accident. It was his decision. His contemporaries Marlowe and Jonson left traces of themselves all over the contemporary records. They gave long interviews to the *Sunday Times* of their day; they had their pictures in the glossies of their day attending the premières of their day; they wrote themselves into their own plays and posterity. This was not the Shakespearean way. He wrote the plays. They appeared, they disappeared. He made his money from them, and that is all he took away. He left no trace of himself. He was not the story. The admonition on stone in Holy Trinity, Stratford, which began our week, is not an idle one.

The curves of the Thames we are twisting through are the curves of British history. Eton Chapel's Harry Potter Gothic weirdness looms up on our left above a reedy marsh; ahead in the distance is Windsor Castle; beyond, the island of Runnymede, where King John signed Magna Carta. Our eventual destination by the end of the day is Hampton Court. The Queen remembered once on television sailing up the river towards Westminster with Winston Churchill shortly after her coronation. She said, in her strangulated accent, 'I remember Churchill looking down on the Thames and speaking of it as "the silver thread that runs through history", and I looked out on this dirty, commercial river and thought, "Can this really be true?"' Well there is poetry in some souls, and not in others.

Windsor Castle looms closer in all its Disneyland perfection, and it is no strain for the imagination to fill with boats and horses and ancient royal progress. We cut into town for a quick coffee and, more crucially, pac-a-macs, because it is clear from the long black cloud bearing down that the sun is about to lose the argument with rain in a spectacular way. We have regained some of our rogue and vagabond swagger and sit drinking our coffee with the sort of open-chested pleasure you gain after three hours' steady walking. Windsor is packed with tourists, and a profoundly useless magician attempts to entertain the squashed quasi-piazza we are in. Soon after Quentin's face goes blank and fills with dread. I follow his gaze. Morris dancers. We ask for the bill quickly, but before we are able to escape they have begun their frolicking.

We are chased out of town by one of the great antecedents for our walk. When we thought of this trek from Stratford to London, one of our principal inspirations was Will Kemp's *Nine Daies Wonder* of 1599. Will Kemp had been the main clown in Shakespeare's company, the Chamberlain's Men. Most of the main comic characters of his early work were written with Kemp in mind. But Kemp was as big a star as his author, and a famed liberty-taker. Though he no doubt appreciated the material he was given, it wasn't enough, and he frequently garnished it with some of his own stuff. When Hamlet warns the players:

And let those that play your clowns speak no more than is set down for them; for there be of them that will themselves laugh, to set on some quantity of barren spectators to laugh too, though in the meantime some necessary question of the play be then to be considered. That's villainous, and shows a most pitiful ambition in the fool that uses it.

There is little doubt that Shakespeare is offloading some of his spleen against Kemp. Eventually the clown's liberties and ego became too much and he was forced out of the company, to be replaced by a more serious and subtle comedian, Robert Armin (who eventually extended his range as far as Iago). Kemp, who was king-sized miffed, decided to stage one of the first great actor publicity stunts. He resolved to morris dance all the way to Norwich from London in nine days. He managed this, though he cheated slightly by taking several week-long breaks in between certain days. He took with him a raggle-taggle crowd of thieves and fans and libertines. Wherever they went they created a riot. Kemp wrote the trip up with a self-regarding delight, and finishes his account with vicious swipes at Shakespeare and his erstwhile colleagues. The morris dancing itself comes over as a Bacchanalian sexual rite, full of a euphoric wildness and an unbridled eroticism. Not the thick-spectacled, half-of-cider jape of today.

Shortly after we escape Windsor, we are hit by a full-on thunder-storm. It is a humdinger of an explosion, full-lunged and full-throttle, a Lear storm:

> Blow, winds, and crack your cheeks; rage, blow.
> You cataracts and hurricanoes, spout
> Till you have drenched our steeples, drown'd the cocks.
> You sulph'rous and thought-executing fires,
> Vaunt couriers of oak-cleaving thunderbolts,
> Singe my white head. And thou, all-shaking thunder,
> Strike flat the thick rotundity o' th' world;
> Crack nature's moulds, all germens spill at once,
> That make ingrateful man.

The thick rotundity of Windsor Castle is under spectacular bombardment as etched forks of lightning attack it over and over from above. We tempt our fate with thunderbolts by standing under a broad oak and watch nature's greatest circus animate the arena all around us. The river boils and stirs behind, the castle wobbles ahead, and the great sound system of the sky blasts out its ear-shattering rebuke to human chatter. We stand there decked out in our thin sheets of plastic, our uncertain summer hats plastered flat against our scalps, revelling in it all.

Once the drama of the storm has passed, it leaves behind its less exciting cousin, a torrential downpour. It rains and rains, thick driving sheets of it, so thick we can only see ten-odd yards ahead. We have no choice but to walk through it, Quentin in his boots, me in the sandals I am somehow unable to remove. We lower our heads, lean forwards and pitch ourselves into the wet. For an hour, this is all we know, path, bridge and rain. We pass Runnymede, that great manifestation of English bolshiness, where Magna Carta enshrined the spirit of democracy in our country and in us for the 800 years since. Even in the pouring rain, as my summer clothes turn into a deep-sea diving suit, I consider how deeply I love that English spirit. Our democracy may be fundamentally flawed as a political system, but a deep instinct of 'gerroff', a deep desire not to be told what to do, always bubbles under the surface of English life.

Most of the greatest moments of pleasure in my life have come from living out that spirit of Celtic and Saxon defiance to the bossy centralizing tendency of the Normans. Catching Michael Heseltine slipping in the back door of the Cambridge Union and avoiding the crowd waiting to abuse him round the front. It's just him and me, so I lob a 'Sod off, you vain twat' in his direction, and receive a thin smile in reply. Running along beside the Poll Tax riot, seeing the streets whirl in joyful terror as the police and government lose control. Teaching my daughters to give the finger to world leaders when we ran into a convoy of the pusillanimous prats at the D-Day celebrations. All gestures, all pointless and futile, but necessary all the same. And I think of all the occasions in Shakespeare where I have drawn joy and sustenance from his great single finger to authority. In *King John* itself, the irrepressible rudeness of the bastard Faulconbridge; Hamlet's dazzling critiques of power; Lear's savage unpinning of the illusion of authority; Timon's counterblasts against the evils of money; Toby Belch's great bark at the repressive miserabilism of the Puritans, 'Dost thou think, because thou art virtuous, there shall be no more cakes and ale?' I think of how deep and wild the spirit of democracy runs through every inch of Shakespeare, and how lucky we are to have it underpinning our culture.

The rain clears, after a couple of hours of belting down, just as we cross the river once more to savour the full delights of Staines. We are leaving the river again, since it is indulging in yet another of its lazy loops, and we are going to have to face six or seven miles of residential suburbia before we meet up with it again. We are momentarily dizzy in our new surroundings – buses, cars, traffic lights, shopping centres, people Saturdaying away merrily with the aimless excitement of the weekend. Chain stores, chain restaurants, chain coffee shops, chain youth wearing their various uniforms of non-conformity. We walk around seeking somewhere to eat that isn't attached to a chain. Tucked in behind a bus station, we find a pizzeria and sink into it. Italian beers are sunk for thirst, wine ordered for taste.

We pick up our conversation from the day before, a decent pause to allow the heat of it to ebb away. There is little chance of a revival of the same fire. We are no longer lost in a great wood searching for the sun to show us the way out; we are eating pizza surrounded by youth, slurping fizzy drinks and romancing each other with grunts. It's not an environment for impassioned debate. I pick up Quentin's gobbet from two or three days before about Jung's genii being born special and fully formed. It's hard to disagree with that, hard to contend that some special genetic code marks out the Mozarts and the Mohammeds, the Platos and the Shakespeares. But whatever the special type of inner self they are born with, they need the right sort of nature around them, and the right sort of nurture to bring them to their peak. They have a capacity, but only the world can bring it to fruition. And they make mistakes, they make mistakes over and over again. Clumsiness and gaucheness and filth are part and parcel of who they are.

Salieri was a clean-living, austere, classically educated, learned musicologist and he could hardly write an interesting sequence of notes. Mozart was a randy, demented, scatological fruitcake and he couldn't write a boring sequence. As with Salieri, Ben Jonson understood what he was doing with his plays. He was deliberate, he followed through his own intellectual and artistic intentions. Yet Shakespeare was the genius, a fact which Ben Jonson was gracious enough to acknowledge. Shakespeare was not without learning, but part of his special genius, as explored recently by Jonathan Bate, was in taking previous texts and messing them up, complicating them. He took maps and scribbled on them. The rudeness and the lack of formal sense are not the by-products of genius, not the fall-out from it, they are the reason for it.

Quentin tacks off in a different direction. He is not going to let his Ted Hughes-inspired cosmology crumble. He has ordered his spheres in one way; I have disordered mine in another. He continues to maintain that Shakespeare's great work was to put the lusting id back into the right relationship with the loving self, to reconnect the ego with the soul. Whatever the mother goddess is, whether it's Mary in the Catholic iconography or some large-breasted, fat-bellied, prominently vaginaed figurine dug up in some prehistoric site, whatever it is, it is Quentin's contention that Elizabethan England was the last time on these shores that we were nursed by the universal assurance of such a figure's eternal love, and the first time we felt the apparent certainty of the destruction of such a figure. This was the crime of the Reformation, Auden's 'offence from Luther until now / That has driven a culture mad'. It was the original crime of civilization, the inevitable crime of consciousness. The collapse of the Catholic church within Shakespeare's own time was a loss he could not bear, and, for Quentin, much of his life's work was in reviving the values that had been lost in a new medium, the theatre.

This is weighty stuff to absorb over an American Hot and a second bottle of Chianti, but it's persuasive and has the poetic ring of truth. It is also borne out by many of the plays, most notably *As You Like It*, *Hamlet* and *The Tempest*, whose structure observes a usurped authority trying to return to power and restore health to the world they have been exiled from. We are now nicely pissed, and veer away from our symposium into gossip and laughter.

The path ahead is by far the grimmest of the week. We are away from the country, and away from the Thames. We have no choice but to pound the pavements for three or four hours, cars, buses and lorries grinding by, aeroplanes roaring along their flight path overhead. We will be passing through Staines, Feltham and Sunbury, places which I am sure are full of hidden magic, but which do not reveal their inner grace immediately to the unfamiliar eye. The greatest change to our modus operandi is that Quentin is beginning to struggle. When I say struggle, a more exact definition would be that he is now moving at the same pace as me, but for him that's practically a call for hospitalization. A country soul at heart, he is finding pavements and dirty air far from conducive. It's clear that his spirit is dipping slightly as well.

To sustain it, he performs one of the greatest acts of soul heroism I've ever witnessed. He walks through the long miles of semi-detached sun-warmed suburbia, through a zone as dead as dead can be, barking 'Venus and Adonis' at the top of his voice as if through a megaphone. 'Venus and Adonis' is a deeply filthy poem, a fact confirmed by several renditions through the week, and Quentin is determined to force its sexuality into South-west London. When he gets to the passage where the two horses copulate, he throws his head back and belts it out:

> Away he springs, and hasteth to his horse.
>
> But, lo! From forth a copse that neighbours by,
> A breeding jennet, lusty, young, and proud,
> Adonis' trampling courser doth espy,
> And forth she rushes, snorts and neighs aloud;
> The strong-necked steed, being tied unto a tree,
> Breaketh his rein, and to her straight goes he.
>
> Imperiously he leaps, he neighs, he bounds,
> And now his woven girths he breaks asunder;
> The bearing earth with his hard hoof he wounds,
> Whose hollow womb resounds like heaven's thunder;
> The iron bit he crushes 'tween his teeth,
> Controlling what he was controlled with.

His ears up-prick'd; his braided hanging mane
Upon his compass'd crest now stand on end;
His nostrils drink the air, and forth again,
As from a furnace, vapours doth he send:
His eye, which scornfully glisters like fire,
Shows his hot courage and his high desire.

It is a heroic effort. It gains us little but looks of bemusement and dismissal and horror, but it pushes a little poetry and a little sex into the ether, and that's no crime.

By the time we reconnect with the Thames we are both beyond speech, Quentin from his pain and his barking, me from the old pains, including the return of that B movie, *The Curse of the Swollen Gonad*. I make another of my navigational *faux pas* and leave us temporarily deserted on a little island, which doesn't amuse. We start to hope rather pathetically that a boatman will appear, and we declare that hitching a lift on a boat would be completely within the rules of engagement. By pure chance we walk past the house of the pioneer of the Shakespeare industry, David Garrick, the eighteenth-century actor and showman. A little further along, there is the shrine to Shakespeare he built by the river, one of the first manifestations of bardolatry, to which we are so completely in thrall today. At any other moment we would have marvelled at the synchronicity of this and might have stepped in and paid obeisance. But we are so royally fucked by exhaustion and faintness and jelly legs that we plough on.

We have booked tickets for *Romeo and Juliet* that night in Hampton Court, in one of the large halls reserved for drama in the days of Henry VIII and Elizabeth. It is being presented in original style by the Globe Theatre company. It is a treat we have been looking forward to all week. Quentin cries off. His feet are going and he has family business to attend to. I am determined to make something of it. So I struggle in, lame, sweaty, wild-eyed and filthy. I find our seats, and spread myself out over both of them, unable to cross my legs or fold them into the correct space. I slowly unpeel my sandals to reveal feet that are yellow with bruising, red with bleeding, green and brown from our country walking, and with a brand new layer of grime from the appropriately named Staines. They have also slowly flattened themselves out like pancakes, so I look like a filthy duck. I groan frequently. The other audience members start to give me filthy looks. The ushers at the theatre start to exchange glances. It could be Laurence Olivier performing and it wouldn't have gained my attention. At the interval, half from kindness and half selfishness, I struggle out into Hampton Court Palace and hobble off to the station in search of a taxi.

Sunday

Sleep lays on its usual restorative hands, and the next morning joints are eased, muscles are supple and feet have somehow shed the hundred nails that were driving into them the night before. It does not prove quite so therapeutic for Quentin, whose feet are still haunted by the impress of the pavements of Sunbury. 'You're in your natural habitat now, Dom. The pavement. I'm outside mine.' My feet are scaffolded out with a strange mix of supportive tapes and plasters, and we cab out to Hampton Court to begin the final stretch. Again the light is crisp, the sun is up, and the morning is full of its habitual delusional hope. Several people had promised to join us for this last stretch, but none of them makes it to Hampton at eight in the morning. This leaves me feeling a bit No Mates, and Quentin feeling a little under-entertained. He was determined to find someone in the course of the week to teach him Brush Up Your Shakespeare, and we have failed him. We are beyond speech or thought in the early part of the morning and trog along silently. We are walking in our dreams now. Our waking state and our sleeping state shadow each other for a while, before one emerges cleanly from the other.

We skirt round the bottom of Hampton Court Palace, along the river, past the bank where Elizabeth would have embarked on her great flotilla of boats, and sailed in rococo pomp up river to dazzle her subjects. We note the artificial symmetries and geometries of the Elizabethan garden, and move on to the more rugged fakery of Capability Brown's reinvention of the park. Brown has harried us along our way, his smoothly curvaceous definition of true nature looking less and less convincing since we have spent so much time with the real thing.

To prick our brains into action I suggest a gambling quiz. Taking out the *Complete Works*, I propose that I will read the first lines of each of the plays. If Quentin guesses the play he wins a pound; if he fails, I win a pound. Quentin complains that this is not fair, since he knows the plays less well than I do. I concede that I will read from the plays in their order in the *Works*, which makes life easier, since *The Tempest* is always at the front, and the history plays are in chronological order. His knowledge of history should set him immediately ten pounds ahead. He still baulks at the idea of this, suspecting it as a sophisticated con. So I further concede that we will then reverse positions, and he can test me for the same stakes on all the last lines. This is well nigh impossible, since most of the plays finish with an indistinguishable couplet about everyone feeling hypothetically cheerful and buggering off to a feast. This is enough for Quentin, and we are allowed to continue. He proceeds to get nearly every play right, revealing an ability for intuitive guessing that is almost druidic, or the fact that he's been concealing the depth of his Shakespearean knowledge all week. I do less well with rather indeterminate last lines such as 'You that way, we this way' (*Love's Labour's Lost*). Quentin seems to be enjoying my discomfiture a bit too much, and we start to get childishly argumentative over the score, and the rules. Fellow ramblers passing us see two men squabbling over how much they owe, and whether it's fair to read a line out in a silly accent. The walk is not, this morning, proving the path to spiritual health we imagined it might be.

We cross a bridge at Kingston and walk through the briefest passage of suburban drab and drear before disappearing into the vastness of Richmond Park. We are in the property of the royals again, and back in the great greenery of English history. We agree to stop the game, since it's throwing Quentin's yin and yang well out of kilter, and magnifying my rather unpleasant inner child. However, just before we finish, Quentin tests me on the last lines of *Richard III*. (He was delighted when I tested him on the first line of the same. Not only because he barked the answer out before I'd got beyond 'Now is the wint . . .', but also because it gave him the opportunity for a supplementary question to me, 'Which northern camping store promotes its annual sale with the slogan *Now is the discount of our winter tents?*') Quentin's eye is distracted beyond the last line to the whole of Richmond's last speech, the same speech I made an unholy mess of twenty years before in a cattle auction barn in North Yorkshire with my Cheapstreet Theatre Co. After his whole week of advancing the cause of conflict resolution, it is as if a giant peach has rolled into his garden:

> We will unite the white rose and the red;
> Smile, heaven, upon this fair conjunction,
> That long have frown'd upon their enmity!
> What traitor hears me, and says not amen?
> England hath long been mad, and scarr'd herself;
> The brother blindly shed the brother's blood,
> The father slaughter'd his own son,
> The son, compell'd, been butcher to the sire:
> All this divided York and Lancaster,
> Divided in their dire division,
> O! now, let Richmond and Elizabeth,
> The true succeeders of each royal house,
> By God's fair ordinance conjoin together;
> And let their heirs – God, if they will be so, –
> Enrich the time to come with smooth-fac'd peace,
> With smiling plenty and fair prosperous days!

This is not Shakespeare's most richly complex description of resolution of opposites, but it is one of his most triumphant. Quentin is on to his theme again, wrapping the bloody scars of English history together with the pain of more intimate forms of separation. Civil war and the pain a child feels when it is taken away from its mother's breast are all part of the same dance for him. He says quite rightly that the Wars of the Roses were a family squabble, fought to the death until finally resolved by marriage. The memory of the bloodshed and the chaos and the dread shifting allegiances would have been fresh in the minds of the conflict's grandchildren, just as no one in Bosnia is going to forget which side their family was on for a while. The need for healing was urgent, as was the sense that any resolution was still fragile, the next great civil war being only forty odd years away. Quentin claims that in Will's great tragedies, the old prophet of Catholic redemption saw cloisters of attachment crumbling, and the new prophet of Puritan supremacy saw foundations of separation being dug. And how noble it was in such an atmosphere, thick with the anticipation of massacre and martyrdom, to struggle for smiling plenty and fair prosperous days.

I can't quite buy this, since I still refuse to see Shakespeare as a man with a mission, or any mission beyond the desire to create. But it is persuasive. Everything about my understanding of the English has led me to see a civil war in the centre of their spirit. Whether Celt against Saxon, or both against Norman, or White Rose against Red, or Fenian against Prod, or Roundhead against Cavalier, or Whig against Tory, or Romantic against Classicist, or socialist against conservative, or bohemian against Victorian, or bounder against straight, or cool against square, or pro-European against pro-American, or whatever, whatever the formulation, there have always been two English gangs forming so that people can join up and biff each other in print or in the pub. These fights, under different names, and with different costumes, are general to all the world, but they are fiercely alive within the English. It is what makes us so compelling, the way we keep our oppositions so stoked up within us. The argument that these conflicts were of fundamental interest to Shakespeare is undeniable. I still feel he didn't aim to resolve them. His task was more precisely to show us how ridiculous and petty such strong positions are in such a wild, random and beautiful universe. Quentin pictures two warriors walking towards each other and embracing into one. I have two warriors being dropped alone into the middle of the Grand Canyon and realizing the futility of their opposition.

We get mildly lost in the expanse of Richmond Park, but it's not as bad as our moment in the wood, and we are soon back on track. It's a low-key atmosphere today. Returning home has distracted us from the singleness of purpose we knew before. Our minds are less trapped within our own arguments, our concentration less fierce. As we rise up the hill of the park, we have another gentle epiphany. We walk under the shade of a small clump of oaks and find that we have company. Sitting with almost pretentious stillness is a gathering of about nine stags. They look as if they are posing for an artist. They have a wonderful arrogance about them, as if they know they are better in the life than any picture could ever capture. Their antlers are stately, erect and poised. We look at them, they look back. As we pass, they slowly, and with perfect communal timing, turn their heads to follow us, the horizontal line of their antlers never wobbling for a second. It is a moment of accidental grace.

We rejoin the looping Thames and walk silently along its side into Putney. Quentin asks what the point of the whole walk has been. A moment of clarity that has escaped us thus far, apart from Mark's mad scream at the fields on Tuesday night. I say I'm not sure, but I am thinking of writing a book about Shakespeare. Whatever I'm approaching, whether it's a book or a play, I like to begin it with some act of respect to its author, some search for a truth, even if it's heading off in the wrong direction. For a man with no shortage of ego, it is important to try and wrestle myself into some state of modesty. I am always looking for a nod from the author, some brief glimpse that tells me I'm on the right track. 'Like the dream of Chekhov,' Quentin says. 'Like the dream of Chekhov,' I reply. Quentin castigates himself for not being modest, for banging on about Shakespeare without sufficient knowledge. I reproach that he has more than enough modesty before any subject. His very zeal and his enthusiasm is an enormous modesty in itself. I fail more grievously on the modesty front in my desire to make a Shakespeare like me, and in my determination to write about him from my perspective rather than his own. 'But who could write from his but him?' asks Quentin. That settles that. My bruised, bloodied and swollen feet, my shrunken waistline and my spinning head are small marks of my respect.

We cross Putney Bridge and stop for pints in a pub. My family joins us here, my three girls running up and jumping on us with their customary exuberance. Quentin has to leave the walk for a while to go and visit a sick relative. We resolve to meet up again later by the Houses of Parliament. My family and I seek out an Italian restaurant and sit for pizza and pasta. It's hard to break the rhythm and be a father when the week has been so distant, so the conversation falters, and there's a weird and unsatisfactory argument over the bill. I part company from them with promises to meet later, and head off up the King's Road. For the first time in the week I am alone. No Quentin, no family, no anybody else, alone, pursuing this invented pilgrimage for a while. There is very little going through my head but the need to put one foot in front of another, and to get to the end. About halfway up the King's Road in a stretch of smart bookshops and antique emporia, I suddenly look up and across the road. My eye meets Shakespeare's. I stop and stare. In the window of a shop across the road, there is a bust of Shakespeare, carved with simplicity and grace out of blackened wood. It has the familiar lineaments of his classic figure, but done with a rough and bald honesty that looks more truthful than any other I have seen. And I caught its eye. I smile and move on. It is a small nod.

I cross back over the river to walk through Battersea Park, still trying to keep as much green under my feet as possible. Mark has been lying in wait on the other side. It is a delight to meet him, and we walk together. He is still a car crash of twisted feet and swollen thighs, even five days after he finished walking, so he hobbles energetically beside my now more confident stride. I meet up with my family again, and pick up one daughter, my second, to walk the last stretch with me. Mark, after his brief burst, gives up again. My daughter asks wonderful big innocent questions as we walk along towards Westminster. Quentin is waiting to rejoin us, sitting on a bench with a lordly air outside the Houses of Parliament. We walk across Westminster Bridge and stop briefly in the middle to look up and down the Thames. I make one last point of the week, and gently. The spirit of the walk is falling away from us as we approach our end point. There is little vigour left in our movement, or our arguments. We are not striding towards a brass band and a ticker tape. We are trailing towards an indeterminate fade away, and back into the rest of our lives.

Our problem at the moment is that we sentimentalize our shamen so grotesquely. The Jungian genii that Quentin brought up earlier in the week are sanctified into such excessively infallible kitsch figures. Jesus as unique and perfect, a poem of wilting sorrow to some, a musclebound warrior of virtue to others. Mohammed seen through the same blinkers, the wise and ferocious prophet, all his impurities blasted off him by the winds of the desert. These men were beautiful and unique and once in an epoch original, but they were also men.

And, like all men, muddled and human. Many have tried to deify Shakespeare in the same way. The Stratford industry depends on it, together with a million school and university courses, and much of the British identity. They all congregate to make Shakespeare not human. To say his plays were all part of some deliberate, divine design. But they weren't. They were plays written by a Stratford boy, who became a man in a London exploding like a firework display. He wrote at a moment when England was taking a corner at speed and he yielded – thrilled – to the force that threw him. That historical moment enabled his gift to produce work that brings together all the concerns of mankind in one newly created world. His work is full of errors, lazy bad errors, the man himself was full of contradictions and failures, but we must accept all those as part of who he is. His gift of sight and of creation did not separate him from humanity, it bound him into it.

I finish and we move on. We descend down into the great fairground that is the South Bank. Crowds bustle and heave in the effort to squeeze into all the madness on offer. Sharks and piranhas and tropical kaleidoscopes of fish in the aquarium under the old County Hall. The surreal warped landscapes of Salvador Dali in an exhibition. Slow trips in glass pods up above the horizon in the London Eye. And all around, as Quentin says, musicians, magicians, mountebanks, fortune-tellers, pick-pockets and other sponges of the groundling crowd. Peruvian bands with their irritating pipes. Bad sub-Dylan buskers. Kids carving shapes in the air and rewriting the space around them with their skateboards and their roller blades. We walk on, Quentin, my daughter and I, through all this mayhem, past the Festival Hall, past the National Theatre, under Blackfriars Bridge and past Tate Modern. And there, nestled within the shelter of larger buildings, snug yet proud, is the Globe, the end of our walk.

The rest of my family is there to greet us together with the hobbling Mark. We have not a lot to say. Quentin and I are too blasted and bewildered to make a speech. He asks what we should have read. I consult the *Complete Works* for the last time, and pass it to my Sasha. I say I cannot read it or I will cry, but as she begins the tears start to sparkle in my eyes.

When that I was and a little tiny boy
With hey, ho, the wind and the rain;
A foolish thing was but a toy,
For the rain it raineth every day.

But when I came to man's estate,
With hey, ho, the wind and the rain;
'Gainst knaves and thieves men shut their gates,
For the rain it raineth every day.

But when I came, alas! to wive
With hey, ho, the wind and the rain;
By swaggering could I never thrive,
For the rain it raineth every day.

But when I came unto my beds,
With hey, ho, the wind and the rain;
With toss-pots still had drunken heads,
For the rain it raineth every day.

A great while ago the world begun,
With hey, ho, the wind and the rain;
But that's all one, our play is done,
And we'll strive to please you every day.

Acknowledgements

My walking companion, Quentin Seddon, is owed the most visible debt for much of this book. He didn't only walk with me, he also talked at great length and helped to crystallize many of my thoughts on Shakespeare and much else, as he has done for a couple of decades now. I have stolen mercilessly from a poetic account of the walk he wrote. If you want to see how deep the theft is, he has posted the poem on a website, www.brushupyourshakespeare.com. I recommend a visit, since it's a fine piece of work. Beyond all that, I and my family will always owe Quentin, and his long-term walking companion Rowena, a great debt of love. On the walk we also had the delightful presence of Mark Rosenblatt, the ebullient presence of Will Mannering and the fleeting presence of Michael Taylor to be grateful for, as well as the hospitality of the Knights and the Joneses.

My great thanks go to all the good people at Penguin who appear to be giving me their rather deluxe treatment; my good friend Eric Schlosser, who put me in touch with them in the first place; Pen Vogler, who is doing her best to shift copies; and most of all my editor, Helen Conford, who is remarkably accomplished at bullying middle-aged men for one so young. She has the acumen to make me think more seriously about my writing and the good grace not to complain when I have forced her to shout through letterboxes when alarm clocks have failed to wake me.

Several people have helped me sifting through the manuscript. At this stage in a Shakespeare book, there is normally a list of the international scholars whom the author has discussed recondite textual matters with. I am afraid I will fail on that account. I sent it to my family. My sister Jessica was extremely helpful, as she always is, with matters of tone, with extra material and with a large helping of extra jokes. My brother, Sean, practised benign neglect. My mother, Jen, was hugely encouraging. And my father, Pat, practised a little benign censorship. My great thanks go to my mother and father for being very open about their own Shakespearean histories, and for immensely stimulating conversations about the possibilities of the book.

I also had the good fortune to have a little help from Maddy Costa, a lot of questions from Sasha Hails, and the constant pruning influence of Helen Conford. Also, gratitude for jokes goes to Yvonne Pioline and John Dougall.

Many people have contributed moments and stories to the book: old school friends, fellow university graduates, colleagues and lovers. I hope I haven't intruded on anyone's privacy – I have tried not to – and I am aware that what I have written is not the truth, it is my truth, and as fallible as anything so partial.

I have studiously avoided, as far as I could, writing about the greatest story of my life, meeting my Sasha, and the arrival in the world of my three daughters, Siofra, Grainne and Cara. I simply do not know the words to describe how lovely they are, how much they mean to me, or how little I would be capable of without them. They know that anything I produce, in the theatre or in print, is as greatly theirs as it is mine.